"*Body Autonomy* deserves a place next to *Pleasure Activism* in the canon of 21st century sex politics books that are deeply grassroots in both content and form. Justice Rivera and the assembled contributors have made the exact book I've been longing for: a contemporary collection of tools both pragmatic and personal, literary and political, for creating and maintaining solidarity in justice movements. This book has skyrocketed to the top of my recommended reading list for those who need vital info and perspectives on sex labor, harm reduction, and intersectional liberation, where I expect it to stay for all of time."

—**Tina Horn, author of *Why Are People Into That?!* and *SfSx***

"Unveil the collective power of BIPOC voices in *Body Autonomy: Decolonizing Sex Work and Harm Reduction*. This groundbreaking text, penned exclusively by authors of color, delves into the complex world of the sex trade, the ravages of the War on Drugs, and the relentless quest for bodily sovereignty. Including Justice Rivera's sharp analysis of sex work and a richly detailed collaborative timeline, the book shines with chapters like 'Sacred Stripper,' which intertwines spirituality and consent in sex work, and 'Drug Policy for Breaking Intergenerational Curses,' an eco-futurist perspective on substance use and healing. Crafted by thinkers like Kate D'Adamo, Jasmine Tyler, and Jade Laughlin, each chapter stands as a beacon of resistance and resilience. This patchwork of narratives challenges the status quo, championing a radical reimagining of a world where the sanctity of bodily rights is universally upheld."

—**Ayize Jama-Everett, MDiv, MA, MFA, director of *A Table of Our Own***

"Harm reduction means listening to the voices of sex workers and people who use drugs and changing the policies that cause damage. Justice Rivera inspires us to act by bringing these stories together, along with historical insight and practical information on how to move past racist, counterproductive, and oppressive 'wars' on drugs and trafficking."

—**Maia Szalavitz, *New York Times* bestselling author of *Undoing Drugs: How Harm Reduction Is Changing the Future of Drugs and Addiction***

"The only true autonomy that we have is that of the body. We live in a space and time where even that is under attack. It is important to reclaim ourselves. There is no need to justify how you have a relationship with you. This book represents an important conversation."

—**Maurice Byrd, LMFT, director of Training and Business Operations, Harm Reduction Therapy**

"An illuminating read that establishes a solid groundwork for understanding sex work, this book skillfully places it and its criminalization within the broader sociopolitical landscape. The authors draw indisputable connections between the wars on drugs and sex work in the timeline, and continue to offer us a narrative that is both informative and eye-opening throughout the rest of the book. Most importantly, there are resources provided, and this work amplifies the voices of those directly impacted, offering a frontline perspective on the consequences of prohibition and the satisfaction of indulgence within both of these domains."

—**Courtney Watson, LMFT and AASECT Certified Sex Therapist, owner of Doorway Therapeutic Services**

"*Body Autonomy* should be required reading for everyone, especially those working in professions that serve the public. The amount of wisdom, data, wit, and heart in this book is beyond words! I am grateful that such an amazing guide to decolonizing sex work and drug use exists, uplifting the voices of so many QTBIPOC luminaries in the space. May this information reach every corner of the world, far and wide!"
—**Leia Friedwoman, MS, The Psychedologist**

"*Body Autonomy* is a welcome contribution to the growing harm reduction literature that contributes to a new emerging paradigm for understanding sex work and drug use as multiply determined activities that often serve vital, positive functions in people's lives. The concept was born from queer and trans sex workers and drug users doing what they had to do to survive and improve the quality of their lives. The book brings together voices of people who represent communities that are most devastated by state violence and is committed to 'breathing a new, safer, and more just world into being.' *Body Autonomy*'s vision for our communities is positive, passionate, creative, hopeful, and inspiring. I highly recommend this book to anyone who cares about creating a more free and just world."
—**Andrew Tatarsky, PhD, author of *Harm Reduction Psychotherapy: A New Treatment for Drug and Alcohol Problems*, director of Clinical Programing for The Freedom Institute, New York City**

"This collection maps out perspectives that are not commonly heard in mainstream bodily autonomy discourse, leaving us space to grapple with considerations across the intersections of transforming harm at interpersonal and structural levels and how healing and pleasure can live amongst this. The collection illustrates the ways in which folks are broadening our understanding of what we must reckon with in order to move towards worlds that fiercely interrupt the cycles of violence around sex work and substance use—whilst lovingly moving towards wholeness and embracing the complexity of human life."
—**Dr. Stephanie Davis and Farzana Khan, Healing Justice London**

"*Body Autonomy* sheds light on the critical intersectionality between the War on Drugs and the criminalization of the sex trade, emphasizing the need for mutual aid and collaboration between these two movements. The book presents compelling ideas about how principles of harm reduction can be applied to replace our current carceral approach. In this collection of essays written by people working within these stigmatized industries who have been disproportionately impacted by systems of oppression, we find moving personal narratives that present new paradigms about personal liberation, ancestral healing, connection to indigeneity, and a fierce insistence in accessing joy and pleasure."
—**Rebecca Kronman, LCSW, founder of Plant Parenthood**

"Despite being a victim of the War on Drugs and witnessing the profound impact of our cultural DNA on systemic issues, I had not considered how root causes of this war manifest in parallel through a misunderstood war on sex work—not until reading *Body Autonomy*. Justice Rivera brings to light an undeniable common struggle between the two. Armed with evidence, insight, and a path forward, this anthology helped me recognize that while we fight many battles, we fight the same war—one of pushing against reactive systems destined to perpetuate misguided harm. Highly recommended for anyone engaged in the work of drug policy and systems change. It's a meticulous dissection of ideologies likely to make one more precise in their political advocacy and compassionate to the nuanced struggles of sex work."

—Kwasi Adusei, DNP, PMHNP

"*Body Autonomy* is a powerful look at the myriad forces that have led to the stigmatization of both sex work and drug use, dating back to the philosophies of the Founding Fathers. Through drawing parallels between how both have been criminalized—and the consequences of that criminalization—it illuminates the importance of uprooting everything from mainstream narratives to the legal system if we want to reimagine a society that centers human care and compassion. I recommend this book for anyone that hopes to be a part of that reimagining."

—Shelby Hartman, cofounder of *DoubleBlind* magazine

"For too long our individual and collective bodies have borne the brunt of neocolonial policy and systemic oppression. Bringing forth powerful voices from across diverse fields, traditions, and cultures, *Body Autonomy* is a well of collective wisdom that is essential guidance for us all now at a very pivotal time. This collection brings us into deeper reflection on our harmful history, more compassionate connection in the present with our bodies, and the process of envisioning and creating a shared future in which pleasure, healing, and liberation are woven into the fabric of our policies and practices."

—Joseph Ryan McCowan, PsyD, supervisor and educator at Multidisciplinary Association for Psychedelic Studies (MAPS)

"Wow! This is an incredible collection of powerful essays and an urgent and important contribution to our evolving understanding of the oldest profession."

—Kaytlin Bailey, founder and executive director at Old Pros

"Justice Rivera's *Body Autonomy* comprehensively dissects the many currents that lay at the foundation of why the negative consequences of drug use and sex work are social constructs, and not a result of drug use or sex work themselves. Her elaboration on how community organizing and policy changes can reduce harmful outcomes creates an essential blueprint for change that not only is long overdue, but also methodically links the drug policy reform and sex worker rights movements in novel ways. A vital read!" **—Juliana Mulligan, LMSW, Inner Vision Ibogaine**

"Some things we wish for will never be invented. A pair of glasses with a small dial on the side that I can turn while looking out at a busy city street and see what it looked like 200 years ago—*twist*—1,000 years ago—*twist*—10,000 years ago! Pulling the glasses off my face, it would be back to pedestrian foot traffic on concrete sidewalks and exhaust fumes in a mad fury of halted productivity. Yet, I would have a greater understanding, one could even call it a *layered* understanding, of what this place had been. Complex, systemic issues are like these layers of time. You can see the street and lament the present, or you can undergo the painful process of knowing that it was once a rich marshland, hold that soil in your hand, and ask the heavens where the hell to start growing something new with knowledge of old. We can change reality but we can't deny it in the process. Not if we're going to see clearly. This book feels like putting on those glasses, but instead of looking out at a city, we're looking at humanity."

—Nicolle Hodges, journalist, author, and founder of Men Who Take Baths

"*Body Autonomy: Decolonizing Sex Work and Drug Use* is an unapologetic collection of literary works woven in the intersection of erotic labor and reproductive justice that is timely required reading with the historical classic staying power of your favorite banned book." —**Sophie Saint Thomas, author of *Sex Witch***

"*Body Autonomy* offers us a powerful glimpse into the radical and transformative grassroots work being done by two of the most heavily stigmatized and criminalized groups in society: sex workers and drug users. Detailing community-based solutions and practical policy changes alongside crucial historical analysis and illuminating personal narratives, this anthology invites us to break cycles of structural violence and criminalization through harm reduction practices both ancient and emergent and points to a much larger societal transformation that wants to unfold. Grounded in lived experience and fierce advocacy, *Body Autonomy* is an inspiring vision for collective liberation in the world to come—and how with compassion and connection we can dream, trip, and pleasure our way there."

—**Britta Love, somatic sex educator, writer, and healer**

"Brilliant, revolutionary, profound, and inciting, *Body Autonomy* is an essential and comprehensive manual for anyone seeking to design a compassionate future in which autonomy, justice, and human rights are written into the fabric of our culture. In order to accomplish this work together, we must dismantle the harmful paternalism, extractivism, and purity-morality cultures of white supremacy that use criminalization of the exploration of consciousness and sensuality as a tool of oppression and control. In Rivera's collaborative anthology, we learn that in order to effectively accomplish this shift, it is critical to understand the structures rooted in hierarchy and exploitation that control our present, to discern the nature and motivations of the opponents that threaten our well-being, to stand on the history and lessons of our collective resistance, and to collaboratively dream our sacred joy into being."

—**Angela Carter, ND, chair, Oregon Psilocybin Advisory Board**

"This anthology, special in its voice being fully BIPOC, is a reminder that Love is an action. Our beloveds, everywhere. Love, the answer. Tenderly, I read these words and remember my own origins—loving those disrupters, those on the edge, those who challenge the status quo. Today, we call this loving harm reduction, decolonization, collective liberation. Tomorrow, with this act of loving practiced, we will know an ancient future. Justice brings her namesake to those who exist on the fringes, illuminating paths of liberation through practical applications of the action of love, followed by prayers of pleasure towards healing, towards joy—in Love. Undeniably required, radical reading."

—**Danielle M. Herrera, harm reduction and psychedelic psychotherapist**

BODY
AUTONOMY

BODY AUTONOMY

Decolonizing Sex Work and Drug Use

JUSTICE RIVERA

FOREWORD BY CAMILLE BARTON

AFTERWORD BY SINNAMON LOVE

SYNERGETIC PRESS
SANTA FE • LONDON

Published by Synergetic Press
1 Blue Bird Court, Santa Fe, New Mexico 87508
& 24 Old Gloucester St. London, WCIN 3AL, England

Library of Congress Control Number: 2024933083

ISBN 9781957869148 (paperback)
ISBN 9781957869155 (ebook)

Cover design and illustrations by Lindsey Cleworth
Interior design by Howie Severson
Typesetting by Jonathan Hahn
Managing Editor: Noelle Armstrong
Production Editor: Allison Felus

Printed in the United States of America

I stewarded this book as an offering to my ancestors who wrote survival into my veins, to all who I have lost in the struggle for freedom and liberation, and to all who continue to raise the collective consciousness. May these words provide knowledge and healing so that all who read them are activated to move forward with awareness, openness, sincerity, and love.

Contents

SECTION 3: HARM-REDUCTION TOOLKITS

SECTION 4: PLEASURE-ORIENTED FUTURES

Foreword

CAMILLE BARTON

BODY AUTONOMY IS A VITAL EXPLORATION OF SOME OF THE WAYS THE state has sought to criminalize, control, and repress the bodies of people in the global majority, Indigenous people, women, queer and trans folks, and all those who have been disproportionately impacted by Western, imperialist state violence for the last 500 years in order to reproduce the status quo. It is an inspiring call to action to build coalitions that center care, pleasure, embodied agency, and dignity for all beings. This generous book traverses the nuanced world(s) of sex work and drug use, highlighting the entanglements between these realms and the oppressive socio-political conditions that determine our lives. None of us consented to being born into a system of racialized, economic bondage, where we are forced to exchange our labor power in order to meet our survival needs. People are trying their best to navigate through this coercive context with varied results. *Body Autonomy* will nourish, support, and validate substance users, sex workers, those who pay for sexual services, psychedelic therapists, and public health workers, as well as people who are keen to infuse more pleasure into their lives. Equally, if you find yourself with a stigma toward sex work or drug use, this book may beautifully illuminate the failings of the War on Drugs and the war against trafficking, demonstrating the need to create new systems that create safety, dignity, and belonging for people, while allowing us the space to explore our bodies and consciousness.

Paying for sex and using drugs are often presented as deviant desires that can be suppressed by most upstanding members of society. However, what if these desires emerge from needs, not wants? In the contemporary Western world, it can be hard for people to discern between their wants and their needs. We recognize that water, food, and shelter are examples of core needs that can have deadly consequences if not met. But what about touch? Scientific studies have shown that healthy human infants will die if they do not receive touch within their first years of life.[1] If we become touch starved as adults, this can negatively impact our health with symptoms including depression, anxiety, increased stress, and higher blood pressure, as well as immune system and digestive issues.[2] I wonder what society would look like if we treated the need for (consensual) touch as just as essential to our functioning as water or food? Unfortunately, in the West forms of touch including massage, cuddles, and sexual connection are often presented as luxuries only available to those in monogamous relationships or to people who have wealth or bodies deemed to be beautiful or deserving enough, rather than something we all require.

Sex workers are some of the only people who provide touch, intimacy, and sexual connection to those who need it outside of hetero-patriarchal logics. This work is sacred and much needed. While sex work is criminalized in the United States, we can look to history and find places where it was seen as a spiritual offering and held with reverence—such as the Babylonian temples in ancient Mesopotamia.[3] There are also modern day examples, like the Netherlands, where touch is considered more of a priority than many other countries in the West—sex work is legal, and some Dutch municipalities pay for *sekszorg*, or sex care, enabling disabled people to have a monthly session with a sex worker to ensure that touch is accessible to those who desire it.[4] Given our need for touch as social animals, why is sex work so stigmatized and prohibited in many contexts around the world? *Body Autonomy* powerfully illustrates how and why sex work has been prohibited in the United States and what it would look like to create a context in which sex work could be regulated in a way that supports sex workers and enables people to access touch without shame or stigma.

Another need that is underexplored in the West is the need to alter our consciousness. Many traditional and Indigenous cultures use practices including meditation, sensory deprivation, body modification, dance, and plant medicines to alter consciousness in ways that connect them to their ancestors, ecosystems, and cosmology. Rather than a rarity, scientist Ronald K. Siegel argues that drug-induced intoxication is a "primary motivational force" for many living beings and therefore common.[5] In *Animals and Psychedelics*, ethnobotanist Giorgio Samorini documents how widespread drug-induced intoxication is across the animal kingdom, leading him to argue that the need to alter consciousness is an inherent part of being alive and precedes the origins of humans. "Drugging oneself is a behavior that reaches across the entire process of animal evolution, from insects to mammals to women and men."[6] Given the moral panic about drugs that has been perpetuated by the War on Drugs, and colonization before that, many see drugs as evil or something that only brings pain and anguish. Samorini argues that addiction and negative dynamics associated with drugs often result from detrimental conditions in society rather than from drugs in and of themselves.[7] If altered states are also a need, well documented throughout the animal kingdom, then why are drugs still stigmatized and prohibited in many parts of the world?

Going into altered states can provide us with a way to reflect upon society, imagine, and create change in the collective. As we have transitioned into industrial capitalism, our bodies have been conditioned to become more and more like machines, with the purpose of increasing productivity and wealth accumulation for the economic elite.[8] Bodies have been heavily regulated by the state, and emotions that are not deemed productive, such as grief, mental-health crises, or drug–induced altered states, are often stigmatized. Many argue that the normalization of drugs like caffeine and alcohol in the West is precisely because they facilitate productivity and numbness respectively, without the kind of self-reflection that could lead to shifting societal conditions.

Body Autonomy documents the ways that prohibitions of sex work and drug use are both forms of social control, looking at the historical context predominantly in the United States and how racism has been intertwined with both the War on Drugs and the war on trafficking, with the brunt of the state violence from these failed projects landing on the bodies of Black, Indigenous, Brown, and Queer people, as well as the land.

If we cannot imagine having autonomy over our bodies (as long as we are not harming others), how can we imagine having the right to agency in our world? How can we imagine the right to clean water, healthy soil, and an environment that can support liveable futures for the next seven generations to come? An environment that makes us feel welcome, enables us to stay present and receive care rather than needing to escape for our own protection? *Body Autonomy* is an important piece of the puzzle in creating the coalitions and the movements we need in order to work toward this future. This book points to the longing that we feel to be in community, to feel deep care, to commune with our ancestors, and to explore pleasure and the ecstatic. It can provide a first step toward feeling that we have a right to a liveable planet and tapping into the agency to grow that with others. Are you willing to share your gifts for this broader vision?

The following are some of my prayers for this book and the ripples it will create in the collective:

> May we honor the sacredness of touch and altered states, while learning how to facilitate these moments of intimacy with harm reduction, consent, and deep care. May we compost the coercive, violent systems that have ripped us from communion with our bodies, the land, and a sense of wonder. May we create a world in which all beings can access safety, dignity, and belonging.

A Guide for Readers

THE ESSAYS, POEMS, AND ARTICLES HEREIN ARE ORGANIZED INTO FOUR sections which correspond to themes from my memoir, *Candy Coated*. The anthology accompanies the memoir but can be read separately. Most essays were written in 2019–2021; some older articles have been included to spark discussion, and others act as worksheets. I encourage readers to approach this collection like a Choose Your Own Adventure novel. The progression of essays moves from explanatory to visionary, tactical to ideological. So start with what is most interesting to you and hop around. If you don't like the content in one article, move on, but don't stop until you have wrestled with something. No matter what, you win.

The content between these two covers is critically insightful and powerful, and I can't say enough how amazing this anthology's contributors are. All authors are BIPOC. Other contributors including editors and design support are either BIPOC, transgender, drug users, sex workers, and/or felons. Put simply, this collection is brought to you by people most affected by interpersonal and state violence and exploitation; people who are invested in disrupting the status quo and breathing a new, safer, and more just world into being. Please read, follow, and support their work.

About the Authors and Contributors

Amira Barakat Al-Baladi—Author of "Sacred Stripper"

Amira Barakat Al-Baladi is an artist, writer, lover, and dreamer. Her podcast, Majnooni Confessions, highlights life from her point of view. As a queer Arab SWer and official Brown Girl Genius, she creates to insert a narrative that she rarely sees anywhere else. She draws upon her DNA-level knowing and extensive training and study of self-healing and community healing techniques to support other healers in developing their gifts through Heaven On Earth, a supportive spiritual community centering sex workers and survivors, featuring Reiki training for her community. Honoring her nomadic lineage, she has traveled and lived all over occupied Turtle Island before rooting down in New Orleans. You may know her by many names, just like any other Goddess. Follow her at www.hoesarehealers.com, on twitter @arabxgoddess, and IG @hoesarehealers.

Adiel Suarez-Murias—Editor of "Mechanics of the Sex Trade" and "Stimulant Stigma"

Adiel Suarez-Murias (she/her/ella) is a queer, Cuban communications brujx from South Florida who is committed to using her powers in service of social justice, liberation, and human rights. She brings to her work a guiding belief in the role of strategic communications and storytelling for good, and a background in rhetoric and comms theory. Adiel often sees her role as fire tender: keeping dialogues around communications alive within movements—as culture, context, and current events evolve.

Camille Barton—Foreword author

Camille Sapara Barton is a *Social Imagineer*, author, and embodied social justice facilitator dedicated to creating networks of care and livable futures. Since 2017, they have worked to ensure that psychedelic therapy will be accessible to BIPOC and other communities disproportionately impacted by the War on Drugs. Camille has taught within various programs for psychedelic therapists in training on topics including somatic grounding, embodied ethics, and intersectionality. Former clients include Alma Institute, Synthesis, CIIS, and MAPS. Their debut book, *Tending Grief: Embodied Rituals for Holding Our Sorrow and Growing Cultures of Care in Community*, is available now.

Ismail Lourido Ali—Coauthor of "Drug Policy to Break Intergenerational Curses"

Ismail Lourido Ali, JD, is committed to building the infrastructure for a just, equitable, and generative post-prohibition world. As Director of Policy at the Multidisciplinary Association for Psychedelic Studies (MAPS), Ismail advocates to eliminate barriers to psychedelic therapy and research, develops and implements legal and policy strategy, and supports MAPS' governance, nonprofit, and ethics work. Ismail is a founding board member of the Psychedelic Bar Association, currently serves on the board of directors for Sage Institute, and has previously served as Chair of the board of directors for Students for Sensible Drug Policy. He is also part of Chacruna Institute's Council for the Protection of Sacred Plants and on the advisory council for the Ayahuasca Defense Fund. Follow @sage_izzy and @MAPS for the latest and greatest psychedelic science and news.

Jade Joughin—Contributor to "Wars on Bodily Autonomy: A Timeline"

Jade Joughin is an adult performer and activist who works to advance the health and rights of GLBTQ people in the sex trade. Her work includes research, editing, and formatting.

Jasmine Tyler—Contributor to "Wars on Bodily Autonomy: A Timeline"

Jasmine L. Tyler is an Associate Professor of the Practice of Racial and Social Justice in the McCourt School of Public Policy at Georgetown University. Jasmine is also the Principal and Founder of Solidarity and Solutions, LLC, a boutique DC-based analytical consulting firm providing human rights and racial justice advocacy services as well as expertise and thought partnership in organizing, movement and coalition building, narrative shaping, and political strategy. Throughout her career, she has worked for several prominent nonprofit think tanks and advocacy organizations including Justice Policy Institute, Drug Policy Alliance, Open Society Foundations, and Human Rights Watch. Professor Tyler grew up visiting her father in prison, developing a keen early understanding of structural oppression in the US. She holds an MA from Brown University and a BS from James Madison University, both in sociology. She serves on boards for Free Minds Book Club and Writing Workshop and Students for Sensible Drug Policy. Follow Students for Sensible Drug Policy @SSDPofficial.

Jessica Peñaranda—Reviewer for "Healing-Centered Harm Reduction"

Jessica Peñaranda is a Queer (im)migrant woman of color, a human rights advocate, organizer, strategist, creative, and caretaker. Jessica has worked for over 14 years providing direct services, strategic leadership, program management, community building, and co-struggling with communities at intersecting identities impacted by systemic and interpersonal violence. Jessica is passionate about collective leadership and birthing communities of care through an intersectional and anti-oppressive healing justice frame-work with an emphasis on connection, cultural humility, mutual aid, and transformative justice. Jessica holds a master's degree in Human Rights from New York University and a BA degree in Women Studies from The College of New Jersey.

J Leigh Oshiro-Brantly—Author of "Pleasure as an Access Point"

J Leigh Oshiro-Brantly (they/them) is a longtime sex worker and survivor existing at the intersection of people, policy, research, and creativity. As a multi-racial Ryukyuan non-binary person who has lived with disabili-ties, poverty, food/housing instability, and violence, these experiences have informed their research, art, and advocacy. Serving at trans and sex worker rights organizations has been their career since 2016. They were an advisor for the Museum of the City of New York's Transgender Activism Exhibit and received the 2019 Marsha P. Johnson Community Leader Award from New York Transgender Advocacy Group, where they served as the president of the NY State Gender Diversity Coalition from 2019 to 2022. They have also curated sex worker film programming and spoken with media outlets such as *Time* magazine, *Vice* News, *TimeOUT NY*, and *Six Feet Apart with*

Alex Wagner. In addition to being a sexuality consultant for TV shows like Showtime's *Billions* and Fox's *The Following*, J Leigh loves surfing, their ancestors, Brazilian Jiu Jitsu, making epic charcuterie plates, and decolonizing their own pleasure.

Justice Rivera—Content collectrix; author of "Mechanics of the Sex Trade," "Exploitation Is to Sex Work as Overdose is to Drug Use," "Overview of Harm Reduction in the Sex Trade," and "Stimulant Stigma"; coauthor of "Wars on Bodily Autonomy Timeline"; and interviewer for "Bigger Picture of Trafficking."

Justice Rivera (she/they; ella/elle) is a writer, social justice consultant, harm reductionist, and pleasure activist based in San Juan, Puerto Rico. Justice's professional and artistic work is grounded in principles of harm reduction, anti-oppression, and healing justice. Her expressions, which come in many forms, seek to deconstruct carceral and punishment-driven paradigms to race, gender, and bodily autonomy. Justice has worked to provide direct services, organizing leadership, and capacity building support to people in the sex trade, survivors of trafficking, and people who use drugs in Denver, Washington DC, Seattle, and nationally. She is now a Partner with the QPOC-led harm reduction consulting company Reframe Health and Justice. This anthology was compiled in part through her 2019 Open Society Foundation Soros Justice Media Fellowship. When she isn't working, Justice loves to travel, cook, volunteer, and play with her cat, friends, and family. Follow Justice on twitter @justice_writes and IG @justicerivera_writes. Follow Reframe Health and Justice on Instagram @harmreductionfemmes.

Kate D'Adamo—Coauthor of "Wars on Bodily Autonomy: A Timeline"

Kate D'Adamo is a long-time sex worker rights advocate with a focus on economic justice, anti-policing and incarceration, and public health. Previously, she was the National Policy Advocate at the Sex Workers Project at the Urban Justice Center focusing on laws, policies, and advocacy impacting folks who trade sex, including the criminalization of sex work, anti-trafficking policies, and HIV-specific laws. Prior to joining the Sex Workers Project, Kate was a community organizer and advocate with the Sex Workers Outreach Project (SWOP) and Sex Workers Action New York. In this role, she developed programming to promote community building and provided peer support and advanced political advocacy to support the rights and well-being of people engaged in the sex trade both on and off the job. Kate cofounded Reframe Health and Justice in 2018 to help organizations with heart shift paradigms surrounding race, gender, bodily autonomy, and labor. She holds degrees from California Polytechnic State University and The New School. Follow Kate (@katedadamo) and Reframe (@reframehj) on twitter for current information on sex worker-centered harm reduction and healing justice.

Melodie Garcia—Author of "Fuck Myself into Heaven," coauthor of section openers

Melodie Garcia is an erotic service provider, harm reductionist, and writer hailing from the Pacific Northwest. Melodie draws on artistic concepts and lessons learned from psychedelia to inform her practice: spread love and deconstruct norms.

Monique Tula—Reviewer for "Healing-Centered Harm Reduction"

Monique Tula (she/her) is the former Executive Director of the National Harm Reduction Coalition. Monique has devoted her career to lifting the voices of people pushed into society's margins caused by capitalism and racial inequity. Central to her belief system is the deep awareness of our interconnectedness, regardless of individual circumstances. Her life's work is a conscious manifestation of the belief that harm to one is harm to us all. She aims to live each day in the moment, in pursuit of balance, personal growth, and discovery—some days are harder to do this than others. Mother of Christian, grandmother of Malcolm, and life partner of Adam, she lives in Los Angeles with her family and their two aggro black cats, Necro and Mancer.

Paula Kahn—Coauthor of "Drug Policy to Break Inter-generational Curses"

Paula is an artist, movement strategist, MPH candidate, and hxstory nerd working at the intersections of Indigenous rights; racial, migrant, environmental, and healing justice; drug policy; feminism; historical memory; and decarceration and demilitarization. Paula is interested in the roles of plants, psychoactives, ceremony, ritual and collective experiences in building historical memory, designing and implementing disarmament, demobilization, reintegration, and genocide prevention initiatives. They currently focus on abolishing the mass incarceration of immigrants in the US and enjoy building transnational networks for planetary rematriation. Born and raised in the working-class suburbs of Los Angeles, Paula descends from Mayan, Ashkenazi Jewish, and Iberian ancestries. Find out more about Paula @plurproductions on Instagram.

Presto Crespo—Author of "Black Trans Joy: A Love Letter to Poppy"

Presto Crespo (any/all) is a Black Latiné TGNC burgeoning pharmacological scientist, self-described "radical-combatant," storyteller, and advocate for drug users as well as those living with chronic pain. Heavily influenced by his birthplace/still current home in the Bronx, he identifies as a former and current lumpenized individual-former drug dealer and current drug user. Presto is an initiate of Ifa and uses the spiritual practice/science to guide their communal work and connections. Presto currently works in harm reduction with NEXT Distro, the New York State Department of Health Office of Drug User Health/The AIDS Institute, and as a freelance stylist.

Richael Faithful—Author of "Ancestral Healing for Liberation"

Richael Faithful (they/them/theirs) is a multidisciplinary folk healing artist and healing justice practitioner rooted in the African diasporic tradition of conjure. They were born in Washington, DC, and raised in Virginia, with a strong affinity to their southern family line in Georgia, Alabama, and Texas. Faithful supports national and local activists of all backgrounds, particularly leaders of Black Liberation movements. They are known for creating spaces to help activists identify and process trauma and invest into healing justice frameworks. Their work has been featured in national publications, including in Colorlines, The Root, Everyday Feminism, and HuffPost, among others. They also publish their own words in several books and law review articles. Faithful is former Shaman-in-Residence at Freed Bodyworks. Before formal shamanic initiation, Richael was a healing-oriented community organizer and peoples' lawyer. Learn about Ricahel's offerings at www.richaelfaithful.com.

Sasanka Jinadasa—Author of "Compassionate Sex Trade Approaches" and editor of "Healing-Centered Harm Reduction"

Sasanka Jinadasa is a strategist in Durham, North Carolina, working to end the oppression and criminalization of people who experience stigma and violence. As a consultant with Reframe Health and Justice, Sasanka has developed racial equity curricula, trained health departments on safer drug use, built capacity for nonprofits on reducing risks for people trading sex, and facilitated inter-movement conversations on healing justice, harm reduction, racial equity, and criminalization. They are committed to developing noncarceral solutions to addressing social injustices, particularly for Black and brown people, queer and trans people, and women and femmes. Sasanka received their undergraduate degree in Studies of Women, Gender, and Sexuality from Harvard University. Follow them on twitter @sasankajinadasa.

Shaan LaShun—Editor for "Overview of Harm Reduction in the Sex Trade"

Shaan Lashun (they/he) helps create resources to support sex workers, kinksters, and queer and trans people of color. He's cofounder of Molly House Project, a sex worker rights advocacy group for masc* providers. Lurk his thoughts and doings at shaanlashun.com.

Sinnamon Love—Afterword author

Sinnamon Love is a visual storyteller, community organizer, Black Feminist Pornographer, and Executive Director of BIPOC Collective, an organization providing financial assistance and increased access to mental health and wellness resources for Black and Brown sex workers. Sinnamon lives with a traumatic brain injury and identifies as a kinky, pansexual, solo-polyamorous grown-up, full-service sex worker, professional Dominatrix, and lifestyle switch. Love is a vibe curator, yogi, Hip Hop and House head, writer, cannabis enthusiast, recovering serial monogamist, #naturallygrey, and happily #singleinbrooklyn.

Victoria (Tory) Howell—Initial anthology formatting and design + website

Tory (she/her) is a graphic designer, web developer, and harm reductionist who believes design has the power to build movements that bring us closer to our liberation. She is eternally grateful to have worked with national and local organizations like National Harm Reduction Coalition, Sonoran Prevention Works, Smoke Works, and Poder in Action. Send her a book recommendation on instagram at @yucca_tory and find out more about her work at www.toryhowell.com.

zara raven—Author of "Abolishing Modern Day Slavery: When Aspects of the Afterlives of Slavery are Repackaged as Freedom"

zara raven is a Caribbean queer mama working to build safety through healing and transformative justice practice. zara is cocreator of many projects and campaigns working to interrupt state and interpersonal violence, including the DecrimNow DC and Decrim NY campaigns to end the criminalization of the sex trades in Washington, DC, and New York. zara's writing has been featured in *Teen Vogue, them,* and the *Washington Post,* and zara's work has been profiled in Slate, Upworthy, mic.com, *Rolling Stone, Hustler* magazine, and more.

Acknowledgments

THIS COLLECTION COULD NOT HAVE HAPPENED WITHOUT THE SUPPORT OF an Open Society Foundation Soros Justice Fellowship, which gave me the gifts of time and community investment. I also want to thank my business partners at Reframe Health and Justice Consulting (Reframe) for allowing me that time, my amazing partner and family for putting up with me, all the substances that helped me focus and chill out accordingly (psilocybin mushrooms, kratom, Vyvanse, Adderall, ibuprofen, caffeine, ketamine, alcohol, MDMA), the land that holds me which was stolen from the Duwamish people, my body that moves me, my panel of psychospiritual specialists that keep me clear and grounded, my ancestors living and past, and all of you for reading this. Salud.

In solidarity,
Justice Rivera

Introduction

LIKE MANY CREATIVE OR GESTATION PROCESSES, COLLECTING AND CON-
tributing to this anthology has taught me patience and flexibility. This
metamorphosis-centered community grew to include a vital constellation
of voices. And while the process was long and often messy, it was worth
it, because one thing remained clear: this book needed to be written. Its
urgency makes it imperfect—it couldn't include everything I wanted—but
the intersecting fallout from the current sociopolitical response to the sex
trade and the impacts of the War on Drugs cannot be ignored.

The mainstream media, heavily influenced by police, prosecutors, and
carceral feminists,[1] tells us that the presence of the sex trade causes exploitation and is, in-and-of itself, exploitative. It cites the demand for sex and sex
buyers as the problem. Their solution is to increase penalties and policing of
men (largely men of color) who buy or purvey sex, thereby regaining power,
filling jail/prison beds, and refinancing criminal legal system budgets that
have been reduced from drug policy reform gains. This carceral approach to
the sex trade disguised as a war on sex trafficking not only has devastating
impacts on marginalized communities but is also rooted in capitalist principles that ignore the daily realities of people in the sex trade.

Criminalization effectively creates an underground criminal market
which, in turn, lends itself to exploitation through the prison industrial
complex.[2] In *The New Jim Crow*, Michelle Alexander highlights how language in the 14th amendment of the US constitution continues the legacy
of Antebellum slavery using prison labor, the War on Drugs, and similar
criminal legal crusades.[3] The current US strategy to reduce exploitation is
exploitative, and it is harmful. The irony is that it harms those that it osten-
sibly seeks to protect.

In this anthology, I seek to engage others who have come to a similar
understanding of the ways that pervasive drug war tactics are being used to
further surveil and control marginalized populations through the war on
sex trafficking. These wars on bodily autonomy are rooted in the gendered,
racial, and economic biases encoded in our country's DNA, supported by a
constitution that has never evolved in a meaningful way.[4]

Body Autonomy underscores gendered and racialized *his*tory while highlighting the ways that it currently manifests in systems and policies that disproportionately and often unfairly impact BIPOC, women, queer and trans people, immigrants, and other traditionally marginalized communities. The concept of Body Autonomy was born from queer and trans sex workers and drug users of color, and communities who understand this intimately. It was born of people doing what they needed to do to survive and who have been punished because they have persisted.

Body Autonomy is intersectional. At its core, it is the understanding that our liberations are tied. It asks us to envision a world in which every person has what they need to thrive. Adiel Suarez-Murias, one of this anthology's community-based editors, explains, "In practice that would be systems that prioritize care, because that's how we all get free. This book is a window into ways in which that world is possible and what it can look like and feel like. So much of what it means to move towards bodily autonomy is to really practice it. This book is brought to you by people who are practicing liberation every day."

WHAT DOES IT MEAN TO SURVIVE? WHAT DOES SURVIVAL LOOK LIKE?

These questions are at the core of many issues at the nexus of economics, public safety, and public health—and the answers vary widely based on one's vantage point within the social hierarchy. Privilege refers to identities and experiences that are normalized in society, thereby providing control of systems and processes to people with these identities and experiences because they are seen as "good" and "normal." Someone who has grown up with access to resources, whether it be a good education, preferential treatment within social and professional networks, or direct financial support, is more likely to have what they need to endure and overcome hard times than someone who hasn't had similar access. Thus, it can be difficult for people with privilege, especially multiple privileges, to truly understand what daily basic survival means and looks like.

Understanding and honoring survival is necessary to create programs and policies that address and prevent violence and exploitation including human trafficking. Without the struggle to survive, people would rarely encounter or engage in exploitative situations. If poverty didn't exist, human trafficking would be rare. Media and political messages and propaganda tell a different story in order to reinforce the status quo.

Without critical examination, it is easy to believe that sex trafficking is rampant, and that increased state surveillance is necessary to keep suburban children safe from organized crime operations mainly comprised of men of color. Such messages are reminiscent of drug war propaganda suggesting that "just say no" policies and law enforcement intervention will save white people from drugs used and pushed by people of color in urban cities. The presence and impact of the modern-day overdose epidemic within white rural and suburban communities shines light on the erroneous and racist extent of such messaging.

WHAT DOES IT MEAN TO HEAL? WHAT DO WE NEED TO HEAL?

Healing, recovering, and expanding are incredibly personal. There is no one cookie-cutter way to heal. Healing is also political; communities of color hid or buried traditional cultural healing modalities for centuries to minimize the ways in which colonial interests weaponize and/or appropriate indigenous healing methods.[5] How we are allowed to heal and what "good healing" looks like continues to be literally prescribed by people with the most power and privilege, determining which forms of healing are legitimate and who gets access to them.

This book unpacks what it means to heal in America through the lens of Healing Justice—a liberatory approach that asks us to center individual and collective healing in our fights for survival, freedom, and restitution.[6] I offer the contents of this book to those who are ready to complicate their understanding of survival and healing, to all who are seeking to know more about underground economies, and to everyone who knows that punishment doesn't lead to liberation and wants something different but might not know where to start, or how to continue, or where to end.

SECTION ONE

Wars on Body Autonomy

This section illustrates how ideological wars in the US are all rooted in and continue to perpetuate racism and xenophobia. When one ideological war ceases to be effective for population control and expansion of federal powers, another is used. This is a primer on the sex trade and an examination of ways in which the wars on drugs and sex trafficking continue in parallel, grounding 200 years of history in the sociopolitical context of the 2020s.

Mechanics of the Sex Trade: An Introduction

JUSTICE RIVERA

UNDERSTANDING THE SEX TRADE REQUIRES RECOGNIZING THE MANY moving parts of the industry as well as the variety of ways people participate in it, which are directly influenced by economic and sociopolitical dynamics. This essay explains key elements of the sex trade including different types of sex work, the continuum of sex work, sex trade push factors, coercion within the sex trade, the legal anti-trafficking framework, and the umbrella of criminalization surrounding the sex trade. To begin, I would like to offer a definition of sex work as "a commercial exchange of a sexual service for money or other benefits like housing, transportation, and other survival needs" (Sex Workers Outreach Project Chicago, 2016).

The term "sex work" was coined in the 1970s by Carol Leigh, a sex worker and labor rights activist, who wanted to call attention to the reality that sexual service is labor. Sex work is used to refer to a broad range of transactions and is a term that has been adopted by health, labor, and human rights organizations including Amnesty International and the World Health Organization. "Sex worker" is used to refer to people of all genders, ages, and backgrounds who are involved in the supply side of the sex trade (Reframe Health and Justice, 2018).

"Prostitution" is a defined crime which encompasses some forms of sex work, but its meaning may shift based on jurisdiction or enforcement pattern. It is a better practice to use the term "prostitution" when referring to laws and criminal-legal practices and use the term "sex work" when describing the broader practice or issue. Individuals who engage in these exchanges may individually refer to themselves through different terminology, and "sex workers" includes many people who do not personally adopt that term as one of identity or practice.

The definition above highlights that sex work is an exchange between two or more people where one party provides a service that is sexual in nature and the other provides something of economic value in return. Some may choose to trade sexual services for necessities such as shelter, food, drugs, and clothing. These individuals may or may not recognize themselves as participating in the sex trade and are referred to as "survival sex workers."

Thus, the sex trade can be formal or informal. Formal sex work refers to someone who acknowledges their participation in the sex trade or themselves as sex workers. Informal sex work refers to people who participate in the sex trade but don't recognize their actions as such or themselves as a sex worker due to the nature of patriarchy, stigma, or other factors. Formal sex work is often safer because it enables individuals to practice safety measures including violence prevention, safe sex practices, and intentional mental hygiene.

The use of "formal" and "informal" also applies to segments of the economy that people work and exist in. The formal economy refers to parts of the sex trade which are legal and regulated such as stripping and webcam modeling. Informal economies, also known as underground or shadow economies,[1] exist apart from the formal capitalist market and are a byproduct of decreasing access to the formal market through criminalization. Informal sex work includes full-service sex work in most of the United States.

There are many different types of sex work, each with different benefits and drawbacks. It is not uncommon for someone to try different involvements in the sex trade before finding the type of sex work that fits best with their needs or lifestyle or simply deciding sex work isn't for them. In this way, the sex trade isn't dissimilar from the restaurant industry, or many other industries. Someone might start as a hostess and like the hours and nature of the work but dislike the brief customer interactions and pay. They then become a waitress and appreciate the social interaction and physical movement, but customers can be rude and working with the kitchen staff isn't their favorite. Next, they become a bartender where they make more money and appreciate the nature of customer interactions. The drawback is that they are expected to work late hours, and bartending can be dangerous.

A comparable trajectory in the sex trade might look like someone starting as a stripper where they like the money and ease of access to the local club but don't like the hours or working for third-party management. Next, they try camming because they want to control their own hours but find the tech and clothing that is required to do well hindersome. They save up enough to start their own business as an independent erotic masseuse where they now can control their own schedule, have authentic relationships with return clients, and make enough money to live comfortably. The drawback is that their work is criminalized, and stigma prevents them from being honest with their loved ones about what they do.

Many of the drawbacks and risks associated with sex work are a result of the current sociopolitical response to sex work, which relies on criminalization, policing, and incarceration to temper underground economies. These approaches create conditions that lead to violence, exploitation, and infectious disease by pushing the sex trade further underground. Illegal forms of sex work are the easiest to enter but often the most dangerous, partly because criminalization reduces workers' safety options. Without being able to openly work, people have a hard time accessing safe sex supplies or safe spaces to work. As a result, workers are often left without the information or tools to prevent sexually transmitted infections, sexual assault, and exploitative encounters. In these ways, criminal legal approaches to the sex trade are counterproductive.

Within legal forms of sex work like stripping, camming, and porn, over-regulation limits accessibility, making it more difficult for people without means to participate. People must have an ID, computer, internet access, a space to work out of, and specialty clothing or toys to strip or cam. Even in legal regimes, there are still traditional workplace problems such as high fees to participate, lack of worker protections, and restrictions on what workers can or cannot do or say. For example, strip clubs often require workers to pay by the day, and management might not treat sexual harassment in clubs seriously.

Despite the limited accessibility, legal sex work is the part of the industry where workers can better avoid arrest and exposure to sexually transmitted infections. The chart and descriptions below explain different types of sex work, the legality of each, and the primary associated potential benefits and drawbacks.

TYPES OF SEX WORK

Full-service sex work means that a range of direct-contact sexual services are offered such as oral and penetrative sex. Each individual service provider sets their own limits on what acts they will or will not engage in, as

Full service	Massage	Phone Sex Operator	Camming
Dancing/Stripping	Fetish	Porn	Sugaring

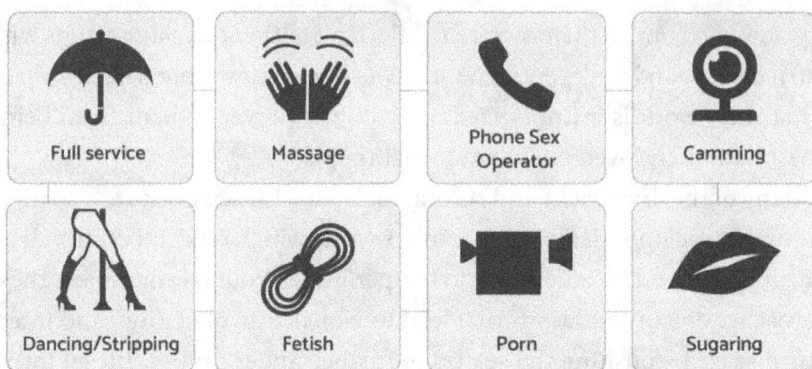

well as their own price structure or menu. Full-service sex work includes escorts who advertise online and street-based sex workers, many of whom are being paid for their time and emotional support for clients in addition to sexual services. Full-service sex work is currently illegal everywhere in the United States except for ten counties in Nevada where escorts must work out of licensed brothels to avoid the risks of criminalization.[2]

Full-service work can be done independently, through the management of an agency or manager, or collectively. (I don't like the word "pimp" because it is racialized. If you don't believe me, do a Google image search right now.) When done independently, the draw to full-service sex work is the accessibility and money potential. Workers don't need to apply or show ID to get the job, people with disabilities and chaotic schedules can do well, and workers get paid immediately as opposed to waiting for a check in two weeks. The drawbacks of full-service sex work include the greatest stigma, exposure to STIs, increased risk of physical and sexual violence, increased potential of trafficking, and the greatest exposure to police surveillance. All these risks are compounded by criminalization.

The draw to work for a third party is that the management usually takes care of administrative and marketing tasks, which can be very time consuming for individuals, and offers a knowledge base they don't possess, including taking pictures, posting ads, screening clients, scheduling, and maintaining a place to work. The third party can also offer some degree of protection, but in return takes a cut of the worker's earnings.

Full Body Sensual Massage (FBSM) and tantra are specialty services that are most commonly not full service. FBSM is widely known as a massage with a "happy ending." Because of its aspects of sexual exchange, FBSM is criminalized like full-service sex work, which means it is illegal outside of brothels in Nevada. Tantra is an erotic practice that helps people connect to and control their sexual energy through breath work, visualization, and other techniques. Tantric practices exist in a gray area of legality, as tantra consists of many spiritual principles and practices; however, where erotic touch and guidance is offered for pay, it is illegal.

The draws to being an erotic masseuse and/or tantrica are that these services are known as healing services; they pay well but don't require penetration therefore reducing the potential of STIs and pregnancy; and a license isn't currently required to do the work, allowing for easier access. Drawbacks include navigating the isolation and fear that accompanies sex work and that both massage and tantra provision are labor intensive.

Sometimes, full-service sex workers also offer specialty services. Another specialty service that may or may not be full-service is **Bondage and Discipline, Domination and Submission, Sadism and Masochism (BDSM)** and **fetish work**. Here, Dominatrixes, Pro-submissives, and switches help clients break free from sexual and societal norms through activities such as power play, pain, pegging, and intentional role play. BDSM and fetish work is arguably the most skilled work as it requires knowledge of a variety of techniques and equipment. The draw toward this type of work is the power and healing that it provides both the client and provider and that it is less competitive than the **girlfriend experience** (GFE, which escorts often provide). The drawbacks include the amount of time it takes to become a competent fetish provider, the amount of money needed to get equipment necessary to do well, and the potential liability involved if someone sustains a non-intentional injury.

Sugaring refers to a sugar baby and sugar daddy/sugar mommy relationship. There are a handful of websites and apps where people can find someone who will buy them nice things and give them an allowance in return for an ongoing—often sexual—relationship. Typically, sugar babies get paid a monthly allowance or pay-per-meet (PPM) rate, rather than an hourly rate like those charged by full-service escorts. Sugaring is in a legal gray area. Sugaring sites can stay in existence because they promise to connect sugar daddies and mommies to sugar babies who will provide companionship— these sites are less scrutinized than full-service advertising boards but still could get shut down easily.

To prevent closure, site administration prohibits people from discussing money directly on the site and leads to the expulsion of sugar babies from sites for "escorting behavior" if they push that boundary. The draw for sugar babies is that sugaring offers the possibility of a long-term arrangement that can meet their basic needs, including potential direct support for housing and transportation, etc. The main drawback is that many people, especially sugar daddies and mommies, don't see these arrangements as sex work, so sugar babies have little negotiating power surrounding money and safe sex practices.

Phone sex operators provide auditory sexual fantasies. Phone sex operation is legal in the United States and most providers work through a company or third-party host. The draws towards being a phone sex operator are the legal nature of the work, flexible hours, and the fact that there is no direct sexual contact or visual requirement. Phone sex operators can also work confidentially from the comfort and safety of their own homes. The drawback is that it pays less than other forms of sex work, so it is often used in conjunction with other forms of sex work or as an auxiliary form of employment.

Camming, shorthand for webcam modeling, is a legal form of sex work where someone with a web cam streams sexual or suggestive content to viewers. Many cam models work for a company or third party, and others work for themselves by hosting content from their own site. The draws to camming are similar to those of phone sex operation, though cam models relinquish privacy by inviting viewers to see their faces and bodies. In exchange, cam models typically make more per minute, though drawbacks include needing reliable access to computer equipment and internet access, private space, and a bank account for direct deposits.

Stripping is a legal form of sex work where the stripper performs promiscuous dances with little to no clothing on. Most dances are done to music on a stage with a pole, and clients can request private dances. The draws toward stripping are that it is legal, offers nighttime hours, and that the club does its own marketing and potentially offers protection from sexual assault. The drawbacks are often the reverse side of the same coin: irregular hours and pay, stage fees and tipouts that reduce net profits, often inebriated clientele, and potentially abusive or negligent third-party management.

Pornography is the filming of actors and actresses, called porn stars, in sexual acts. The filming and distribution of porn is protected by the first amendment, making it legal if everyone involved is a consenting adult (though local exemptions and inclusions complicate this in different states). Porn can be made through a third-party or independently, called amateur porn. Pornographic acting is attractive to people wishing to use sexuality as an artistic medium, often within a regulated environment. The drawback is that it can be a very hard industry to break into professionally and make a living wage. Additionally, even though porn stars use a stage name, most show their face on film, which can then easily be found on the internet and potentially lead to shame and moral ostracization despite the legal nature of the work.

Each of these types of sex work also carries with it a distinct screening burden. Screening refers to the ways in which a sex worker checks out clients to protect themselves against violence and arrest. Independent, full-service sex workers are most likely to institute screening, as they are the most vulnerable to individual and structural violence, and the criminalized nature of their work prevents other safeguards. Screening for a street-based sex worker includes talking with a client outside of the car to get a gut-check on the person before getting in. Whereas for an internet-based escort, screening includes asking for referrals from other providers the client has seen before. Screening is utilized less for forms of sex work that require less direct contact. Finally, one of the benefits of working for a third-party is the potential of built-in screening and protection.

CONTINUUM OF SEX WORK

The type of work that someone is doing within the sex industry and where a person is working are two main factors that help determine a worker's profit, safety, and well-being. The third factor is how someone is approaching the work, or the mindset they are in when they are doing it. To introduce this concept, I like to refer to Norman Zinberg's theory of drug, set, setting[3] in which he discusses three interdependent variables that, combined, determine the outcome of a person's drug use.

This concept can be applied to the sex trade. One primary distinction when doing so is that sex work, unlike drug use, is driven by economic push factors. Ultimately, people sell sex or the illusion of sex because their sexuality makes money. The ease with which people can access that money and their autonomy in doing so are important distinctions in understanding how sex work differs from sex trafficking, and the foundation for a continuum of consent known within the sex workers rights movement as Choice, Circumstance, and Coercion, or the 3 Cs model (Sex Workers Outreach Project):

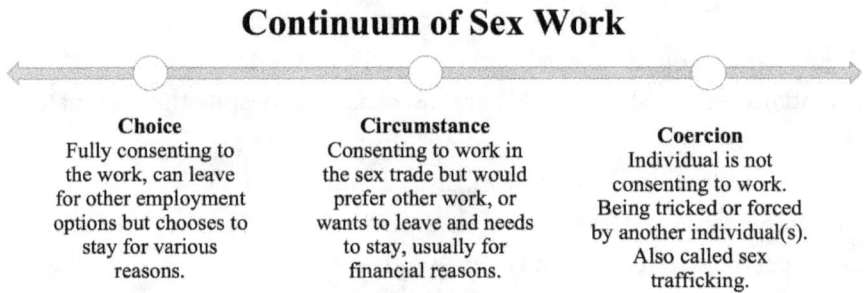

Continuum of Sex Work

Choice	Circumstance	Coercion
Fully consenting to the work, can leave for other employment options but chooses to stay for various reasons.	Consenting to work in the sex trade but would prefer other work, or wants to leave and needs to stay, usually for financial reasons.	Individual is not consenting to work. Being tricked or forced by another individual(s). Also called sex trafficking.

The graphic above (Reframe Health and Justice, 2018) helps explicate how economic push factors affect people's mindset to work. Choice-based sex work describes periods where a person has significant access to a variety of resources. They could do other work but choose sex work because it is the best option for them at the time for a variety of reasons and priorities. This continuum also refers to pathways of entry into the sex trade. Someone who starts in the industry as a choice-based sex worker can leave or refuse a date and still have other accessible survival options. This security often means that a person has less exposure to violence and infectious disease by allowing them to enforce their rates, safety practices, and screening processes without making compromises motivated by economic need.

Circumstantial sex work describes periods where someone has limited access to resources but continues to have a high degree of autonomy in their work and life. Despite wanting other work, they might not be able to get a living-wage job in the formal economy for a variety of reasons, so sex work is the best option to meet their survival needs at that time. To further paint a picture of how workers in each category engage in their work and the broader systemic issues at play, the following are some circumstances that make sex work work. Since sex work is directly impacted by economic push factors, here's what you need to know about the ways each of these groups might engage in sex work and why:

Age: For young adults without support or access to resources, a limited job history impedes their access to profitable labor. The sex trade provides an opportunity to make better money than most entry-level positions without obtaining expensive and time-consuming degrees or certificates. Minors without the support of a guardian are denied jobs in the formal economy and have no choice but to turn to the informal economy to support themselves.[4]

Gender presentation and sexual orientation: Surveys of people in the sex trade show that a disproportionate number of transgender women are involved in the sex trade.[5] Transphobia leads both to transgender youth being kicked out of their homes and to widespread discrimination in hiring or social services. In her book *Redefining Realness*,[6] Janet Mock talks about hormone replacement therapy and confirmation surgery as her primary survival need and push factor into sex work. Her story echoes that of many other trans women whose gender presentation is a barrier in finding sustainable work and housing.

Similarly, a survey done in 2013 through Street Wise and Safe and the John Jay School of Criminology[7] illustrates that queer-identifying people have the highest rates of involvement in the sex trade and that young queer women are most at risk of exploitation within the sex trade due to reduced access to upward mobility through formal-economy employment or marriage. A survey of Sex Worker Outreach Project members conducted in 2019 shows that over 80 percent of sex-work organizers are LGBTQ. Transgender workers are most likely to experience isolated acts of extreme physical and sexual violence, as opposed to exploitation, because to exploit someone, their worth must first be recognized. Every year on December 17, sex workers who have been lost to non-natural deaths are recognized across the world as part of the International Day to End Violence Against Sex Workers. Databases such as the one kept by SWOP USA[8] show disparities in which identities experience the most murder.

Dependents (children, parents): Taking care of dependents is both time consuming and expensive. The sex trade offers flexible hours and good money. Being a sex worker and a parent is a delicate matter since Child Protective Services sees a parent's sex work as harmful to children, even when the parent is providing for all the child's needs and the child is unaware of the parent's work or sexual activity.[9] Furthermore, in child custody battles, a mother's status as a sex worker has been seen as more egregious than a father's unemployment, promiscuity, or record of abuse.[10]

Criminal record: Once charged with a felony, the collateral consequences of a criminal conviction impede people's ability to find housing and employment. Felon discrimination is practiced by employers and housing providers across the United States, though a rising number of cities are joining the movement to "ban the box," suggesting that people's merits should be considered before past experiences with the criminal justice system.[11] Such policies recognize that, without a way to make ends meet, people with records are often left with few options but to return to underground, criminalized labor.

Even with misdemeanors, repeat offenses (often survival offenses such as petty theft), failure-to-appear charges, and three strike rules[12] create a cycle of arrest and incarceration that can be difficult to break out of. A 2018 CNN report highlighted that two-thirds of people in jails aren't convicted, meaning that most prisoners cannot afford bail and incur incarceration-related debt.[13] Such policies effectively criminalize poverty by placing certain economic expectations on people who clearly can't meet them.[14]

The stigma associated with a prostitution charge is so severe that it is undifferentiated from the systemic discrimination of a felony charge. For example, an employer or leasing agency that finds a prostitution record isn't empowered to turn down the person based on their record but will likely discriminate based on the record and choose someone else instead. Furthermore, sex workers may receive trafficking-related felonies due to the expanded liability of working collectively, as well as poor training among law enforcement to distinguish between trafficking and the sex trade more broadly. Trafficking felonies carry deep stigma and, in some places, require sex-offender registration.[15] In this way, people are punished for doing sex work and then pushed back into sex work, only to be punished for it again.

Documentation status: In her book *Revolting Prostitutes*,[16] Juno Mac discusses the myriad of ways that the criminalization of sex work and the war on sex trafficking are really about controlling migration. Harsh immigration laws push undocumented people toward sex work because gaining access to a formal-economy job without documentation can be nearly impossible without committing other crimes such as fraud. Additionally, there are few pathways toward citizenship in the United States, and those pathways take many months and often years to complete when they are available. Desperation and fear of deportation leave undocumented people vulnerable to sexual, financial, and physical exploitation, especially trafficking into other forms of labor.[17]

Disability status: People with physical and mental disabilities experience employment discrimination despite the Americans with Disabilities Act (ADA) protections that mandate and even give tax breaks for organizations that provide people with the necessary tools they need to complete a job. Furthermore, some people with disabilities are unable to work full-time jobs, but accessing disability benefits can take years, and are often not enough to survive on. The sex trade might be an attractive option for people with disabilities who desire to make more money per hour than they can in other forms of work, make their own hours, and disclose their disability status if and how they want.

Access to stable housing: Housing is consistently named as the most immediate need for street-based and survival sex workers.[18] Unstable housing means that many homeless femmes and Men who have Sex with Men (MSM) are put in positions where they begin trading sex for shelter. This puts them at risk of exploitation by their housing provider or creates a glass ceiling where people are "motel homeless"—paying weekly to keep a room, sometimes for years. In this situation, people work to keep their motel room but are rarely able to make enough money to secure more stable housing. Saving enough to put down a security deposit and first month's rent for an apartment remains beyond reach financially—and often impossible for other reasons (see criminal record, gender, and documentation status points above). Despite being chronically homeless, sex workers who are motel homeless are often missed by homeless service organizations, most of which are designed to reach people sleeping on the streets.

Access to living-wage employment: Minimum wage hasn't been a living wage since the 1960s. As Andrew Bloomenthal notes in "Can a Family Survive on the US Minimum Wage?":

> Full-time employees earning the federal minimum annually pocket just $15,080, placing them well below the $23,850 poverty line—even for families of two. And minimum-wage

earners with families of four fall almost $9,000 below the poverty line. Pay is not the only problem. Many companies don't offer full-time hours, even when workers want them. Fluctuating schedules, split shifts, and the dreaded "clopening" (closing the store at night, then reporting back to work early the next morning to open it), make it difficult for employees to work second jobs, attend college classes, or arrange child care.[19]

The current sociopolitical market creates a vacuum where entering the underground economy is the best or only option many people have to survive.

Race and Ethnicity: The legacy of slavery in the United States is one in which white people have significant advantage in accessing wealth through inheritance, education, hiring, and promotion. Even today, the wealth gap between white Americans and Black Americans is widening, and for every $100 in white family wealth, Black families hold just $5.04.[20] For this reason, a large percentage of people in the sex trade, especially the survival sex trade, are people of color. Femmes of color also experience higher rates of sexual assault, police violence, and sex trafficking than white counterparts due to racialized perceptions of who is a victim versus who is a criminal.[21]

Racial profiling combined with racialized narratives about what a trafficker looks like mean that most people who are arrested for "soliciting a prostitute" and third-party charges are men of color. The sad irony about the prison industrial complex is that laws are used to reinforce the loophole in the 14th amendment that says that slavery is illegal except for as punishment for a crime. Thus, people of color are funneled into jails and prisons where they are forced to work, making license plates, underwear, to-go coffee cups, and many of the products that Americans commonly and unknowingly purchase and use daily. The same people who insensitively and erroneously call human trafficking "modern day slavery" somehow believe that "slavery" can be eradicated by using slavery, that the remedy for violence and exploitation is a violent and exploitative criminal legal system.

Status as student, educational background: The enormity of student loan debt, as well as difficulty making ends meet living solely off student loans—for those who have access to them—means that an increasing number of students are turning to sex work to support their living expenses.[22] Many face stigmas in doing so and choose to remain silent about their work. Despite not needing an education to enter or succeed in the sex trade, educated sex workers are largely able to charge more and get higher paying clients who are looking for sophisticated companions. Sometimes, highly educated people become career sex workers because of the flexibility and pay provided.

Geographic location, transportation needs: Similar to the way people end up trading sex for housing and shelter, people who are hitchhiking or in need of transportation are sometimes solicited for sexual services in exchange for transportation. People in geographically isolated areas and with lower socioeconomic status are more likely to exchange sex for transportation.

Currently on social benefits: Social Security Disability Insurance (SSDI), Temporary Assistance of Needy Families (TANF), food stamps, Medicaid, and other forms of social and public benefits all impose income caps, and SSDI imposes hourly work caps. Benefits alone are rarely enough to live on, and a wide gap exists between being impoverished enough to receive public benefits and earning a living wage. Sometimes, people who receive benefits must find other unrecorded ways to make money that don't jeopardize their benefits. Sex work is one such option.

THE POLITICS OF CIRCUMSTANCE

Circumstantial sex workers often do sex work for a period of time to get by. People can move back and forth along the Choice, Circumstance, and Coercion continuum during their time in the industry. There are countless ways this might happen. Someone who is doing sex work circumstantially could get connected with friends in the industry who support their professional development, thereby increasing their profit, safety, and contentment with their work and moving them closer to Choice on the continuum. Alternatively, sex work can help someone survive until they get a job that is a better fit for them, moving them off the continuum altogether.

The lack of resources and access to resources inherent in circumstantial sex work mean that a person in this situation has increased exposure to infectious disease, violence, exploitation, and arrest. For example, while unprotected sex is nearly unheard of among higher-paid escorts, someone engaging in circumstantial sex work who has greater unmet needs and therefore a necessity to take more clients and do more per session, may choose to take the risk. This dynamic could also play out when negotiating sexual services with someone who isn't willing to provide screening information—someone with fewer financial options might be willing to take this risk as well because of the pressing need for immediate income, putting them at infinitely higher risk of sexual assault, most often without recourse.

As laws pass across the United States that limit people's ability to work anonymously online,[23] many formerly choice-based sex workers are left with few options but to hit the streets, increasing their chances of getting arrested or assaulted.[24] These policies, often masked as anti-trafficking measures, actually increase these workers' vulnerability to sex trafficking by making them targets. In 2018, one study of 260 sex workers following the seizure of Backpage.com, a global adult advertising site, showed that 60 percent of sex workers reported an increase in advances and threats by someone looking to manage and potentially exploit or hurt them.[25] By limiting the autonomy of sex workers, these laws create an environment ripe for exploitation and coercion.

COERCION AND TRAFFICKING

In the 3 Cs model, coercion refers to points and periods of time where someone has little to no autonomy over the work they do, and a third party is controlling their movements and resources. The presence of coercion does not automatically mean that trafficking is occurring, as coercion is much broader. Trafficking is a legal definition for an experience of exploitation through force, fraud, or coercion by a third party which has multiple elements required for its proof. Similar to other issues of harm and injustice, trafficking is a legal limit which exists within a broader sphere, like the legal definition of rape exists within the broader scope of sexual assault or harm. It is also important to note that coercion does not necessarily mean that the person being coerced does not have access to resources, as evidenced by Jasmine, a self-described sex trafficking survivor and advocate I spoke to who publicly shares her story of being pimped out from a mansion and driving a Mercedes that her pimp bought her.[26] In many cases, despite being exploitative, a coercive situation meets a worker's resource needs, and might be the best option out of a range of terrible options.

Choice, circumstance, and coercion

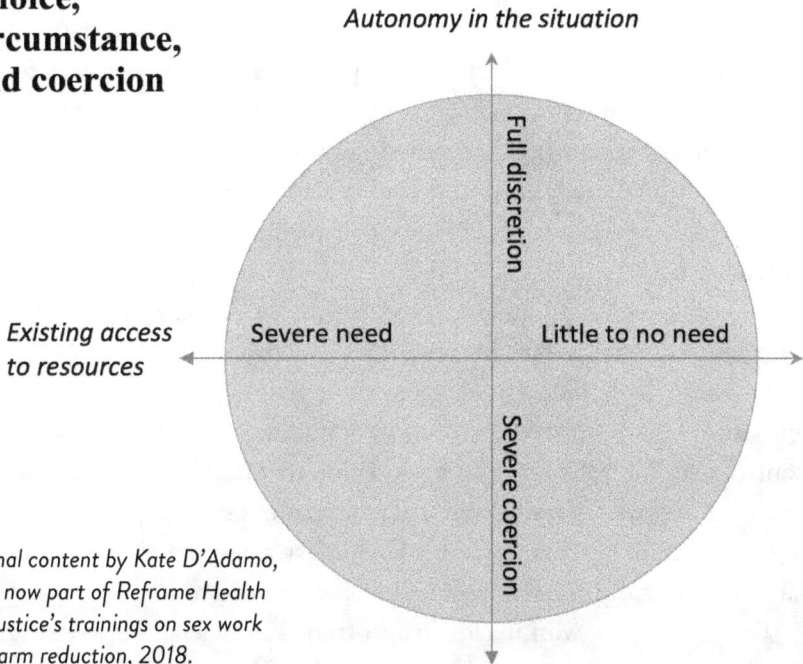

Autonomy in the situation

Full discretion

Existing access to resources ← Severe need | Little to no need →

Severe coercion

Original content by Kate D'Adamo, 2017; now part of Reframe Health and Justice's trainings on sex work and harm reduction, 2018.

The graphic above is a tool to help ascertain what constitutes coercion. The upper righthand quadrant represents a circumstance where someone can find, screen, and see clients in the way they choose. They are in control of their circumstances, even if they have a manager or coworker.

Exploitation includes everything below the horizontal line. Exploitation does not, however, automatically mean coercion. In her article, "Five Faces of Oppression," Iris Young states:

> Exploitation uses capitalism to oppress. The economic theory of capitalism states that people are free to exchange goods freely. Yet, whenever this has happened throughout history, it has created different classes of people: wealthy and poor . . . Therefore, exploitation creates a system that perpetuates class differences, keeping the rich richer and the poor poorer.[27]

The lower righthand quadrant represents a circumstance where another person is in full control of the worker's situation, circumstances, and how much money they make from trading sex. This might be a manager, partner, or friend. This quadrant helps explain that not all third-party management is exploitative. Most forms of sex work that are currently legal in the United States put power in the hand of third-party management, as well as faith in these companies and managers to honor and protect workers' bodies (though it's worth noting that sometimes this doesn't happen). Once legality is removed, there is an almost automatic assumption that underground third-party management is coercive or violent, but both these things can be true or not.

The upper lefthand quadrant of the graphic represents those workers with high autonomy but low resources. An example of someone in this situation might include a single mom and exotic dancer struggling to make ends meet. She is worried that she might not make rent this month but has control over her schedule and a good club to work at. The lower lefthand quadrant represents trafficking. Lack of resources is the primary trafficking vulnerability factor. Someone who doesn't desperately need money is harder to trick or threaten into doing what you want.

During my time working for an anti-trafficking agency between 2011 and 2014, I worked with many young adults who went in and out of homelessness. At some point, handfuls of them met someone who provided them housing (often this was a family member). For example, instead of paying rent, one of my participants, Nick, provided sex acts to clients that the person he was living with found for him. The person offering housing did all the negotiation, so Nick didn't have much control over those interactions. After Nick made rent, he could keep everything else he made, but it wasn't much. Nick had the option to leave, but then he would be living on the street again.

Sometimes, someone's entry into the sex trade is through coercive means, but after leaving the exploitative situation, that person comes back to the sex trade to work independently. Returning to the idea of the continuum of sex work as "set" in sex work, set, setting: the 3 Cs can be applied to someone's entry into the sex trade, where they are at economically on the continuum generally, and where they are economically during a specific day or interaction within the sex trade. When considered as "set," and combined with type of work and setting, it is easier to understand an individual or type of person's needs—knowledge which is particularly helpful for professionals who are working directly with people in the sex trade or creating policies that impact people in the sex trade.

As indicated earlier, coercion is broader than trafficking, though the two are often used interchangeably.[28] To understand how the legal definition of trafficking is applied—and how it can be helpful or harmful for people in the sex trade—it is important to begin by unpacking the federal definition of human trafficking found in the Trafficking Victims Protection Act of 2000:[29]

> **Sex trafficking:** (a) Whoever knowingly—(1) in or affecting interstate or foreign commerce, or within the special maritime and territorial jurisdiction of the United States, recruits, entices, harbors, transports, provides, obtains, advertises, maintains, patronizes, or solicits by any means a person; or
>
> (2) benefits, financially or by receiving anything of value, from participation in a venture which has engaged in an act described in violation of paragraph (1), knowing, or, except where the act constituting the violation of paragraph (1) is advertising, in reckless disregard of the fact, that means of force, threats of force, fraud, coercion described in subsection (e)(2), or any combination of such means will be used to cause the person to engage in a commercial sex act, or that the person has not attained the age of 18 years and will be caused to engage in a commercial sex act, shall be punished as provided in subsection (b).
>
> **Labor Trafficking:** the recruitment, harboring, transportation, provision, or obtaining of a person for labor or services, through the use of force, fraud, or coercion for the purpose of subjection to involuntary servitude, peonage, debt bondage, or slavery.

Here, we see that sexual labor is separated from other forms of labor trafficking and is defined, in part, by age. Adults in the sex trade experience trafficking when another person uses force, fraud, or coercion to compel the victim to perform sex work, thereby making money off the sex worker's labor. The primary indicator of trafficking is the means by which the exploiter compels the victim to engage in the sex trade. The elements of force, fraud, or coercion must be present for a situation to be considered trafficking. In other words, trafficking involves an action (recruiting, enticing, harboring, transporting, providing, obtaining, advertising, maintaining, patronizing, or soliciting), a means (force, fraud, or coercion), and a purpose (benefiting financially or receiving anything of value).

By this definition, sex work is, in and of itself, different than sex trafficking . . . unless the sex worker is a minor. The second part of this definition begins to conflate sex work with trafficking by stating that anyone involved in the sex trade who is under the age of 18, with or without the presence of a third party, is a victim of trafficking. This language is an attempt by social workers and child advocates to place minors involved in the sex trade in social services rather than juvenile detention. To reinforce this provision, Safe Harbor laws, passed in 34 states, mandate that minors in the sex trade be detained and connected to a child protection services agent rather than booked into jail on a prostitution offense.[30] According to a participatory action study by the Young Women's Empowerment Project, these laws put too much faith in a broken and often abusive child welfare system:

> Girls are denied help from systems such as DCFS, police and the legal system, hospitals, shelters, and drug treatment programs because of their involvement in the sex trade, because they are trans girls or because they are queer, because they are young, because they are homeless, and because they use drugs. Girls in the sex trade face exclusion and neglect when accessing shelter and other services. Abuse in foster care is both systemic and personal—as girls reported being physically and emotionally abused by foster parents and threats that DCFS would take their children away.
>
> In examining the data sets, we found the threads of violence and trauma throughout. But these girls don't see themselves or want to be seen as victims. They are survivors of violence and they resist the systems of oppression that define their lives, and use their own methods of resiliency. The more they resist by standing up for themselves with police or service providers—getting to know their rights—the more resilient they become in all aspects of their lives. And the more they engage in self care and harm reduction and building support networks—the

more they are able to resist the violence that permeates their lives.[31]

Human trafficking is a legal construct. First, it is a way to prosecute crimes. There are very few trafficking convictions, however, because it is hard to prove fraud or coercion, and force is rarely used due to this method's inefficiency in keeping exploited people around. Despite Hollywood's adoration of *Taken*[32] narratives, the reality is that people who are physically forced to work run as soon as they can. In contrast, it only takes 72 hours to get someone under your psychological control, and trauma bonding is a way more effective way of making money off someone else.[33] Also known as Stockholm Syndrome, trauma bonding is a means of psychological control that distorts and plays upon a victim's love for the abuser. Furthermore, it is harder to get caught or be held accountable for perpetrating psychological abuse.

Around 2013, instead of exploring transformative justice measures,[34] lawmakers began expanding trafficking-related charges and the definition of who is a trafficker to make more trafficking prosecutions. The outcome is overly broad and vague legal language that positions sex workers and their peers, community, and family members as traffickers.[35]

Trafficking as a legal construct can also be used to access victim benefits such as a T-Visa, victims of crime compensation, restitution, vacating convictions, case management or other service provision, or if a survivor needs law enforcement involvement. The margins for being able to access these benefits are very narrow, requiring cooperation in bringing charges against the exploiter(s), working with law enforcement, and repeatedly telling stories of victimization. Many people don't want to participate in this process for fear of retaliation from their exploiter(s) or community.

Furthermore, many victims of trafficking have had negative experiences with law enforcement, making this process even more difficult. Many other victims try to cooperate but don't make it all the way through legal proceedings, then having nothing to show for days or months of laborious talks with police, lawyers, and case managers and, if someone is undocumented, may themselves face potential deportation. This broken trafficking victim support system is the result of the legal application of trafficking. If it doesn't benefit someone, there might not be any reason for them to identify as a survivor.

VIOLENCE AGAINST SEX WORKERS

The fact of the matter is that exploitation, although harmful and traumatic, is not most sex workers' primary concern: violence and arrest are.[36] In a 30-year study of 1,969 street-based sex workers in the United States, violence and drug use were the predominant causes of death.[37] The sources of violence include street violence, intimate partner violence, violence from clients and pimps, and police violence. A survey of youth and young adults in the sex trade in Chicago reveals that young sex workers there experience the foster care system and social service system as the most violent actors in their lives.[38]

Under the current sociopolitical paradigm where sex work is criminalized and stigmatized, sex workers often are left with little recourse when experiencing violence, since reporting a crime would mean exposing oneself to arrest and prosecution. Serial rapists know this, which allows them to target sex workers. Gary Ridgeway, known as the Green River Killer, raped and murdered 49 sex workers in the Pacific Northwest during the 1980s and '90s. When caught and asked about his choice to target sex workers, he said that he knew that no one would care about "dead hookers." He could get away with it; and he did for nearly two decades. He was right.[39]

The threat and experience of external harm can begin to manifest internally, exhibiting as high rates of self-harm. Sex workers experience mental health issues such as depression and anxiety two times higher than the general public.[40] Twenty percent of sex workers experience complex Post Traumatic Stress Disorder (PTSD).[41] Sadly, the burden and isolation of having to navigate dual identities, stigma, criminalization, and trauma correlate to higher rates of suicide. Violence against sex workers is a problem of such vast proportions that communities across the globe come together annually on December 17 to hold space for peers and loved ones who have been lost to murder and suicide. Attending a local International Day to End Violence Against Sex Workers event near you is a great first step toward being an ally with sex workers.[42]

HOW YOUNG WOMEN WERE INVOLVED IN THE SEX TRADE

A participatory action study of over 200 young women in the sex trade revealed that boyfriends, johns, and family members are larger sources of

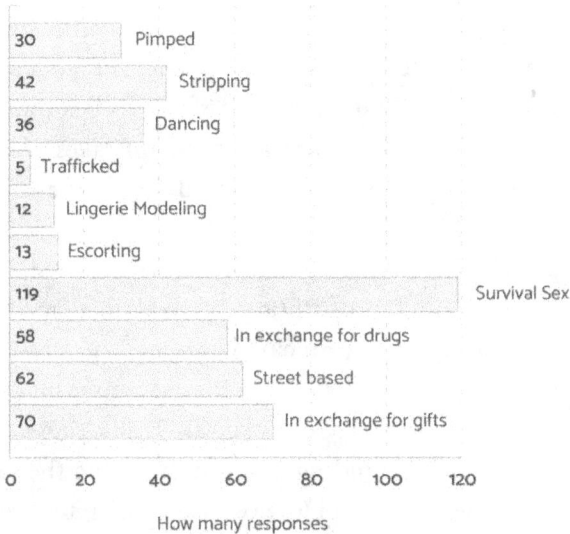

30	Pimped
42	Stripping
36	Dancing
5	Trafficked
12	Lingerie Modeling
13	Escorting
119	Survival Sex
58	In exchange for drugs
62	Street based
70	In exchange for gifts

How many responses

violence than pimps. The majority of harm that youth reported came from child service systems: "violence included emotional and verbal abuse as well as exclusion from, or mistreatment by, services. Traditional places of safety and protection are not available to them" (Girls Do What They Have to Do to Survive, Young Women's Empowerment Project, 2009).

THE CRIMINALIZATION OF SEX WORK

Violence and exploitation can be a possible negative consequence of the sex trade, or even a possible negative consequence of the sociopolitical response to the sex trade. In this way, exploitation is much like overdose is to drug use: not all drug use leads to overdose. Rather, the way someone uses is influenced by social norms, limited access to sound drug education, and criminalization, which can result in putting too much of a drug in your system, thereby shutting it down.[43]

Exploitation can be thought of similarly: not all sex work is or leads to sex trafficking. Rather, someone's working conditions are influenced by social norms, limited access to resources, and criminalization, which can result in someone else coercing them to trade sex, stripping them of their agency and fair labor compensation. Overdose and exploitation happen, but we know after 40 years of the drug war that trying to eradicate drug use through criminalization exacerbates overdose.[44] Substance use prevention, harm reduction, and treatment, in combination with other social and medical services, are an infinitely more effective means of reducing overdose.[45] My hope is that this lesson[46] can be applied to the sex trade and approaches to reducing exploitation to avoid repeating the mistakes of the drug war: perpetuating violence and disease, ruining and ending lives, and separating families.

"The pressure to crack down on human trafficking has led to a resurgence in policing and prosecuting prostitution. As explained above, sometimes the issues of sex work and sex trafficking can overlap. However, attempting to curb human trafficking by criminalizing consensual sex work can inadvertently harm consensual sex workers."[47] Trafficking laws are one of four categories of laws surrounding and criminalizing the sex trade. The list below (via Reframe Health and Justice, 2018) illustrates this umbrella of criminalization, as well as its impact.

THE CRIMINALIZATION OF SEX WORK

Laws	Policing	Supervision
Prostitution/loitering (including prostitution-free zones)	Asset forfeiture	Court fees and fines
	Confiscation of condoms/condom possession is used as evidence of prostitution	Deportation
Patronizing		Post-conviction requirements including sex offender registries and banishment
Pimping/pandering/ promoting	Police harassment and sexual harassment of sex workers	
Trafficking		Problems associated with having a conviction including exemption from rape shield laws and victim's compensation funding
		Inability to enforce labor laws

There are many types of prostitution-related charges, which vary from state to state and municipality to municipality.[48] While language varies widely, all municipalities in the United States (save 10 counties in Nevada which have high-barrier and management-heavy brothels) criminalize consensual and un-filmed, full-contact sexual transactions between adults. Both buyer and seller charges fall under the category of prostitution. Buyers receive a charge for patronizing a prostitute, but many municipalities record both sides as prostitution or solicitation, so data can be hard to aggregate.

In addition to solicitation charges, there are a handful of charges that expand surveillance of the sex trade while simultaneously decreasing the burden of proof that police need to make an arrest. One example of these charges is loitering for the purposes of prostitution. Prostitution surveillance, like drug surveillance, is one of the areas of the law exempt from entrapment charges. Across the board, loitering charges have been identified as increasing police racial profiling and brutality.[49] Other examples include gesturing for the purposes of prostitution, walking in a prostitution-free zone, and travel bans on entering countries for the purposes of prostitution. This is just one type of law that increases criminalization and decreases burden of proof geographically. Others include violating a Stay Out of Areas of Prostitution (SOAP) order and prostitution in/near a military base.[50] Prostitution-related charges like these sanction racial and gender-based profiling and police harassment of sex workers.

Increasingly, across the country, the legal terms for prostitution-related charges are being changed, and associated punishments are being intensified to further criminalize buyers and increasingly associate buying sex with trafficking. One such example is that Seattle/King County renamed the charge of "patronizing" to "sexual exploitation" in 2015 and increased the associated penalty to a $5,000 fine, among other punishments. The fact that this charge now sounds like a trafficking charge and carries a significant financial impact has harmful reverberations on work and family lives (most people picked up on patronizing in Seattle are men of color and indigent, despite the city being overwhelmingly white and the median household income nearly $100,000).[51]

This "tough on the buyer" tactic is an abolitionist approach to the sex trade, spearheaded by oil tycoon heiress Swanee Hunt and her foundation, Demand Abolition.[52] The "End Demand" approach is exclusively rooted in ending the sex trade. It applies a supply-based economic theory to ending sex trafficking that suggests that sex trafficking in women exists solely because the sex trade exists and the reason why the sex trade exists is because men buy sexual services. Therefore, by ending the demand for sexual services, sex trafficking will no longer occur. This approach completely ignores social and economic push factors into the sex trade, the myriad of reasons why people buy sex, gender variation across sellers and buyers, and the failure of anti-drug approaches to end addiction.[53]

Utilizing punishments such as increased financial penalties, asset forfeiture, and mandatory minimums, the End Demand approach to anti-trafficking increases carceral control over marginalized communities by creating a narrative where all sex workers are victims and buyers and third parties are traffickers and victimizers. A recent proliferation of End Demand legislation throughout Europe and now in Canada claims to decriminalize the supply side of the sex trade (because they see all sex workers or "sellers" as victims) while increasing or imposing criminalization for the demand side.

Sweden was the first to codify this approach in 1999 and claims that numbers of sex-trafficking incidents have declined due to this legislation. However, members of sex work and various research communities across the globe point to the flawed methodology of Sweden's claim, including a lack of research on trafficking prior to its passage and increased services and awareness in the years following.[54] Sex workers in Sweden also raise concerns about their increased vulnerability to violence and exploitation due to less work, changing power dynamics with clients who require more personal security, increased police surveillance, coercive police behavior, increased arrests for other charges, and underfunded service provision. While resources are poured into stopping buyers, thereby reducing sellers' income, sex workers haven't been given additional social service support mechanisms, including healthcare and shelter, to offset the impact of the Swedish model.

Despite the lack of research and disagreement surrounding the Swedish sex trafficking law (referred to as the Swedish or Nordic Model), at least 18 other countries have implemented some version of this law, though only three countries actually decriminalized the sale of sexual services. To add harm to injury, sex trafficking victims are the only crime victims who are arrested and coerced into services "for their own good," a practice that contradicts the notion that they are victims in the first place. Examples of coercive services include programs that offer basic needs such as housing or a cell phone to people who act like a "good victim" or "formerly prostituted woman" and do as they say.

"Pimping," "pandering," and "promoting" are all third-party charges. Even when force, fraud, and coercion aren't present, sex trade management in the underground economy is illegal and therefore punished through jail/prison time, asset forfeiture, hefty fines, and state supervision. Pandering and promoting charges are "assistant pimping" charges which state that someone who assists in or materially benefits from another person's prostitution are therefore managing them. This includes driving someone to a date, acting as a safety buddy for a worker's protection during a date, or helping someone book appointments. Promoting laws threaten to shut down any place of business where sex work is knowingly happening.

Pandering and promoting laws are the most broad and vague category of law surrounding the sex trade, thus, these laws have been the easiest to inflate to trafficking charges and felonies. What used to be a high-level solicitation misdemeanor is now a low-level trafficking felony. When trafficking charges can't be brought, promoting or pandering charges usually can be.

The frightening truth about pandering charges is that they criminalize harm-reduction practices. Now, workers who formerly used a safety buddy or assistant to increase safety and sanity must choose between working in isolation or placing their friends at risk of receiving a trafficking felony. Sadly, sex workers themselves represent a significant portion of those being charged with pandering felonies. I have provided direct services to handfuls of young women of color who received both prostitution and pandering charges for working with other women. Their trafficking felony is regarded as similar to a sex offense, further restricting their participation in housing projects and diversion programs, and often directly impacting their parental rights.

My friend is a trans migrant sex worker from the Philippines who moved to America in her early 20s.[55] After leaving an abusive marriage, she began working as a nurse. My friend loved her job, but in order to send money back home to her family, as well as visit sometimes, she began doing sex work on the side. She learned how to advertise and screen from her friends, other trans, Asian migrant sex workers. To share costs and protect one another, they worked from hotel rooms which they rented together. One night, they were all busted in a sting operation. Everyone was charged with prostitution, and because my friend had been the one to rent the hotel room, she was charged with pandering as well. This misdemeanor means she can no longer work as a nurse, and now she must rely more heavily on sex work as a means of making money. However, her biggest concern is how this criminal record might affect her citizenship application. While she acknowledges the privilege she has in working with a good lawyer—something many in similar positions don't have access to—she is concerned that she will be denied citizenship despite years of living in the US and working on her application.

The policing of prostitution is also rife with police oppression and abuse.[56] Research done out of Johns Hopkins School of Public Health shows that police violence is correlated with client violence—the more workers encounter police, the more likely it is that they will experience violent or exploitative encounters with clients.[57] This is, in part, because civil asset forfeiture practices[58] and the use of condoms as evidence of prostitution[59] leave workers in a worse place than they started after a "catch-and-release" encounter with law enforcement.

Human rights approaches to the sex trade must call for police reform along with policy reform. Isolated policy interventions that reduce incarceration but increase or ignore police surveillance also ignore the myriad of ways that police harass and abuse sex workers. Much of this behavior is sanctioned forms of abuse, such as taking all the worker's money and letting them go (civil asset forfeiture) or taking all of their condoms away (condoms as evidence).

"In a 2002 study of sex workers in Chicago, twenty-four percent of street workers who reported being raped stated that the perpetrator was a police officer. The same study found that approximately twenty percent of sexual violence against sex workers was attributed to police officers. In another study done in New York City, thirty percent of sex workers interviewed reported that a police officer had threatened them with violence."[60] In 2018, 50 percent of sex workers who use drugs in Seattle reported experiencing police harassment and abuse in their lifetimes, with the most common forms of harassment being verbal abuse, shaming public displays such as making them lie on the sidewalk in lingerie and handcuffs, offers to trade sex to avoid arrest (and then many times still being arrested anyway), and use of unnecessary physical force.[61] The most severe accounts of police harassment are from older workers, workers of color, transgender workers, and workers who use drugs—all of whom police see as less "savable."

Clients of sex workers also experience civil asset forfeiture in the form of seizure of cash and cars. For a member of a single-car family, this seizure means that the whole family is left without a car. When arrested and charged with a prostitution-related offense, both buyers and sellers are subject to fines, classes, mandated HIV testing, and probation. Fines vary by municipality but are usually higher for clients than sex workers, whereas jail sentences are more commonly higher for workers than their clients. Clients are also more likely to be able to bail themselves out of jail or complete court-sanctioned classes, allowing them the opportunity to get the charge dismissed from their records.[62] Inability to pay, for either party, can result in jail time.

Court-mandated classes often consist of education on sexual health and coercion. Some have a counseling portion. The goal of "buyers' classes," facilitated from an anti-prostitution lens, is to help people with their "prostitution addiction" using binary narratives of sex work as either shameful or victimized. Classes for sex workers are increasingly part of post-booking prostitution diversion programs, lengthy criminal-legal-social service system partnerships that provide people with limited resources and an opportunity to dismiss their record. These programs are an attractive option for sex workers who don't want to go to jail and a good option for people who thrive under highly structured, restrictive environments.

To succeed in a prostitution diversion program, a person must abide by curfews, random drug testing, the requirement to maintain a minimum of part-time employment, involvement in religious programming such as attending mass within a specific Christian denomination or church, and involvement in 12-step programs. Many others impose no dating/sex rules, require that participants pay or surrender their social benefits up to the house/program, and encourage "snitching" on each other.[63] Standards don't exist for these programs—some require that participants pray together. Many people cannot exist under these conditions for weeks to months and drop out, leading to their eventual arrest and jail time that is now longer because of the additional absconding charge.

Several jurisdictions also include mandatory HIV testing for solicitation charges. If a sex worker is determined to be living with HIV, they could also face broader charges such as attempted murder or assault[64] regardless of whether transmission could have occurred or not. Someone living with HIV who is on probation might also have their medications and medical experiences dictated or monitored. The experience of being on probation is like that of being in a post-booking diversion program but without access to resources or the possibility of erasing any record of the charge. Requirement of probation might include orders to stay out of certain areas (Stay Out of Areas of Prostitution/SOAP or Stay Out of Areas of Drug Use/SODA orders), randomized drug tests, classes, wearing an ankle bracelet, check-ins with the probation officer, and unannounced home visits from the probation officer. Often, such state supervision makes it difficult to maintain a formal-economy job when probationers must leave work multiple times a week, often without significant notice, to go pee in a cup or meet with their probation officer.

Other problems associated with having a prostitution conviction include a charge triggering deportation proceedings for undocumented workers and the fact that sex workers may be exempt from victim compensation funds and excluded from the protection of rape shield laws. The Victims of Crime Act Victim's (VOCA) Compensation Grant Program provides federal funding, made up of fines from criminal penalties and bond forfeitures, through the Justice Department Victims of Crime Office to state victim compensation programs that support persons who have endured financial hardship due to victimization.[65] VOCA guidelines prevent federal victim compensation dollars from being provided to people who "have committed a criminal act or some substantially wrongful act that caused or contributed to the crime," including people who trade sex and people under the influence of illicit drugs.[66]

The 1994 Violence Against Women Act created a federal rape shield law that limits the extent to which a complainant's past sexual behavior or sexual reputation can be used within cross-examination or evidence. Similar to the federal code, most states' interpretation of the rape shield statute allows past arrests for prostitution and related crimes to be entered into the court record, as they are part of a person's criminal history and not their sexual history.[67] While the intention of the law was to reduce stigma and support the reporting of crimes, this exemption supports narratives that sex workers cannot be raped, bring violence upon themselves, and aren't good or deserving victims, thereby increasing stigmatization and discrimination.

Exemptions such as these are just one way that reporting a crime can be a traumatic event for someone in the sex trade. Reporting thereby triggers the possibility of exposure, traumatic investigations, and having a complaint completely ignored.

ONE SEX WORKER IS ONE SEX WORKER

There isn't one way that sex work looks, because we are talking about work that spans the economic continuum. In "A Harm Reduction Approach to Prostitution Using Safe Injection Sites as a Guide," Emani Walks writes that "street-based sex work is overrepresented in media and tends to be what people think of when they consider prostitution and prostitution reform, but it is estimated that eighty-five percent of sex work in the United States today is indoor sex work."[68] Generalizations about the sex trade are often indistinguishable from class and poverty.

For example, I provided a training on the Harm Reduction Approach to Working with People in the Sex Trade to a homeless service organization (Reframe Health and Justice, 2018). Afterward, someone came up to me and said that she appreciated the nuance I presented but couldn't stop seeing the sex trade as harmful because every sex worker she worked with experienced extreme violence and hardship. My response was to ask how many homeless women she worked with were experiencing extreme violence, whether or not they were a part of the sex trade. Poverty and its proximity to violence is harmful and upsetting, but to blame the sex trade for the areas where it intersects with poverty is mistaking a coping mechanism for the problem itself.

Understanding the sex trade requires a critical analysis of so many things: economic variables, bodily regulation, generational and institutional oppression, and more. This chapter has introduced you to the core language and main concepts. I invite you to recognize where you feel discomfort in your body and the places you feel yourself shutting down. Send love to those places and know that this is what it feels like to open. You don't have to drink the Kool-Aid—please challenge anything that doesn't feel right in your gut. If it feels good to you, get up, shake it off, and do something nourishing for yourself before digging back in (at least, that's what I am going to do right now).

Casualties of War: The Wars on Drugs and Trafficking

JUSTICE RIVERA

AFTER SEVERAL YEARS OF WORKING IN NONPROFIT AGENCIES THAT TAKE a harm reduction approach to working with drug users and sex workers, I've observed many similarities between the War on Drugs and the war on trafficking. As the drug war has lost popularity, the war on trafficking has gained momentum. Both the War on Drugs and the war on trafficking are housed within the criminal justice system, operating through punishment and incarceration. Both wars seek to eliminate their abstract opponents by attacking communities of drug users and sex workers, composed mainly of poor people of color.

INCREASED SANCTIONS

One way in which both the War on Drugs and the war on trafficking operate is through the use of increased sanctions. The criminal justice system imposes harsh penalties on drug- and sex-related crimes, which in turn leads to mass incarceration, blocking upward mobility for those targeted. The best known example of this phenomenon is the crack versus cocaine disparity.[1] This discrepancy punishes crack cocaine users, most commonly Black people, with mandatory minimum sentencing many times longer than convicted powder cocaine users, most commonly white people, for an equivalent amount of what is chemically the same drug. This sentencing guideline continued for 25 years until Congress passed the Fair Sentencing Act of 2010. The act did not eliminate the disparity between sentences for crack and cocaine trafficking, but it did reduce the crack versus cocaine

Originally published in a slightly different form on *Tits and Sass*, edited by Caty Simon (June 30, 2015, https://titsandsass.com/casualties-of-war-the-wars-on -drugs-and-trafficking/). Reprinted by permission of the author and the publisher.

sentencing ratio from 100:1 to 18:1. It also eliminated the mandatory mini-mum sentence for crack possession.

In 2015, President Obama signed the Justice for Victims of Trafficking Act. Just as the Anti-Drug Abuse Act did with drug charges, this piece of federal legislation created mandatory minimums for trafficking-related charges.[2] The California state legislature passed comparable anti-trafficking legislation in 2013, and states across the nation are now adopting similar laws. California's Proposition 35 increases police surveillance of the sex trade and funnels money and resources into the criminal justice system rather than to victims of trafficking and service providers by redefining crimes and increasing penalties.

As Melissa Gira Grant observes,[3] Prop 35 is overly broad, defining traf-ficking in a way that could potentially target anyone involved in the sex trade. Prop 35 also increases penalties for trafficking-related charges to include large fines of up to $1 million, prison sentences ranging from five years to life, and sex offender registration. As a result of Prop 35 and sim-ilar legislation, sex workers are often charged with trafficking in addition to prostitution when they engage in consensual adult sexual encounters for money. Last year, I met with a 20-year-old woman who'd been charged with pandering[4] as well as prostitution because she worked in solidarity with a 17-year-old; she'd formed this partnership with her coworker without knowing she was underage to keep them both safe.

Another notable sanction that both the War on Drugs and the war on trafficking use as a tool of control and punishment is asset forfeiture, which often occurs during drug raids and prostitution stings. By law, when police officers perceive a person's belongings are involved in a crime, they seize the item and sell it. Police seize cash, cars, and homes. Impound companies

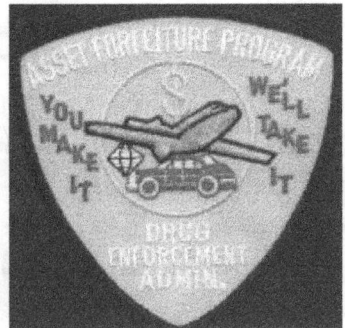

charge fines for holding vehicles[5], and many sex workers, sex work clients, and drug users do not have the means to get their cars out of impound lots. What ends up happening most of the time is that law enforcement agencies sell the impounded cars, keep the money, and use those funds to make more drug and prostitution-related arrests.[6]

SAFETY SUPPLIES BECOME PARAPHERNALIA

Drug paraphernalia is illegal in many states, and possession carries different penalties depending on which drugs they are meant to be used with. For example, a marijuana pipe often triggers a ticket and a fine, while a syringe triggers several days in county jail, including a booking fee. Police officers use paraphernalia as probable cause to search a person for drugs. Many people do not know their rights, and police will often use paraphernalia to justify a search of their environment as well as their person, despite actually needing a warrant to conduct such searches.

Similarly, condoms are considered evidence of prostitution in some jurisdictions either by law or in practice. In 2013, New York reformed a law that established possession of more than three condoms as evidence of prostitution.[7] Opponents of the law stated that criminalizing condoms is bad public health policy because it discourages people from carrying and using condoms. Despite the law's reform, police still threaten to use condoms as evidence when arresting someone they perceive as a sex worker in an attempt to get them to admit guilt.[8] During Know Your Rights trainings, which the last organization I worked at provides to sex workers, participants would often tell me that the officer who arrested them stated that possession of so many condoms was probable cause for a prostitution arrest. But that "evidence" was not formally submitted on their ticket because the law in Colorado does not actually recognize condoms as evidence. Such practices push drug use and sex work, as well as sex trafficking, underground, creating more violence and isolation by depriving people of the means to reduce risks in their drug use and sex work.

FEDERAL FUNDING BANS

In 1988, Congress placed a federal funding ban on needle exchange in the Public Health and Welfare Act.[9] No federal dollars could be used on this highly effective HIV prevention intervention until 2009 when the Obama administration and Congress removed the ban in the appropriation process. Two years later it was added again as an appropriation rider. Then, in 2016 after over 200 mostly white injection drug users in rural Indiana contracted HIV, a mostly Republican Congress relaxed the ban.[10] At the time this chapter was updated in 2022, a ban on funding needles still existed.

However, current language allows for federal money to be spent on staff, infrastructure, and other supplies at syringe access programs.

Federal funding bans extend beyond limiting organizations' sustainability and growth to imperiling individual health and prosperity. People with drug felonies and sex offenses are denied access to federal assistance, including food stamps and Section 8 housing. This creates a cycle of release and reincarceration as felons are not able to meet their basic needs after re-entering society. People with drug- and prostitution-related charges on their records often return to the street economy in order to take care of themselves and their families, violating their parole/probation and sometimes catching additional charges. Tax payers' dollars are spent funneling people in, out, and back into jails and prisons rather than helping people with felonies become stable.

In 2003, the President's Emergency Plan for AIDS relief (PEPFAR) created national and international strategies aimed at ending the AIDS epidemic. PEPFAR imposes bans on federal funding dollars to syringe exchange programs, as well as organizations that support the decriminalization of prostitution, limiting the impact that harm reduction agencies can have on preventing the spread of HIV/AIDS. Such funding restrictions also impede community-based organizations' ability to provide sexual health services and education to drug users and sex workers.

In 2013, the American Foundations for AIDS research (amfAR) released a fact sheet calling on the federal government to lift these bans.[11] The fact sheet outlines how lifting federal funding restrictions on syringe exchanges and sex worker–positive organizations would be more cost effective to the US, as harm reduction and prevention are significantly cheaper than providing health care to people with HIV. One syringe costs an organization 10 cents whereas viral treatment costs thousands of dollars over a lifetime. In 2013, the US Supreme Court found the anti-prostitution pledge to be unconstitutional.[12] However, the federal government still withholds its funding dollars from sex worker–positive organizations, directing them toward abstinence-based organizations instead.

DISPROPORTIONATE EFFECTS ON MARGINALIZED COMMUNITIES

Michelle Alexander, author of *The New Jim Crow*, a primer on racial disparity in the drug war, writes that "[a]ny movement to end mass incarceration must deal with mass incarceration as a racial caste system, not as a system of crime control."[13] The 13th Amendment of the US Constitution states that slavery is illegal except as punishment for a crime. But after slavery was outlawed, many states adopted Jim Crow laws, perpetuating the mass arrest of Black men in order to utilize their prison labor.[14] Shortly after Jim Crow laws were overturned, the War on Drugs began, and it continues to do the work Jim Crow laws did by incarcerating huge numbers of Black men.

Dr. Carl Hart, a neuroscientist who specializes in debunking drug war myths, writes about the role that media sensationalism plays in perpetuating drug war hysteria. Anti-meth ads show extreme cases of meth use and declare that all meth use looks like that. In fact, that is what extreme sleep deprivation and malnutrition look like. Anti-trafficking ads also use sensationalism to incite pity and fear in the American public. Foreign children are shown trapped in cages, despite the fact that traffickers use fraud and coercion much more commonly than force. Lurid images like these do little to educate anyone about the nuances of drug use and trafficking in the sex industry, but they do plenty to affirm people's existing prejudices.

Media attention surrounding the war on trafficking warns American parents to keep close watch on their children and stay wary of men of color. This is reminiscent of media surrounding the War on Drugs in the 1980s and 1990s. During the '80s, the spotlight turned to Black men and welfare mothers, ignoring drug use in suburban white neighborhoods. Law enforcement shifted most of its resources to monitoring poor inner-city neighborhoods. This colored portrayal of drug use led to the imprisonment of high rates of Black people in America, much higher than any other race. The media also promotes racial stereotypes of sex workers and sex trafficking victims. Law enforcement uses racial profiling when arresting Black female sex workers and "saving" white young women in the sex trade.[15] Thus, poor women of color are arrested and incarcerated at much higher rates for prostitution-related crimes. Instead of being treated with compassion, sex trafficking survivors are often arrested, criminalized, and mistreated by the criminal justice system. Even attempts at diversion—treating sex workers as "victims" instead of "criminals"—usually leave workers with open records and still conduct them through the criminal justice system,[16] which leads to deportation for migrant trafficking victims.[17]

In 2013, Monica Jones, a Black transgender woman, was arrested for prostitution while accepting a ride home.[18] She was found guilty, but she appealed her case in the Arizona State Court, drawing attention to police profiling of transgender women of color as sex workers. Trans women are less likely to be hired by employers in the legitimate economy, which often forces them into underground market work. But even when trans women of color are breaking no laws, they are often arrested for simply "walking while trans."[19] After prostitution and drug arrests, transgender women who have not had gender confirmation surgery (which many transgender people do not get done due to cost, access, or personal preference) are booked into men's pods, leaving them vulnerable to sexual harassment and physical assault. Furthermore, court-mandated treatment centers as well as many community-based nonprofits deny care to transgender people.

Sex solicitation arrestees present disparities in gender as well as race.[20] For many years, sex buyers were penalized less severely than sex sellers. The recent emergence of End Demand initiatives that seek to harshly punish and shame sex buyers has reduced this gender gap somewhat.[21] However, demand cannot be "ended" without cutting off supply, meaning that sex workers are still being penalized economically if not legally. And sex workers are still being arrested more often than sex buyers. At a Demand Abolition meeting in September 2013, a vice sergeant from the FBI's Innocence Lost Task Force told attendees that their arrests were composed of 60 percent sellers that year.

Sex and drug sellers are punished for selling pleasure to white middle- and upper-class consumers. Then, white middle- and upper-class corporate workers profit off their punishment through industries such as private prisons and for-profit treatment centers. And as long as people are poor and have few options, they will turn to underground work to survive, feeding these industries.

FUTURE VISIONS: SOLIDARITY BETWEEN MOVEMENTS

Today, many people refer to human trafficking as "modern-day slavery." Others within the anti-trafficking movement disagree with this language, arguing that human trafficking does not have the institutional backing that defined slavery in the old American South. Prison abolition activists

This photo by Flickr user Ira Gelb of a frail white woman marked as a "slave" has been used on many anti-trafficking websites and articles.

recognize the institutional backing given to the criminal justice system of incarceration, which holds people against their will and reaps the benefits of their unpaid or underpaid labor. Mass incarceration is also called "modern day slavery." No matter what camp you belong to, it's easy to see that we cannot eradicate slavery-like conditions with slavery-like conditions. We cannot incarcerate exploitation and violence away when incarceration itself is exploitative and violent.

The wars on drugs and sex trafficking have had negative public health consequences, including the exacerbation of the HIV/HCV epidemics, fatal drug overdoses, and the proliferation of post-traumatic stress disorder. Community members and activists have been calling for an end to the War on Drugs for decades, and as a result, public health solutions to drug abuse have begun to emerge by way of drug policy reform and criminal justice reform. These measures could have utility within policies surrounding the sex trade to reduce the immediate negative impact of criminalization.

One such measure that twenty states throughout the US support is some form of decriminalization of drug paraphernalia. Essentially, this policy recognizes that people who are connected to community care and harm reduction materials, such as clean syringes, should not be punished for possessing the very materials that the organization gives them. Policies that exempt participants of community-based nonprofits from arrest allow for the proper disposal of syringes and ensure that police officers will not be stuck by used syringes during searches. This affirmative defense is a realistic goal activists can work for in their states while also advocating for the end of the drug war. Local governments could explore partial decriminalization of prostitution in ways that don't decriminalize one party while further criminalizing another, such as adopting an affirmative defense to prostitution for sex workers accessing services from a recognized harm reduction organization.

Activists can push for similar middle paths when approaching the war on trafficking while also advocating for the complete decriminalization of sex work. On the way to ending America's ideological wars, municipalities across the US should fund sex worker–centered harm reduction outreach, drop-in centers, and services in neighborhoods most affected by the War on Drugs and the war on trafficking. At the same time, court and community care systems can employ alternative justice methods such as restorative and transformative justice models. Most importantly, alliances between drug policy reform advocates and sex worker rights advocates need to be made to ensure the United States reduces its overreliance on the criminal justice system.

Wars on Bodily Autonomy: A Timeline

KATE D'ADAMO AND JUSTICE RIVERA WITH DEVELOPING

CONTRIBUTION FROM JASMINE TYLER AND JADE LAUGHLIN

THE STORY OF GOVERNMENT CONTROL OVER BODILY AUTONOMY IS THE story of the building of an American national identity. Europeans who had violently colonized what would become the United States were trying to create something new and unrelated to the land they stood on. They sought to do this in a way that would understand and reinforce the power structures that they believed in—secularity, land, white supremacy, and hetero-patriarchy as the backbone of what it meant to be an American. But without social structures to rely on, such as the church or thousands of years-long developed notions of identity, contemporary structures would need to be built which naturalized these identities and punished those who deviated. Our founding fathers allowed just enough self-determination for the next generations of Americans to expand the country while always being in the precarious position of, at some point, needing to fall in line.

For there to be an American, there had to be a counterpart, a non-American. Until the late 18th century, that was the slave. After the 14th amendment abolished slavery, except for prison labor, in 1868, the need for an outsider turned to Asian immigrants. This is when we start to see the development of criminalization as the primary tool of maintaining white supremacy. The story of sex and substance regulation—two of those powerful drivers of embodied self-determination and expansion of personal liberty—has always existed in American society. Their policing and regulation have been a story about trying to understand narrative, federalism, and the bounds of a state ruled by police to enforce culture. Over the past 200 years, slavery, colonization, and imperialism have weaponized substances and non-Christian sexuality against non-white communities during periods of heightened immigration and to expand or maintain federal powers after war. When a prohibitionist approach to one is losing traction, the other ramps up.

The below timeline illustrates how the wars on bodily autonomy borrow from and feed into one another. Racialized anti-drug, anti-sex work, anti-reproductive health, and anti-queer laws and institutional policies serve to protect the straight, white, moral order that our founding fathers raped and pillaged for.

Note: We aren't historians. Rather, we're femmes of color and activists who have an interest in the historical context of our lives, and policy wonks who geek out on political history. We wish to understand this country's lineage and evolutionary motivations. We look backwards so we can create a future with ourselves in it. There are stories of resistance, survival, revolution, decolonization, and revolt that shape the culture and possibility that exists today that aren't included in this timeline. Their non-inclusion here does not reflect their importance, but rather our limitations. We invite you to fill the gaps in this story—and the empty space on these pages—with the moments that hold relevance to you and your story.

Also note: we chose to use the term "marijuana" to reclaim it as an Indigenous medicine and to free it from the stigma that still follows it from 100 years ago.

1800–1869: FORMATION OF THE STATE AND NEED FOR "PROTECTION"

The early 18th century is the birth of policing. Many people trust the State and are policed with consent. Sex work in this era offers economic liberation to women in a world of Western Expansion and almost no economic opportunities. Patronizing a sex worker and using substances in this era exists as an accompaniment to the daily operation of Western Expansion. Substance distribution becomes an economic opportunity for those men who don't have the means, legitimacy, or capacity to become doctors. Because drugs are a product that usually involve some form of inter-state commerce, their regulation is primarily federal. Sex work, specifically prostitution, is a service, lending it to local and civil regulation. Federal policies seek to restrict rather than regulate sexual labor across state lines. Wars on substance use and sex work both have roots in the temperance movement and carceral feminism—the need to protect white femininity and the idea that prohibitionist policies, policing, and prisons can do that.

KEY THEMES

- This is a period of state formation where individual states are building an identity through state-based regulations and local institutions such as police departments. Because they are local, the laws are all local.

- During this period, prostitution is generally regulated instead of outright criminalized, though we see the roots of anti-prostitution and anti-sodomy laws begin with the suppression of vice. Regulation focuses on zoning and keeping prostitution out of sight rather than policing bodies.

- Next comes the roots of alcohol prohibition along with Irish and Jewish immigration.

- Drug regulation begins with the enactment of pharmaceutical standards, but drugs aren't seen as a crime of morality yet.

TIME LINE

YEAR	CATEGORY	EVENT
1770–early 19th century	Sex work	The largest area of prostitution—known as "Holy Ground"—occurred around the Church at the intersection of Vesey and Barclay in New York City.
1805	Sex work	Louisiana enacts its first criminal code, which included an explicit prohibition of the "abominable and detestable Crime Against Nature, committed with mankind or beast." This will become a prostitution ordinance.
1829	Parallel enforcement mechanisms	The Metropolitan Police Act is passed in the UK, offering Nine Policing Principles. These Principles will shape modern, urban policing moving forward, including in the US.

1830s	Parallel enforcement mechanisms	Lynchings, or extrajudicial murders by a group in "service to justice, race, or tradition," begin, primarily targeting Black individuals, though also targeting other racial groups. Lynchings reached their peak in the early 1900s.
1845	Parallel enforcement mechanisms	NYPD is created.
1846	Parallel enforcement mechanisms	Alabama begins its own convict-lease system which lasts until 1928, when Herbert Hoover is vying for the White House. A convict-lease system involves local citizens "renting" incarcerated people from the state for physically demanding labor. In 1883, about 10 percent of Alabama's total revenue was derived from convict leasing. In 1898, nearly 73 percent of total revenue came from this same source.
1847	Drugs	Members of Maine's Total Abstinence Society convinced the state government to pass the Fifteen Gallon Law, the first prohibition law. The legislation banned the sale of alcohol in amounts smaller than 15 gallons, effectively limiting access to alcohol to the wealthy.
1857	Sex work	New Orleans' first explicitly anti-prostitution ordinance, the Lorette Ordinance, passes. The law prohibits prostitution on the first floor of buildings and requires licensing fees. It is soon after declared unconstitutional.
1860	Drugs	Efforts to regulate the sale of pharmaceuticals begin. Laws are introduced on a state-to-state basis that create penalties for mislabeling drugs, adulterating them with undisclosed narcotics, and improper sale of "poisons." Poison laws generally either require labels on the packaging indicating the harmful effects of the drugs or prohibit the sale outside of licensed pharmacies and without a doctor's prescription.

1865	Parallel enforcement mechanisms	Black Codes are enacted, imposing involuntary labor as punishment for minor infractions, setting the stage for the Jim Crow era.
1868	Parallel enforcement mechanisms	14th amendment of the constitution abolishes slavery, except as punishment for a crime.

1870–1903: NEW ACTORS IN REGULATION

The late 18th century sees the reformation of the country's identity post civil war. The American Civil War was a rupture in the American project and necessitated redefining what it meant to be an American, especially a white Christian citizen. The federal state becomes stronger in reaction to both the forming of a white national identity and shifting patterns of immigration. Abolishing the role of the slave had a psychological and financial impact that completely destabilized the hierarchy of American identity. In combination with fears around new patterns of immigration, this leads to a rise in regulatory bodies and a shift in how bodies are controlled. Christian morality and public health rise as control systems. Post-abolition, prisons become warehouses, and exploitative capitalism continues to rely on the labor of Black and brown people. This is the creation of a white Christian country; this is the creation of Modern America.

It is also the perpetuation of social tension in America. Women's liberation movements—the same ones pushing for alcohol and prostitution prohibition—adopt "white slavery" and "abolition" terminology to describe their efforts. The language change claims prostitution as a "slavery" of white women in order to ride the coattails of Antebellum slavery abolition, which had lost supporters upon the shift to Reconstruction. Media (in the form of the press) rises as both a tool of resistance and a vehicle for racist propaganda.

KEY THEMES

- The need for a non-citizen rests on borders. This era sparks a proliferation of hash immigration laws, especially around Asian immigration. Opium use and Chinese prostitution became focal points for racist propaganda, the main drivers of which are doctors and the medical establishment.

- Prostitution bans come before drug bans, mirroring what is happening internationally.

TIME LINE

YEAR	CATEGORY	EVENT
1870s	Drugs	Although created in 1853, the hypodermic syringe is perfected in this era, changing the medical establishment as well as the way people used recreational substances. Teas and tinctures continue to be the most acceptable methods of consumption in this era.
1873	Parallel enforcement mechanisms	Anthony Comstock creates the New York Society for the Suppression of Vice, an institution dedicated to supervising the morality of the public. Comstock influences Congress to pass the Comstock Law, which made illegal the delivery or transport of "obscene, lewd, or lascivious" material and birth control information.
1875	Sex work	US Congress passes the Page Act of 1875, outlawing the "importation" of Chinese women into the United States for the purposes of prostitution.
1880	Drugs	The US and Qing Dynasty China completed an agreement prohibiting the shipment of opium between the two countries, the first of many treaties which unfairly benefitted Western countries. Qing China is still suffering the effects of fighting the Opium War (1839–1842) with Britain.
1882	Parallel enforcement mechanisms	Chinese Exclusion Act suspends Chinese immigration for 10 years under the belief that Chinese opium smoking threatens the moral system of the country. There were concerns about the supposed effects of opium smoking on sexual behavior, arguments that it both heightens male and female desire and endangers the nation's

		reproductive capacity, and fears that opium smoking and Chinese prostitution would encourage miscegenation to the detriment of America's socioeconomic progress.
1883	Parallel enforcement mechanisms	"Eugenics" is coined and gains favor as a movement by 1910. The US movement sought to eliminate negative breeding traits by focusing on traits of "undesirable" minority populations. Leads to forced sterilization (started in 1897 in MI) and "fitter family contests."
1884	Sex work	Waco, Texas, completely outlaws prostitution.
1887	Community resistance	Several madames in Chicago publish *The Sporting and Clubhouse Directory*, a guide to local brothels and sex tourism destinations.
1888	Community resistance	The era of Jack the Ripper. Extreme violence against women was covered in the media which started to change the narrative around sex workers, painting them as vulnerable women.
1889	Sex work	Waco, a city lauded for its multitude of educational institutions and churches, becomes the second city in the United States to legalize prostitution in a red light district. This district, known as the Reservation or Two-Street, brought in thousands of dollars of revenue to the city while serving as a source of controversy for many years.
1891	Community resistance	Brushy Mountain State Coal Miner Strike ended convict leasing in Tennessee after coal miners protested the use of unpaid convict labor in their stead. In resolving the strike, the state banned convict leasing, but also built the Brushy Mountain State Penitentiary, which operated until 2009. The Penitentiary is built with prison labor.
1893	Drugs	Methedrine, aka methamphetamine, is first synthesized. It will be sold as an over-the-counter stimulant in the 1930s and '40s.

1893	Parallel enforcement mechanisms	Anti Saloon League is founded. Their primary platform is to prohibit alcohol consumption, prostitution, and sodomy.
1894	Sex work	In Sioux City, it becomes common practice for prostitutes, madams, gambling house proprietors, and saloon keepers to pay a monthly fine to the police department, with regular payment serving more or less as a license and virtually insuring the payer against arrest.
1899	Parallel enforcement mechanisms	Juvenile courts start in Chicago. These courts combine probation, separate hearings, and special judges in dealing with young offenders.
1900	Drugs	Cocaine is removed from Coca Cola (12 years after Coke was founded) because of fears that it contributes to "Black crime in the South" and white social pressures.
1902	Sex work	The Committee of 15, initially formed to examine how NYC should treat prostitution, releases its report, *The Social Evil*, opposing regulation and recommending improvements to housing, health care, and increasing women's wages. Moral reformers in Sioux City, Iowa formed an alliance with business leaders who did not profit from prostitution and succeeded in closing the Warwick Hotel, a Black-owned hotel which was a major spot for prostitution and other forms of vice in the city.
1903	Sex work	Alaska banishes brothels from the town center but allows them in "Indian Country."

1904–1916: ROLE OF CIVIL SOCIETY IN LAW AND MORALITY AND CREATION OF THE FEDERAL POLICE STATE

At the center of the story behind the wars on bodily autonomy is the formation of the country and the power struggle between federal and state governments. Prior to this era, federal government oversight included immigration, finance, war, and treaties—not policing. The early 19th century ushers in the strengthening of the federal government as cop. It also begins positioning civil society to enforce social purity. Moral reformers recast sex workers from "no good" degenerates to women lured into a life of evil by immigrant men purveying substances like marijuana. Core themes of this era include individual responsibility stipulated by temperance and anti-immigration concerns combined with an image of the ideal American family bolstered by the ideology of eugenics. Furthermore, industrialization brings with it a movement for labor protections and workers' rights, which is continually undermined by the courts. Class and gender tensions are heightened, especially as women enter the workforce.

KEY THEMES

- Strengthening and shaping the role of the federal government comes in the form of the first federal prohibition law (opium), the creation of the FBI, federal jurisdiction to regulate prostitution across state lines, and the formalization of federal regulation of drugs into five schedules.

- The need to create an American identity relies on the federal government as enforcer and punisher of noncitizens. This takes the form of anti-Mexican drug propaganda and policies and anti-Eastern/Southern European "white slave" rhetoric and protections.

- Criminalization of marijuana and prostitution begin on the state level.

- Suppressing birth control information is a Temperance movement/ Christian morality issue until eugenics concerns provoke a desire for population control. Pioneer birth control activist Margaret Sanger promotes contraceptives through a eugenics platform, intentionally partnering with African American churches in the South.

- Strong focus on individual responsibility includes product labels on substances and Red Light Abatement laws, as well as nuisance orders.

- Rise in knowledge of venereal disease leads to forced sterilization of women engaging in, or presumed to engage in, prostitution, and classification of prostitution as a sexual crime rather than a crime of public order.

TIME LINE

YEAR	CATEGORY	EVENT
1905	Sex work	The American Society of Sanitary and Moral Prophylaxis forms to combat venereal diseases and prostitution. The organization recommends that "municipalities can better devote their energies to teaching and warning against her than in regulating her in business. Education is cheaper and more effective."
	Parallel enforcement mechanisms	US military and police adopt the use of fingerprinting, and prisoners make the first fingerprinting cards at Leavenworth.
1906	Drugs	Pure Food and Drug Act requires that certain drugs, including alcohol, cocaine, heroin, morphine, and marijuana, be accurately labeled with contents and dosage. Previously, many drugs had been sold with secret ingredients or misleading labels. Cocaine, heroin, marijuana, and other such drugs continue to be legally available without prescription as long as they were labeled.
1907	Parallel enforcement mechanisms	Indiana enacts a forced sterilization law and applies it to people trading sex, the homeless, unwed mothers, alcoholics, and children with "discipline problems."
1908	Parallel enforcement mechanisms	The Federal Bureau of Investigation (FBI) is created within the Department of Justice. Their mandate includes controlling First Nation communities and border control.

1909	Sex work	Iowa passes the first Red Light Abatement Law which uses civil penalties to push brothels out of the center of cities and towns. Citizens could sue brothels with the argument that brothels were bringing down their property values, which meant property-owning citizens could use legal tools against brothels and workers without relying on police.
	Drugs	The Smoking Opium Exclusion Act bans the possession, importation, and use of opium for smoking. Opium could still be used as a medication. This is the first federal law to ban the non-medical use of a substance. Along with tariffs, this will lead to opium extraction (pills and tinctures versus raw material) and changes the way people use opium. The push for the law's passage involved stereotypes regarding morality of Chinese railroad workers.
1910	Sex work	The Mann Act (White Slave Traffic Act) makes it a crime to transport women across state lines "for the purpose of prostitution or debauchery, or for any other immoral purpose." The nation's first federal anti–sex trafficking law was so broadly worded that courts held it to criminalize many forms of consensual sexual activity. It was also used as a tool for political persecution and blackmail.
1911	Sex work	In Hoke v. United States, the US Supreme Court holds that regulating prostitution is strictly the province of the states, but that Congress could regulate interstate travel for purposes of prostitution or immoral purposes. Nevada, while tolerant of prostitution, adopts state laws which include prostitution prosecutions under nuisance orders.

1913	Sex work	The Bureau of Social Hygiene is incorporated by John D. Rockefeller Jr. as a result of his service on a special grand jury to investigate white slavery in New York City in 1910. The purpose of the Bureau is "the study, amelioration, and prevention of those social conditions, crimes, and diseases which adversely affect the well-being of society, with special reference to prostitution and the evils associated therewith."
	Drugs	California outlaws marijuana through an amendment to the 1907 Poison Act that made the possession of "extracts, tinctures, or other narcotic preparations of hemp, or loco-weed, their preparations and compounds" a misdemeanor. Another amendment in 1915 additionally forbids the sale or possession of "flowering tops and leaves" except with a prescription.
	Parallel enforcement mechanisms	*Traffic in Souls*, an American white slavery propaganda film, is released.
1914	Drugs	For the first time, the United States bans the domestic distribution of drugs through the Harrison Narcotic Act of 1914. The Act regulates and taxes the production, importation, and distribution of opiates and cocaine. The Harrison Narcotic Act medicalizes drugs by requiring doctor's orders, thereby outlawing recreational use. One of the first marijuana drug raids occurs in a Mexican American neighborhood in Los Angeles where police raid two "dream gardens" and confiscate a wagonload of marijuana.
1914–1916	Sex work	The American Hygiene Association visits 80 cities in 25 states, successfully lobbying state governments to change prostitution from a crime of public order to a sexual crime, using Red Light Abatement laws to permanently shut down brothels. Suicide

		rises among women who lost work due to closings, though most women moved to more tolerant cities or hid their work.
1915	Sex work	New York state criminalizes all forms of prostitution.
	Drugs	Mormons who went to Mexico in 1910 return to Utah with the habit of smoking marijuana. The Mormon Church declared smoking marijuana to be a sin, and a month later the legislature passes an anti-marijuana law as part of comprehensive anti-drug legislation. The connection between the two events is disputed.

1917–1950: FEDERAL EXPANSION OF POWERS AND INSTITUTIONALIZATION

This era is marked by alcohol prohibition, the Great Depression, and two World Wars, which serve to formalize an underground economy and deepen the country's reliance on capitalism. At the end of the war, soldiers come home and return to the work force and women are expected to return home to perform domestic labor. This backward-facing culture shift normalizes and promotes the blond-haired and blue-eyed nuclear family. The American image is used to fundraise for American soldiers on a global scale.

Governmental power is expanded during emergency, but then remains expanded. The federal government assumes domestic police powers and a codependent relationship forms between the military, police, and public health initiatives. Public safety and public health are seen as two sides of the same coin, and state funds for public health come from the military. The United Nations is created, solidifying that countries must have a strong federal government to become a world actor.

KEY THEMES

- Federal vs. state tension is exemplified by federal closure of local red light districts, the creation of the Narcs and FDA who target Black and brown communities, national alcohol prohibition and its reversal, as well as marijuana taxation.

- World War II disrupts the international heroin and opium trade, leading drug seekers and users to physicians and drug stores for narcotics. At this time, anti-drug sentiment and criminalization centers around marijuana, meaning its use is punished more harshly than heroin or other narcotics.

- This is an era of unprecedented military expansion. Tobacco, alcohol, amphetamines, and cocaine are accepted and encouraged, and criminalization of women in the sex trade around military bases is funded by the Department of Defense to control venereal disease. Meanwhile, soldiers use substances to cope with pain and the conditions of American exploitation. This contributes to unprecedented rates of what we now know as PTSD in the aftermath of combat.

TIME LINE

YEAR	CATEGORY	EVENT
1917	Sex work	The Federal government sends a message to Waco, Texas, to close their red light district. The city complies.
1919	Sex work	Chamberlain-Kahn Act is passed as part of the Army Appropriations Act. It focuses on the spread of STIs under the assumption that sex workers (and loose women) had syphilis and gonorrhea and were compromising the health of the military. Funding went to universities to research treatment and pushes for quarantining/detaining, locking up, and forcibly testing women.
	Drugs	Federal alcohol prohibition is codified through the 18th Amendment to the US Constitution. Alcohol prohibition is approved by 36 out of 48 states, banning the production, transportation, and sale of alcoholic beverages. It does not outlaw alcohol consumption.

	Parallel enforcement mechanisms	National Motor Vehicle Theft Act passes, making the interstate transportation of stolen vehicles a federal crime and suppressing underground interstate commerce. One of the first federal policies to issue state consortium grants, or seed funding for projects which will not be continued.
1920s	Drugs	Proliferation of state-based marijuana taxes pass in reaction to Mexican immigration and the use of marijuana cigarettes. The campaign is backed by William Randolph Hearst's racialized smear campaign to stigmatize hemp paper so it could be replaced with his (poorer quality) pulp paper.
1921	Sex work	International Convention for the Suppression of the Traffic of Women and Children is hosted through the League of Nations.
1922	Drugs	Jones-Miller Act puts serious restrictions on cocaine manufacturers.
1926	Parallel enforcement mechanisms	The FBI expands from its early form. Formal training will begin in 1928, creating the FBI as we know it today.
1927	Parallel enforcement mechanisms	TV is created, followed by TV stations in the 1920s and 1930s. This creates new avenues for drug propaganda. Early TV and print media broadcast stories about reefer madness and Black people withstanding bullets and associates jazz music with drug use.
1930s	Parallel enforcement mechanisms	Maternity clinics are created, and forced sterilizations increase, targeting people with physical and mental disabilities. General Assemblies are created to oversee sterilizations in the South. The practice of forced sterilizations expands through the early 1980s, targeting women of color. Between 1930 and 1970, one third of Puerto Rico's female population will be sterilized.

1930	Drugs	The Federal Bureau of Narcotics is created in its current form. For the next 32 years it will be headed by Harry J. Anslinger. Anslinger, like many of his colleagues, comes from the Bureau of Prohibition. David Wills, a Quaker missionary, creates the first therapeutic communities (TC) based on "pray your way out." Horrible replication in 1969 within psychiatric hospitals led to modern-day TCs within the prison industrial complex.
1932	Parallel enforcement mechanisms	Tuskegee experiments begin in Alabama to record and find treatment for syphilis among Black people. The 600 male participants were not given informed consent or treatment for their conditions. The experiment is set to last 6 months but will run for 40 years.
1933	Drugs	The 21st Amendment to the US constitution repeals the 18th Amendment, ceasing alcohol prohibition 13 years after it began. The amendment remains the only major act of prohibition to be repealed.
	Parallel enforcement mechanisms	Hitler and Nazis are inspired by the American eugenics movement, especially scientists in California who were funded by the Rockefeller Foundation and other philanthropy.
1937	Drugs	Congress passes the Marijuana Tax Act which imposes a $1 nuisance tax on the distribution of marijuana. This act is passed by Congress on the basis of testimony and public perception that marijuana caused insanity, criminality, and death. It requires anyone distributing marijuana to maintain and submit a detailed account of transactions including inspections, affidavits, and private information regarding the parties involved. Obtaining a tax stamp requires individuals to present their goods, which was then construed as confession.

1938	Drugs	Food, Drug, and Cosmetic Act redefines drugs as "affecting the body even in absence of disease" and affords FDA control over drug safety. The Act establishes a class of drugs available by prescription but allows companies to determine the class status.
1939	Parallel enforcement mechanisms	Harry Anslinger begins targeting Billie Holiday, a renowned musician, former sex worker, and drug user. Anslinger believes that jazz is a drug-infused sin and holds a deep disdain for Black people and women. Holiday fights administrative racism and misogyny, but they were stronger. Anslinger's men planted drugs on Holiday. She serves prison time and is stripped of her performer's license. She still finds ways to sing. On her deathbed, narcs plant drugs on her again and she dies cuffed to a hospital bed. Outrage around her treatment advance community-based treatment for people who use heroin.
1941	Sex work	Congress passes the May Act, intended to prevent prostitution on restricted zones around military bases.
1941–1944	Sex work	Around 250 prostitutes are registered as "entertainers" with the Honolulu Police Department. Each paid $1 a year for her license and is expected to report her earnings and pay taxes on them. Approximately 15 houses of prostitution operate in Honolulu.
1942	Drugs	Dwight D. Eisenhower orders half a million benzedrine tablets for American troops deployed to North Africa.
1944	Sex work	In Mortensen v. United States, the US Supreme Court rules that prostitutes can travel across state lines without violating the Mann Act if the "sole purpose of the journey from beginning to end was to provide innocent recreation" without engaging in prostitution.

1951–1967: CRACKS ARE FORMING, CRACKDOWNS ARE COMING; NEOLIBERALISM

The 1950s through the mid-1960s is an era marked with government corruption and budding community resistance. The American image of the white, nuclear family begins to erode and those invested in it fight unfairly to maintain it. This era is marked by assassinations of progressive leaders and militarized police violence. The Vietnam War begins. By the '60s, many Americans have had enough. Race riots usher in a period of liberalization as existing systems break. This is the Civil Rights era and the beginning of the gay and trans liberation movements. It is a period of possibility, and it is all televised.

KEY THEMES

- The first mandatory minimum penalties are instituted along with the expansion of jails and prison labor.

- Jimmy Carter runs for president on a platform of marijuana decriminalization. He loses, but his platform builds the counter base for Nixon's anti-drug response in the late '60s.

- Non-violent resistance leads to institutional gains. There is a sociopolitical ideology shift related to bodily autonomy, acknowledging that addiction is a disease, porn actors can unionize, people of color can desegregate, and LGBTQ+ people exist.

- Media is influential as both a tool of control and a platform for educating the general public about corruption and abuse that is occurring across the country. By 1960, 90 percent of American households have a TV, compared to 20 percent ten years prior.

TIME LINE

YEAR	CATEGORY	EVENT
1950s	Drugs	Though heroin addiction is on the decline in the aftermath of WWII, crackdowns on street drugs cause street costs to double, thereby leading to more crime to support people's ability to maintain the same level of usage. The US military and CIA research LSD as a possible "truth drug," which could be used to persuade prisoners to talk. After military interest in LSD wanes in favor of other drugs, the psychiatric community begins to research and issue reports on the drug's possible therapeutic benefits for patients with psychiatric issues, depression, and epilepsy. Recreational use of LSD increases throughout the late 1950s and 1960s.
1951	Drugs	Boggs Act increases penalties fourfold and sets mandatory minimums for drug convictions. A first conviction for marijuana possession carries a sentence of up to 10 years and a fine of up to $20,000.
1953	Drugs	Illinois institutes "loitering addict laws" that require narcotics users to register and carry identification cards. This will be ruled unconstitutional.
1956	Drugs	Daniel Act increases penalties by a factor of eight over those specified in the Boggs Act. The rationalization for the law shifts away from marijuana causing insanity and criminality, instead relying on the proposition that marijuana use leads to the use of heroin, creating the gateway drug theory.
1956–1971	Parallel enforcement mechanisms	The FBI conducts a series of covert projects called Cointelpro to surveil, infiltrate, discredit, and disrupt American political organizations including the Black Panther Party, feminist organizations, and anti-Vietnam war groups.

| 1960s | Parallel enforcement mechanisms | Johnson administration supports birth control under a eugenics platform.

Three progressive leaders are assassinated: US President John F. Kennedy in 1963; Malcolm X, Black power activist, in 1965; and Martin Luther King Jr., civil rights movement leader, in 1968. |
|---|---|---|
| 1961 | Community resistance | Freedom Riders ride interstate buses into the segregated South to challenge the non-enforcement of Supreme Court decisions that declared segregated buses unconstitutional. |
| 1962 | Drugs | In Robinson v California, the Supreme Court rules that it is unconstitutional under the 8th Amendment of cruel and unusual punishment to criminalize drug addiction because it is a disease, status, or condition rather than a specific act. While the possession or distribution of illegal drugs may be punished as a crime, the mere status of addiction may not be punished when not connected to a concrete instance of use. This ruling encourages a shift away from the "moral failing" model of drug use toward a medical addiction model. |
| 1963 | Parallel enforcement mechanisms | Bull Conner, Police commissioner in Alabama, releases dogs on protesters including white adult and child protestors. This sends a clear message that whiteness is not protected as much as white supremacy. The attack is broadcast on television causing horror and outrage among the general population. This is a catalyst for change. |
| 1964 | Sex work | HERE brings *Playboy* to the table to sign a contract for Local 705, creating the first union in the sex industry for bunnies at the Playboy Club. |
| | Parallel enforcement mechanisms | The premier national civil rights legislation, the Civil Rights Act, outlaws discrimination on the basis of race, color, religion, sex, or national origin, requiring |

		equal access to public places and employment and enforcing desegregation of schools.
1965	Parallel enforcement mechanisms	The Voting Rights Act prohibits racial discrimination in voting, including the use of literacy tests. The act contains special provisions for the South and mandates bilingual ballots. It has been amended by Congress five times since.
1966	Drugs	The first head shop, Ron and Jay Thelin's Psychedelic Shop, opens on Haight Street offering hippies a spot to purchase marijuana and LSD.
	Community resistance	The Compton's Cafeteria riot occurs in the Tenderloin District of San Francisco and was one of the first LGBTQ riots. Seen as a precursor to the Stonewall Riots, it marks what is widely considered the beginning of collective transgender activism in the United States.

1968–1981: SHIFTING UNDERSTANDINGS OF DRUG USERS AND SEX WORKERS' GRASSROOTS RESISTANCE

This period marks the beginning of America's ideological wars, from the War on Drugs to the fight against Communism, movements that legitimize and maintain federal control. Ideological war warrants a shift from federal drug regulation towards criminalization. The Vietnam War is linked with concerns that drugs are associated with hippies and the anti-war movement, even though the government is giving them to soldiers. Nixon and Rockefeller spearhead the War on Drugs and the modern prison system. The federal response also incentivizes expansion of state and local law enforcement partnerships between justice systems and nonprofits. The Nixon administration is the first and only to grant equal funding to the Drug Enforcement Administration (DEA) and drug abuse treatment. President Reagan's War on Drugs shifts funding and attention toward policing bodies of color.

At the same time, white feminists get a patronizing win when abortion is legalized but Congress won't fund it. Second Wave feminists' next move to gain equal power is to try and strip men of theirs by aligning with carcerality and hyperpolicing. This is the domestic violence and anti-trafficking response as we know it, and a focus on criminalizing sex workers' clients. States try to hold onto regulatory models of certain parts of the sex trade, and grassroots support systems emerge to advocate for rights not punishment.

KEY THEMES

- The modern prison system, created by Nixon and Rockefeller, works in tandem with the Rockefeller drug laws.

- Creation of Nonprofit Industrial Complex and government control over the momentum of social welfare programs.

- Marriage of prison and nonprofits: federal funding is given to drug treatment programs and cities engaging in prostitution diversion programs; victim assistance centers are opened.

- States lose power surrounding drug regulation, but brothels open in Nevada and indoor prostitution is legalized in Rhode Island.

- Development of grassroots support systems, including the formation of sex worker and drug user rights movements as we know today.

TIME LINE

YEAR	CATEGORY	EVENT
1969	Community resistance	Stonewall Inn riots begin, with transfemme sex workers Sylvia Rivera and Marsha P. Johnson at the forefront.
	Drugs	In a special message to Congress, President Richard Nixon identifies drug abuse as "a serious national threat." Citing a dramatic jump in drug-related juvenile arrests and

		street crime between 1960 and 1967, Nixon calls for a national anti-drug policy at the state and federal level.
	Parallel enforcement mechanisms	The Chicago Cook County PD and FBI kill Fred Hampton, a young Black Panther Party leader, by raiding the house while he is sleeping and shooting him and several others in their sleep.
		The Tax Reform Act provides Section 501(c)3 in the Internal Revenue Service Code, which says that every charity in the US that fits certain requirements is a "private foundation." In 1976, Congress passes a bill that allows nonprofits to legally spend up to $1 million per year on lobbying efforts. This gives them greater voice in the government, but also means grassroots and community efforts have to conform to certain structures to receive benefits. This sets the stage for Reagan to tie the War on Drugs to nonprofits in the future and for community resistance to become institutionalized within them.
1970	Community resistance	Street Transvestite Action Revolutionaries (STAR House), which provides housing and support to LGBTQ youth and sex workers in NYC, is founded by Sylvia Rivera.
	Drugs	The Controlled Substances Act (CSA) is enacted into law by Congress. This legislation is the foundation on which the modern drug war exists. It is the federal drug policy under which the manufacture, importation, possession, use, and distribution of certain substances is regulated or criminalized. It outlines five "schedules" of drugs and assigns responsibility for enforcement of this new law to the budding DEA.
	Parallel enforcement mechanisms	Fourteen peaceful student protesters are killed by the national guard in the Kent State massacre. This marks the first time that students are slain in an anti-war gathering.

1970s	Sex work	Cities begin taking money for Diversion Programs for women picked up on prostitution charges.
1971	Community resistance	New York Conference on Prostitution is organized by 30 women belonging to various feminist groups. The conference features workshops and a final discussion panel on "The Elimination of Prostitution." It was one of the earliest confrontations between feminists who had never worked in the sex trade and sex workers. The Attica prisoners riot for four days. Over half of the prisoners in a New York penitentiary take 42 prison staff hostage and seize the prison until their 28 demands for better living conditions and basic human rights are met. Most are agreed to before Governor Nelson Rockefeller orders police to take back control of the prison, resulting in 43 deaths, 33 of which are inmates. As a result of the riot, changes are made in the NY prison system to reduce tension in the system and prevent such incidents in the future. Regardless, many of the complaints and demands from later prison riots are the same as Attica prisoners'.
	Drugs	The Nixon administration coins the term "War on Drugs." President Nixon characterizes the abuse of illicit substances as "public enemy number one in the United States," beginning a 40+ year ideological war that dramatically increases the US incarceration rate.
	Sex work	The Nevada state legislature passes an amendment saying that licenses cannot be extended to brothels in counties with more than 250,000 residents. The Mustang Ranch becomes the first licensed brothel in Nevada.
1972	Drugs	The Shafer Commission, Nixon's National Commission on Marijuana and Drug Abuse, recommends marijuana decrim-

		inalization. The report iss ignored by the White House.
	Parallel enforcement mechanisms	John Burge and the Cook County Police Department begin torturing African American men to obtain confessions using tactics like electric shock and suffocations. The State Attorney's office covers it up for nearly a decade but, eventually, an independent investigation will find Burge guilty in '92, though he will not be fired until the next year. An international investigation will produce several settlements and dismissals of charges for torture survivors. Twenty Black men remain in prison on convictions based in whole or in part upon their coerced confessions.

The first three victim assistance programs in the United States begin, two of which are rape crisis centers in Washington, DC, and the San Francisco Bay area. |
1973	Drugs	Nixon creates the Drug Enforcement Administration (DEA) to coordinate the anti-drug efforts of all other agencies.
	Parallel enforcement mechanisms	Supreme Court decides abortion is federally legal in Roe v Wade. The Hyde Amendment will be added to US Congress' appropriation bill in 1975, blocking federal funding for abortion care.
	Sex work	National sexual labor rights group, Call Off Your Old Tired Ethics (COYOTE), is formed by Margo St. James in California.
1974	Drugs	The Narcotic Addict Treatment Act is signed into law by Congress, creating the methadone clinic structure.
1976	Sex work	RI-based sex worker rights group COYOTE files a lawsuit against Rhode Island, COYOTE v. Roberts, challenging a statute that criminalizes prostitution by raising the question of how much power the state should have to control the sexual activity of

its citizens and alleging discrimination in the statute's application. Data is submitted that demonstrates selective prosecution, as the Providence police were arresting female sex workers far more often than their male customers. COYOTE's lawyer argues that the law is so broad that it fails to even mention money, which could make sexual relations between unmarried adults a crime.

The Conference on Violence Against Women is held in San Francisco. Women Against Violence in Pornography and the Media (WAVPM) is formed as a result. Two years later, WAVPM organizes "Feminist Perspectives on Pornography" featuring workshops, speeches, and a march by 5,000 women demanding an end to pornography.

1978	Community resistance	Carol Leigh, California-based adult industry performer and labor rights activist, coins the term "sex work." The term is meant to draw attention to the work people are performing rather than the criminal legal charge of "prostitution."
1980	Sex work	*Take Back the Night*, an anthology of anti-porn articles, many of which are from the 1978 WAVPM conference, is published. The Rhode Island General Assembly dismisses the lawsuit filed by COYOTE after changing the state law on prostitution. The new law deletes the statute prohibiting the act of prostitution itself, prohibiting street solicitation instead.

1982–1999: ROLL BACK OF PROGRESS

The late 20th century is a tipping point where the states drop to their knees and begin calling the Feds "Daddy." Federal power is held through the appropriations process and states begin to see more money, especially for the expansion of law enforcement (as services become tied to the expansion of policing). Prior homophobic and racist anti-sex and drug policies are a catalyst for the HIV epidemic, which in turn fuels more prohibitionist policies and exclusionary medical practices. The 1980s give us the War on Drugs, gun control, and the feminist sex wars—excuses to over-police Black communities and take away civil liberties. Public opinion is guided through prevention propaganda, and the rise of the 501(c)(3) will serve to later suppress revolutionary activities.

KEY THEMES

- Underground syringe exchange starts as community-based HIV prevention. In response to the first wave of states legalizing syringe exchange, Congress prevents federal funding from going to these programs.

- Civil rights–era progress is halted by the War on Drugs, which increases penalties for drug possession and institutes sentencing disparities. Drug courts begin, which formalizes the relationship between law enforcement and drug treatment programs with new 501(c)(3) status and a need for funding.

- Second-wave and anti-porn feminists begin anti-trafficking organizations and use trafficking rhetoric to enforce victim-perpetrator dichotomies. After the court rules that porn is protected expression, anti-porn feminists turn to increasing criminalization of other forms of sex work.

- Resistance is institutionalized: the movement for drug policy reform begins, sex workers receive services through community-based public health programs, and strip clubs unionize. Resistance groups have to become formal organizations to get access to public and private funding, but funding bans and philanthropic elitism limits their effectiveness.

TIMELINE

YEAR	CATEGORY	EVENT
1982	Community resistance	US PROS Collective forms in San Francisco to fight for decriminalization of sex work.
	Drugs	Nancy Reagan starts her "Just Say No" campaign, touring elementary schools to warn students about the danger of illegal drug use. When one 4th grader at Longfellow Elementary School in Oakland, California, asks Mrs. Reagan what she should do if approached by someone offering drugs, Reagan responds, "Just say no." The slogan and Nancy Reagan's activism on the issue become central to the administration's anti-drug message. By portraying drugs as a threat to children, the administration is able to pursue more aggressive federal anti-drug legislation. Ronald Reagan addresses the nation declaring a "War on Drugs."
	Sex work	Barnard Conference on Sexuality is held in NYC to discuss taboo sexual topics. These discussions are considered the beginning of the feminist sex wars.
1983	Sex work	The Minneapolis city government hires Catherine A. MacKinnon and Andrea Dworkin to draft an anti-pornography civil rights ordinance as an amendment to the Minneapolis city human rights ordinance. The amendment defines pornography as a civil rights violation against women and allows women who claim harm in pornography to sue the producers and distributors for damages in civil court. It also allows viewers who have pornography forced upon them to sue. The law passes twice by the Minneapolis city council but is vetoed by the mayor.
1984	Community resistance	The California Prostitutes Education Project (CAL-PEP) is founded and serves as one of the first HIV education, prevention, and street outreach organizations in the country.

	Drugs	Comprehensive Crime Control Act increases federal penalties for cultivation, possession, or transfer of marijuana.
	Sex work	Anti-porn ordinance based on Minneapolis's passes in Indianapolis, Indiana. It will later be ruled unconstitutional by the Seventh Circuit Court of Appeals, a decision affirmed by the US Supreme Court.
1986	Drugs	Investigation by a sub-committee of the Senate Foreign Relations Committee, the Kerry Committee, finds CIA involvement in Contra cocaine trafficking. Investigation findings are evidence the government funded America's crack/cocaine epidemic. Drug-Free America Act mandates begin requiring drug-free work spaces and schools. The Anti-Drug Abuse Act is enacted into law by Congress. The bill enacts new mandatory minimum sentences for drugs and institutes the crack vs. cocaine disparity, where crack is penalized at a rate 100 times worse than cocaine, primary drivers of the incarceration crisis America faces today. It also changes the system of supervised release from a rehabilitative system into a punitive system.
	Sex work	The final report of the Attorney General's Commission on Pornography (Meese Commission on Porn) claims a connection between sexually violent material and sexually violent actions, and puts forth 92 recommendations that call for federal, state, local, and private actions to crack down on porn. A 1986 amendment protects minors against commercial sexual exploitation and adds protection for adult males. It also replaces "debauchery" and "any other immoral purpose" with "any sexual activity for

1993	Sex work	Heidi Fliess, known as the "Hollywood Madam" for connecting Hollywood actors with escorts, is arrested. She is convicted on three charges of pandering. She will serve three years in prison before the charges are overturned, at which time she will be charged with tax evasion and spend another two years behind bars.
1994	Community resistance	The Lindesmith Center is formed to challenge conventional thinking about drugs, addiction, and drug policy. The Center will become the Drug Policy Alliance in 2000.
	Parallel enforcement mechanisms	The Violent Crime Control and Law Enforcement Act of 1994 is the largest crime bill in US history, adding 100,000 new police officers, $9.7 billion in funding for prisons, and $6.1 billion in funding for prevention programs, which are designed with significant input from experienced police officers. The bill also creates regional drug task forces (COPS and Byrne Jag), which are later associated with racial discrimination in undercover drug busts.
1995	Sex work	The first Johns School, a diversion and education program for men caught soliciting sexual services, begins in San Francisco as a project of Standing Against Global Expansion (SAGE). The group is run by a former sex worker.
1997	Community resistance	Rentboy.com is founded to provide the company of male escorts.
		The first strip club unionizes in San Diego, followed by the famous Lusty Lady in San Francisco.
1999	Community resistance	Community organizing group, New York City AIDS Housing Network, is formed. It will become Voices of Community Activists and Leaders (VOCAL-NY).
		St. James Infirmary, a health clinic run by and for sex workers in San Francisco, opens its doors.

2000–2007: SMOKE AND MIRRORS

By 2000, the War on Drugs has reached its limits in terms of being useful as a form of forced labor and population control. The "moral failing" model of addiction supporting the War on Drugs is challenged by a medical model of addiction, calling for equal parts collaboration from community-based services and law enforcement. This era ushers in the pathologizing of drug users as mentally handicapped and sex workers as victims of circumstance. It is also a wave of the mind/body sovereignty movement in the US that breeds weed libertarians.

Drug war mechanisms continue where useful for federal control and begin to be subsumed by the war on terror (i.e., drug trafficking is a significant funding source for global terrorism, therefore drug enforcement is a fight against terrorism). The War on Terror is used as an excuse to expand the executive branch and global powers. Community resistance evolves as state-based advocacy becomes increasingly necessary.

KEY THEMES

- After a decade without international wars in the '90s, things go global in a different way when Dick Cheney negotiates overseeing foreign policy as vice president. This is when we start to see expansion of executive branch powers.

- Human trafficking is defined on the federal level, and anti-prostitution funding bans are imposed throughout federal funding streams.

- States regains control through prostitution-free zones in DC, as Rhode Island begins efforts to criminalize all sex work again.

- Community resistance both broadens and becomes more specialized: YWEP formed, SWOP USA formed, and the first international day to end violence against sex workers.

YEAR	CATEGORY	EVENT
2000	Sex work	The United Nations passes the Protocol to Prevent, Suppress, and Punish Trafficking in Persons, Especially Women and Children (known as the Trafficking Protocol), a supplement to the Convention Against Transnational Organized Crime and one of the "Polermo Protocols." In the same year, the Trafficking Victims Protection Act (TVPA) passes in the United States. The Act creates three categories for trafficking and defines all minors engaging in sexual exchange as trafficked.
2001	Drugs	The National Research Council Committee on Data and Research for Policy on Illegal Drugs is published. The study reveals that the government had not sufficiently studied its own drug policy, which it called "unconscionable."
	Parallel enforcement mechanisms	A series of coordinated terrorist attacks kills nearly 3,000 Americans on September 11. Part of the US federal response is to pass the Patriot Act, an effort to dramatically tighten US national security. The act expands law enforcement surveillance, including tapping domestic and international phones; eases interagency communication to allow counterterrorism efforts; and increases penalties for terrorism crimes. The Act also expands the list of activities defined as terrorism.
2002	Community resistance	Young Women's Empowerment Project (YWEP) is formed in Chicago as a radical harm-reduction organization serving young women who trade sex. After receiving threats of pandering, arrests from law enforcement for providing harm reduction information to minors in the sex trade (who the law defines as victims of

		trafficking), and other political challenges, the organization will be forced to shut down in 2013.
	Parallel enforcement mechanisms	US detention camp Guantanamo Bay, which is known as a site of "enhanced interrogation techniques" and major human rights violations, is established in Cuba. The CIA destroys tapes depicting extreme torture in this camp in 2005. The Senate has since only published 10 percent of their report on CIA torture. Despite other countries defining enhanced interrogation as torture, the US government orders Guantanamo Bay to stay open indefinitely in 2018.
2003	Community resistance	SWOP organizes and hosts the first International Day to End Violence Against Sex Workers on December 17. The memorial continues annually on December 17 across the world to honor sex workers who have lost their lives to the stigma and violence of whorephobia.
		The Sex Workers Outreach Project (SWOP USA) is formed by Robyn Few to address violence in the sex trade and advocate for the basic human dignity of sex workers. It is now the largest sex worker rights organization in the US with over 25 local chapters across the country.
	Parallel enforcement mechanisms	Vice President Dick Cheney's expanded executive powers allow for the US invasion of Iraq. The US will be the last invading country to remain in Iraq (until 2011) even though most Americans disapprove of the war. In a January 2003 CBS poll, 63 percent of Americans want Bush to find a diplomatic solution rather than go to war, and 62 percent believe the threat of terrorism directed against the US would increase due to war.

2003	Sex work	President's Emergency Plan for AIDS Relief (PEPFAR) is introduced with an "anti-prostitution pledge" requiring organizations receiving HIV/AIDS funding through the program to sign a pledge that they oppose prostitution. The APP is instituted within anti-trafficking funding streams through the TVPA in the same year.
2004	Sex work	On November 2, 2004, the city of Berkeley, California, votes 63.51 percent against decriminalizing prostitution. The same day Churchill County, Nevada, voted 62.78 percent to keep brothels legal even though no brothels exist in the county at the time.
2005	Drugs	Methamphetamine epidemic is declared in the US. Congress, who passes the Combat Methamphetamine Epidemic Act, restricting over-the-counter cold medication. The Act is passed as part of the Patriot Act Reauthorization and calls for the DEA to crack down on available compounds, which leads to the manufacture and use of less safe compounds, including bath salts.
2006	Sex work	Washington, DC, creates "prostitution free zones," essentially removing the requirement of reasonable suspicion for cops to make a prostitution arrest.

2008–2020: CONTROL WHACK-A-MOLE

This era reveals a struggle between policy reform and system change as the drug war loses traction and federal control mechanisms shift toward the war on sex trafficking, justifying the claim that police presence and expansion are still necessary. As opiate overdoses rise, communities call for a bio/psycho/social approach to drug use that expands services without increasing law enforcement power. Advancements in computer and internet technology lend themselves to anti-sex work/trafficking propaganda and legislation. Social media resistance goes viral with #blackivesmatter and #metoo. Neoliberal drug policies are passed on the state level, followed by conservative sex trade policies. Overt racism is officially American again and police continue to kill Black people with impunity.

KEY THEMES

- Drug war loses traction: reduction in crack vs. cocaine disparity, removal of federal mandatory minimums in drug laws, relaxation of the federal syringe exchange funding ban.

- State-based drug policy reform gains traction and so do local carceral responses to the sex trade: marijuana legalization and psilocybin decriminalization versus expansion of third-party charges, mandatory minimums, and enhancements for purchasers.

- The Feds seize and close online advertising venues as civil responsibility to monitor the sex trade resurfaces in a modern online context.

TIMELINE

YEAR	CATEGORY	EVENT
2009	Drugs	Beginning of Hepatitis C epidemic among people who inject drugs. Known as the "silent killer," HCV claims more lives annually than all other nationally notifiable diseases combined. Opiate overdoses become an international epidemic. By 2014, OD is the leading cause of accidental death in the country. By 2016, cumulative deaths pass that of the HIV epidemic and Vietnam War soldier casualties.
	Sex work	Rhode Island signs a law making prostitution a misdemeanor (again).
2010	Drugs	California Proposition 19 (also known as the Regulate, Control and Tax Cannabis Act) is defeated with 53.5 percent of California voters voting No and 46.5 percent voting Yes.

2010	Drugs	Obama passes the Fair Sentencing Act, ending mandatory minimums for crack possession and reducing the crack vs. cocaine disparity to 18:1.
	Parallel enforcement mechanisms	The Affordable Care Act passes, reforming America's healthcare system and further expanding Medicaid to low-income individuals and families.
	Sex work	Craigslist closes its adult services section after years of harassment from anti-sex work organizations.
2011	Community resistance	The first Occupy movement protest begins on Wall Street and spreads to over 600 communities in the US to camp out in front of government and financial institutions demanding economic equality and "real democracy." After the first month of protests, police begin forcibly removing protestors.
	Drugs	Law Enforcement Assisted Diversion (LEAD), a pre-booking model of drug diversion, begins in Seattle, Washington. It will become the model for drug diversion practice and will be replicated and adapted in major cities across the country.
2012	Drugs	Colorado and Washington State passes laws to legalize the consumption, possession, and sale of marijuana.
	Sex work	The CEASE Network is launched by Demand Abolition, an anti-prostitution foundation funded by oil heiress Swanee Hunt, to expand police surveillance of the sex trade. Funding is given to police and prosecutors' offices in 13 major US cities to conflate sex work with sex trafficking and increase criminalization of buyers.
2013	Community resistance	Solutions Not Punishment Coalition (SNaPCo) is formed in response to a proposed Atlanta city council ordinance that would have imposed even steeper fines, fees, and jail time and banished those convicted of street-level sex work.

	Community resistance	The Black Lives Matter movement is started by three radical Black femme organizers after the acquittal of George Zimmerman, the police officer who killed Trayvon Martin, a Black 17-year-old.
	Parallel enforcement mechanisms	Gilead Pharmaceutical Company creates a cure for Hepatitis C. The pill costs $1,000/day for a 90-day cycle, so expensive that insurance companies and state Medicaid programs impose stigmatizing bans on who can receive treatment.
	Sex work	Monica Jones, a Black trans woman, is arrested and charged with manifesting prostitution during a sting operation coordinated alongside a diversion program named "Project ROSE." Jones takes her case to the Arizona supreme court. The case is dismissed in January 2015.
		The Supreme Court invalidates the Anti-Prostitution Pledge within PEPFAR for US-based organizations, but the State Department can still require this for international organizations. Although unconstitutional in PEPFAR funding, the APP remains a requirement in federal anti-trafficking funding streams.
		Women with a Vision successfully challenges the Crimes Against Nature statute in Louisiana (Doe v Caldwell).
2014	Drugs	HIV/HCV outbreak among white rural drug injectors in Indiana facilitates an ideological shift in the way Congress and the general public view addiction (less stigma surrounding opiate use and more funding for white users to access treatment and recovery).

2014	Parallel enforcement mechanisms	Police kill Eric Garner in a choke hold, and a grand jury declines to indict the officer. Protestors hit the streets and flood social media with #Icantbreathe. Several states over, two police officers kill 12-year-old Tamir Rice while he is playing and restrain his sister. Neither officer is fired for murdering a Black child.
	Sex work	Bay Area adult advertising site MyRedbook is seized and sex workers in the Bay Area lose a vital safety tool. Its owners are charged with money laundering and using the internet to facilitate prostitution.
2015	Sex work	Federal agents from the Department of Homeland Security and members of the NYPD raid Rentboy.com's headquarters, seize the website, and arrest seven of its employees.
2016	Drugs	Congress passes the Comprehensive Addiction Recovery Act and 21st Century Cures which provides millions of dollars in funding to substance use prevention and treatment (harm reduction isn't expressly authorized or dismissed). Congress relaxes the federal funding ban on Syringe Services Programs, authorizing Department of Health and Human Services funding under certain conditions. No additional funding is provided.
2017	Community resistance	Following allegations of sexual abuse and misconduct against film producer Harvey Weinstein, #metoo becomes a social justice movement, raising awareness of the pervasiveness of sexual abuse and assault. The anti-violence phrase was originally coined by Tarana Burke in 2006.
	Drugs	Drug supply becomes poisoned with fentanyl.

2018	Community resistance	Decriminalize Nature is founded to improve health and well-being by decriminalizing and expanding access to entheogenic plants and fungi through political and community organizing, education, and advocacy.
		Reframe Health and Justice is founded by queer Asian and Latinx femmes to support organizations in deepening their practices of care and collaboration through healing-centered harm reduction.
	Sex work	Congress passes the Stop Enabling Sex Traffickers Act, commonly known as SESTA-FOSTA, which imposes severe penalties on online platforms that facilitate sex work. The Department of Justice seizes Backpage.com, the largest low-cost global advertising site, before the bill is signed into law. Dozens of online advertising platforms shut down immediately to avoid liability. Backpage's owners are charged with money laundering and promoting prostitution.
	Drugs	The first psilocybin mushroom deprioritization bill passes in Colorado. Decrim hearings are held in Oregon and California.
2019	Sex work	NY introduces a full sex-work decriminalization bill, followed by Vermont, Washington, DC, and Louisiana. The DC decrim bill gets a hearing by the Judiciary Committee of the DC Council and testimony lasts 14 hours. The session ends without the Council voting on the bill.
2020	Community resistance	Social Justice movements band together to put pressure on cities to defund police and move money toward investment in community-based services.
	Parallel enforcement mechanisms	Coronavirus pandemic destabilizes the economy and raises issues about systemic support for people in gig economies and contract workers.
		Police kill Breonna Taylor and George Floyd.

Reframing Harmful Stigmas

This section highlights the incision of social morality into the rhetoric and legislation of a punishment paradigm. Stigma, a result of misunderstanding what it means to be "other," is felt internally, interpersonally, and institutionally. Reframing harmful stigmas surrounding sex work and substance use begins with intentionality, information, and connection.

Human Trafficking: The Bigger Picture

An Interview with Aya Tasaki

JUSTICE RIVERA

THIS INTERVIEW CORRESPONDS WITH A CHAPTER CALLED "EXPLOITATION Nation" in my memoir, *Candy Coated*, where I work under the table for someone who ends up being psychologically abusive and exploitative. I explain the myriad of reasons why I stayed at the time, and how I didn't have any legal recourse or protection once I finally had had enough. My story goes on to show my desperation and desire for revenge that led me to take what was mine from the store owner, later leading to time in jail and a theft felony. *Candy Coated* is a memoir about survival, social justice, and recovery. The story of one young, mixed-race femme's journey toward discovering that compassion is better than punishment and rights are more effective than rescue, it reveals the truth surrounding what society says is good versus bad. Entertaining, intense, and informational, *Candy Coated* is a book that deconstructs the ways Western society views substances, sex, labor, and healing. It is a compelling and human story that invites empathy while offering a realistic look at systems of (in)justice in the US. Readers have called *Candy Coated* "*Orange is the New Black* meets *Party Monster* but more intersectional, magical, and inspirational."

My hope is that retelling these trials and tribulations illustrates how labor exploitation is vastly misunderstood and underfunded.

I love storytelling as an effective way to create change, and I also love hearing from people who are doing on-the-ground work. My goal is for this interview to help readers understand the complexities associated with labor trafficking: what it can look like in form and scope, what resources are/aren't directed to it, why it isn't sexy to talk about like sex trafficking might be, and what is needed to comprehensively understand and address all forms of human trafficking. And, what better person to discuss these things with than Aya Tasaki!

Aya is a queer, bicultural immigrant born and raised in Tokyo and the Midwest, with familial grounding in Hiroshima, where both of her grandmothers were survivors of the atomic bomb. She grew her political and organizing roots working with and alongside radical queer-trans POC and API communities in New York City and across the US and has been involved with gender-based violence movement spaces for 15 years. Aya currently works with the National Network of Abortion Funds and is on the advisory board of Red Canary Song.

Justice Rivera: Hi Aya, I am so excited to have the opportunity to highlight your work and that of Womankind. Will you please tell folks about Womankind, your anti-trafficking programs and approaches, and your role there? I would also love to know more about you and what brought you to/keeps you doing this work?

Aya Tasaki: Womankind is a direct service organization based in New York City serving survivors of sexual violence, domestic violence, and human trafficking for close to four decades.[1] Since its inception as a small, grassroots, volunteer-led group originally called the New York Asian Women's Center, the organization has focused on serving the Asian Pacific Islander (API) community, from children to elders. It currently has two emergency residential spaces, a legal program to support immigration and family law needs, individual counseling and case management, support with social benefits access, and a whole host of programs including many that are holistic healing spaces created and led by survivors. The helpline offers support in 18 Asian languages and dialects, in addition to English and Spanish, and has also introduced a chat and text feature.

Project Free, established in 2005, is Womankind's anti-trafficking program. When the Human Trafficking Intervention Court[2] was established in 2009 in New York City, Womankind was one of the service providers. After being involved for 10 years, Womankind formally left that role, seeing that this court system was not where its resources should be going towards in truly supporting and making a difference in survivors' lives. This long-debated decision was solidified after Womankind joined the DecrimNY[3] steering committee at its inception. Womankind has had an explicitly anti–End Demand approach to human trafficking since joining Freedom Network[4] in

2014, so the trajectory seems natural. Yet, it still remains one of the very few anti-trafficking organizations that has an explicitly decrim stance to sex work.

I was Womankind's first Manager for Policy and Advocacy in 2018 until I transitioned out about a year and a half later. I had also been a legal intern during my first summer in law school.

I am no longer affiliated with Womankind but heavily pull from my experience there as I continue to be involved in the anti-trafficking and sex workers' rights movement work as a board member of Red Canary Song. Red Canary Song is a grassroots collective based in New York City, born in the wake of Yang Song's death. Yang Song was a Chinese massage worker who was killed in a police raid in November 2017. It exists today to support the organizing of Asian and migrant massage parlor workers and sex workers from a labor rights and mutual aid framework.[5]

This work is extremely important to me as part of bigger movement work towards radical liberation for all, and it is also something that sits at the intersection of my personal, academic, and professional experiences. I was born in Japan and moved back and forth between the US and Japan since I was young but spent the majority of my life until 16 in Tokyo. My entire family is Japanese and all live there still. Growing up in Japan was extremely hard for me as a young girl, where sexual harassment and violence of all stripes were rampant and normalized alongside an extremely robust sex and porn industry, but without any space to speak about it, not to mention any conversations about misogyny, patriarchy, intense sexism, etc. (I had no access to the voices of badass sex workers and porn stars).

It was in that environment where I went in and out of the sex trade as a minor, mostly engaging in "enjyo-kosai" or "compensated dating," which was almost a buzz word at the time. Aside from the fact that what I was doing would be considered illegal and make me an automatic victim of rape and pedophilia as a minor, I also experienced multiple instances of violence throughout the time. Coupled with the fact that I had extremely internalized racism and rage towards Japanese people and society, this made me ripe to swallow all of the end-demand, carceral rhetoric of trafficking and sex work I was exposed to through undergrad and grad school (I did both in international affairs).

Organizing with radical queer and trans people of color (QTPOC) community in NYC (particularly the Audre Lorde Project[6] back in the day) really shifted my entire political viewpoint and, seriously, community taught me. I found my own liberation and healing making so much more sense in the Prison Industrial Complex (PIC) abolition, anti-carceral, decrim liberation framework. Movement community saved me in so many ways, they continue to teach and hold me—and I believe everyone should have safe access to a network/community in the same way.

JR: Yas Kween! Thank you for sharing and I couldn't agree more. I am interested in hearing more about your experiences working with survivors of trafficking. What types of violence and exploitation are your clients experiencing? Are there trends in the types of people who are accessing your services and the types of harm that are experienced among the Asian and immigrant community?

AT: The main forms of exploitation and labor trafficking are often found in the hospitality industry and in construction, agriculture, and domestic work. Contrary to the narrative we often hear, many men experience exploitation and trafficking. Labor exploitation and trafficking looks like being subjected to less-than-poverty-level wages and abysmal working conditions, enforced with physical, psychological, and sexual violence in the workplace. A commonality among API and immigrant communities that make the picture complex include having a precarious immigration status that is weaponized against them (including confiscation of immigration and identification documents, high debt accrued through various immigration channels/processes, combined with threats of physical violence against family members in their home country, deportation to a country where the individual fled from fearing violence, etc.). Another complexity is that the person or people who are exploiting or trafficking them are often extended family or community members.

On the point about division of sex/labor—which I also touch on in later answers—there are often instances/situations that could "legally" be categorized as "sex trafficking" or "sexual exploitation," but that live within or alongside labor trafficking or exploitation. Service providers and legal frameworks (with tremendous help from media and dominant social narratives) are set up to obsessively encourage the individual to identify whether or not there was any type of sexual violence or exploitation, when in reality the identification and emphasis of that information does nothing for the individual (i.e., there are no practical additional benefits they would get).

My former colleague Mary Caparas, manager of the anti-trafficking program at Womankind, often says "human trafficking is an experience and not a prescription," and I think this is absolutely spot on. Oftentimes the experience of trafficking is multiple events and types of violence throughout the course of time, and not just a single event. Just because sexual violence or exploitation may have occurred throughout the individual's experience (sexual violence is often used by traffickers/exploiter as a tactic), that does not mean that those are the sites of redress/justice/healing that the individual is seeking or where actual answers live.

There are many survivors who simply have no interest in addressing the sexual violence part, especially when it is irrelevant to or getting in the way of addressing their immediate needs. For example, think about how this all plays out for someone being exploited in or labor trafficked into a bar/nightclub/massage establishment where they are forced to bartend or do custodial work without (or with minimal) pay, no breaks, no days off. Under these circumstances, we often see folks making the choice to engage in various types of sex work (often in inconsistent ways, here and there) in order to make money and to carve out resources as best they can. Even when labor exploitation and trafficking are the issue that needs to be addressed, the incessant fascination with the "sex" part by law enforcement and many service providers leads to criminalization of the survivor or a barrier in truly having their needs met in ways that lift them out of the situation.

JR: This really speaks to the fact that the anti-trafficking movement is a top-down movement. I appreciate you proposing the goal of flexible and compassionate approaches that address people's needs rather than set prescriptive approaches. Will you tell us more about the concerns and needs of the survivors you work with and people who access your services?

AT: The main needs and concerns are really the things fundamental to every human being—safe housing for themselves and their families, food, and immigration status that allows them to not be criminalized or fear deportation, keeps their family together, and allows them to work. What they do *not* need is someone else to make decisions for them, patronize them, or "save" them. When individuals have the basic resources and safety afforded to them—as every single one of us has the right to—that is an investment in their humanity. They then can go ahead and actually access the wisdom that already lives inside to assess what the best course of action/choice is for them. Even if the choices they have are far from ideal, those of us on the outside offering support must always ask: what does it mean to truly honor someone's choice and self-determination?

If anything, it is our duty to make sure that someone is able to live out their choice that they have made at a certain point in their lives in the safest way possible and to support them in getting to a place where they have more options. People do not need to be supplied with some outside "voice for the voiceless." What this needs to look like, especially for survivors who are immigrants, is that they need support and access to resources to be offered in a form where they are allowed to honor the relationships and communities that matter to them for whatever reason. Oftentimes, those that were violent or exploitative towards them are extended family members or members of the only community the survivor has ties to. Support and resources to survivors cannot be tied to demands that sever ties with or criminalize people in their lives.

JR: This is *all so real*. Thank you. Let's talk more about the barriers to care and well-being that you've presented. What local, state, and federal policies leave the communities you represent vulnerable to trafficking and which make their situations worse? Are any of these anti-trafficking laws?

AT: I have to say that so many of the policies that exist, whether they were explicitly created to alleviate issues of human trafficking or not, create more barriers and long-term harm. There continues to be clear over-reliance and heavy investment in punitive, simplified, criminal legal responses to address trafficking, exploitation, and violence, which are structural and systemic social issues. This includes things from federal immigration policies, including public charge, Department of Housing and Urban Development (HUD) proposing rules that would prohibit mixed-status families from being eligible for assistance and housing (which is especially detrimental when lack of safe housing is one of the leading vulnerabilities of folks being exploited and trafficked), states with lack of vacatur laws that allow for a trafficking survivor's criminal record to be wiped, and any and all regulations that give excuses for law enforcement to raid/enter immigrant-owned businesses (e.g., massage establishment ordinances that allow for citations if the business has anything that obscures the view into a window).

So much of the laws and "campaigns" to combat trafficking are a show of unwillingness to engage with its real complex causes. You can see that in the extreme hype around sex trafficking and the idea of labor trafficking as a complete afterthought, when in reality there is so much more of the latter (not to mention how labor exploitation and labor trafficking are so often what puts folks at heightened risk of sex trafficking). Many of the initiatives claiming to combat sex trafficking are jumping straight into the thing that seems easiest to "solve," which is to get rid of "demand"—not demand of sex trafficking, sexual exploitation, sexual violence, but demand of all sexual services and the sex trade.

I really think so many people and organizations are eager to cling onto the idea of End Demand[7] as a "solution" because once you start having to dig a bit deeper, everything you have built your world around (carceral systems, immigration, capitalism, etc.) will crumble, and that is terrifying for most whether we want to admit it or not. Even after decades of surface-level, carceral-based ideas to combat trafficking clearly not working, so many refuse to accept that it is the dominant criminal legal paradigm that is not working and continue to double down on pouring more and more resources into criminalization mechanisms. Many still think that the end will come once they are able to outspend and incarcerate their way through.

What's really painful and frustrating to witness is how these laws and service models that are being given the most funding are so often designed in ways that break up networks and communities—communities who hold critical knowledge of how to truly strike at the true causes of violence and exploitation—and it does so under the banner of fighting trafficking. Bill after bill, resources are poured into new types and categories of criminalization and excuses for increased interaction with law enforcement. Funding for service providers is tied to cooperation with law enforcement (e.g., offering "sensitivity training" for cops, being the social worker on police raids, being a service provider in Human Trafficking Intervention Court, anti-prostitution pledges,[8] etc.).

Criminalization and increased invitation of law enforcement intervention into the picture is the exact opposite of what we need! It has been made clear, time and time again, that the reason individuals do not report their exploitative or abusive working conditions to law enforcement is because of legitimate fear of losing their job (a big deal when that job is literally your lifeline), fear of being detained and deported (because the system continues to criminalize the choices people make to immigrate to a safer and better life), fear of facing violence from law enforcement (we have been seeing for years on end how law enforcement are violent and exploitative towards trafficking survivors, those perceived to be sex workers, and immigrants), and fear of being criminalized for decisions they made in order to survive.[9] Fear has no place in a true solution in fighting trafficking, exploitation, or violence, and placing law enforcement into the picture is always about injecting fear. This criminalization and fear breaks up communities and networks, because it breaks up trust.

The actual cases of trafficking that come through to organizations like Womankind are majority referrals through other community organizations. When there is trust, survivors are able to choose when and how to communicate and disclose their situation to another. Not only do community and trusted networks keep us safe, they know how to stay safe. So why not divest and defund the myriad of bills and regulations that boost law enforcement, and fund communities instead so they can truly resource these safety mechanisms?[10] Why not fund the spaces where solutions are created, where truly life-changing support is offered, where communities can actually be safe enough to create sophisticated analysis and piece together the complex web of solutions? (Yes, looking at spaces led by sex workers, domestic workers, street vendors, etc.)

JR: Preach! And thank you because this is exactly what I think people need to hear. Your organization sits on many coalitions that work to comprehensively address trafficking. What is the division of focus and resources allocated between sex trafficking and other forms of labor trafficking? The last several publications of the annual Trafficking in Person Report[11] highlight the vast extent of non-sexual labor trafficking occurring worldwide; do you feel appropriate time and resources are spent addressing non-sexual forms of labor trafficking? Furthermore, the general public doesn't hear much about non-sexual labor trafficking. Why do you think that is?

AT: Anti-trafficking service providers see the reality on the ground: how funding continues to disproportionately be poured into organizations that focus on sex trafficking and exploitation. Sex trafficking is sensationalized through a multitude of channels, and it's all-hands-on-deck moral panic where every single person thinks they can be and should be equipped to spot and urgently call law enforcement to rescue trafficked individuals perceived to be in situations so dire and on the brink of death. It sells, and is continuing to be sold, as the noble cause for the public to the detriment of those who are actually sex trafficked, vulnerable to being sex trafficked, labor trafficked, and exploited. The mainstream anti-trafficking framework was created from and imposed by a completely outsider savior point of view and continues to be so. It goes hand in hand with being anti-sex work and doubling down on criminal legal systems and immigration control. It fits so neatly into the carceral, clear-cut moralistic ideas of good/bad that most of us were raised with, which makes it easy to sell.

This sensationalized narrative is packaged together with the End Demand measures that purport to prevent trafficking in the sex trade through criminalizing customers. End Demand measures end up harming sex workers and have done virtually nothing to reduce violence, exploitation, or trafficking.[12] This is in part because End Demand refuses to accept the idea that the sex trade needs to be treated in the same way as other industries and workplaces (i.e., as work/labor) where individuals can benefit from measures that focus on ending demand for trafficked and exploited labor across all sectors, and measures that strengthen the bargaining power and safety of workers.

We really need to go back to a labor rights framework approach to all forms of trafficking, because I think the attempted division of sex and labor trafficking has been detrimental to the entire anti-trafficking effort. The infatuation with keeping society captive to sex trafficking and away from labor trafficking is convenient and easy, because tackling labor trafficking is inherently about confronting capitalism—the way we as society view and value labor and the people who do the labor—and it's just too much and too inconvenient of a fight to fight.

The criminal legal system only centers victims when what they want aligns exactly with what the system wants, and I wonder if this is another reason why labor trafficking in construction, agriculture, domestic work, etc. doesn't get enough attention. For example, so many folks who are exploited in those sectors don't have "clean" immigration stories and don't fit into the perfect victim narrative. In a story about sex trafficking where the convenient headline is about "sexual exploitation of naive, innocent, desperate women," whatever complicated immigration stuff can usually be manipulated into that sympathetic helpless victim narrative (and thus, again, enables the attention to be diverted away from things like the harmful immigration system, capitalism, etc.).

There is also something to be said about how there are many survivors who have fallen back into being exploited/trafficked precisely because we have not invested enough in cultivating environments for individuals to act based on their own wisdom and needs and allow access to tools/resources that would honor their autonomy and path to lift out of the cycle. What leads someone to being vulnerable to violence and exploitation in the first place is not the "bad actor" or individual that does harm, it's the lack of access to resources coupled with systemic violence and oppression. This is especially true because the common choices an individual makes when they are in a truly hard situation are the ones that continue to be criminalized (e.g., sex work, selling goods on the street, care work, or any kind of informal work without immigration documents, etc.).

Even if the violence and exploitation are perpetrated by individual employers or even state officials, what is enabling and continuing to sustain it is capitalistic labor migration regimes and neoliberal economic policies. If we do not invest in labor rights, social conditions, housing, decriminalizing sectors of work, etc., we cannot support those who were actually trafficked into this country/within this country to get out, and we cannot prevent those who are in precarious situations from falling into increasingly dangerous situations.

JR: Thank you for explaining why prohibitionist approaches to the sex trade disguised as anti-trafficking policies aren't working. You have touched on what is working, and I love to hear about community-based solutions to addressing violence and exploitation. Some rights-based anti-violence programs are exploring transformative justice approaches to addressing trafficking.[13] Will you please tell me more about it and why this approach is so important?

AT: A lot of this connects to the complexities that I spoke about earlier—how so often the person or people who perpetrated violence, exploited the individual, trafficked the individual, are immediate/extended family members, members of the survivor's own community, or have become the survivor's main community (herein also lies the complexity of how an individual's relationship with the person that is exploiting them is often much more than just that). Transformative Justice (TJ), at its root, is about responding to violence without creating more violence. And it recognizes state violence, including the criminal legal system and criminal-immigration legal system, as the main site and perpetrator of violence and exploitation.

In the carceral and punitive system that the majority of our society relies on, the response to an individual being exploited or harmed would be to call law enforcement. The result of this response is usually criminalization of not just the person who caused harm, but also layered criminalization of the survivor as they are exposed to law enforcement that is systemically racist, anti-immigrant, sexist, transphobic, and homophobic. Even if the survivor ends up getting through it in one piece at the end, that takes years of being entangled in the criminal and immigration system. People have a false understanding that once a survivor "leaves the bad situation" and is going through legal proceedings "on their way to freedom," the survivor is protected and in a safer place.

The reality is that the hurdle of obtaining a T-visa (for human trafficking victims) or a U-visa (for victims of crime) is extremely high for many, requires extensive interaction and "cooperation" with law enforcement, and can take years. The idea of vacating an individual's criminal record that they may have accrued throughout their experience of being trafficked, exploited, or simply trying to survive, still lags way behind, meaning that many survivors are barred from housing, employment, and other benefits in the interim because of it. Even in situations where it is only the person who caused harm that gets punished by the system, it too often leads to survivors being isolated and cut off from the only network they had—a network that may have been their sole source of income, housing, and a type of shield from law enforcement and ICE. This puts the survivor in a heightened place of vulnerability, in a situation where risk of exploitation is even greater. We cannot continue to underplay the importance of the communal ecosystem an individual is embedded in, however complex it may seem. A TJ approach creates space for that to be honored, while the carceral approach actively destroys it.

JR: It is exciting to know that there are solutions outside the criminal legal paradigm! Is there anything else you would like readers to know about how to examine, prevent, or address human trafficking?

AT: I really want to get rid of the words "desperate" and "out of desperation" from the vocabulary bank of anti-trafficking work, or at least limit their use to a bare minimum. These words really rob and minimize the power behind choices individuals make. We see this especially in treating those who make the hard yet valid and valuable choice to trade sex—even if that decision was made under extenuating circumstances—it is no one's to police or rescue. That is still the choice they made as the best in the moment and that needs to be honored. The use of words like "desperate" really flatten the complexity of the individual and deprive them of self-determination and wisdom. Individuals need access to resources (we're talking tangible, fundamental, basic human needs) and support with creating a physical and emotional space that will allow them to make the best decisions for themselves. If an individual decides to trade sex or stay with a violent employer for the time being until they feel safe and ready to leave—these and any other decision need to be honored.

I also want to ban the narrative that paints the gig economy and so-called informal economy as always being the worst, last-ditch choice that individuals with no other options cling to as a form of survival. This works really well to keep these sectors apart from "formal" sectors that are somehow more deserving of labor protections and as sites of collective power. If we want to truly fight against trafficking and exploitation, we need to understand that fighting for housing for all, expanding what constitutes "labor" and strengthening the protections for workers, and fighting for accessible and robust health care and social benefits systems are all major ways to do so. In fact, if we don't rebuild those components of our society, exploitation and trafficking won't ever go away.

Furthermore, use of money for "awareness campaigns" and "raising visibility" is not only useless, but lazy and harmful—the message that everyone can do something to fight trafficking, and that something is "learning how to spot it" plus the number to your local law enforcement. Much of the anti-trafficking work we see in the mainstream may help some individuals but keeps the bigger cycle of trafficking and exploitation going. If your fight against trafficking and exploitation does not center dismantling capitalism and an explicit racial justice analysis, then you are probably doing more harm than good.

JR: Thank you so much, Aya. This has been a deeply educational and moving conversation.

You can follow Aya on Twitter at @asiannomad, WomanKind at @iamwomankind on all social media platforms, and Red Canary Song at @redcanarysong.

Abolition Means No More Policing: When the Afterlives of Slavery Are Repackaged as Freedom

zara raven

ACCORDING TO THE LAW, I'M A SEX TRAFFICKING SURVIVOR. AND YET IF you search for images that represent child sex trafficking, Black, queer, and trans youth rarely show up in the results.

The images on the websites of most anti-trafficking organizations are often young white girls with their hands tied, or pale hands forming stop signs with writing in black sharpie across the palm. The words often say "STOP" or "HELP ME" or "I AM NOT FOR SALE." In this popular narrative of sex trafficking, traffickers are strangers preying on innocent white girls, abducting them from nuclear families, and carrying them across state lines.

This narrative relies on several myths that uphold racial capitalism: strangers as dangerous, Blackness as criminal, and prisons, policing, and borders as protection. When the Trafficking Victims Protection Act (TVPA) defined sex trafficking as "the use of force, fraud, or coercion to compel someone to engage in the exchange of sex for resources" in federal law in 2000, designating all people under the age of 18 who trade sex for resources as child sex trafficking victims, the moral panic around sex trafficking aligned well with the fear-based messaging of the War on Terror: If you see something, say something. In a similar vein, signage across public transportation, airports, schools, and hotels have urged people to spot trafficking and report tips to the human trafficking hotline operated by global anti-trafficking organization Polaris, which works closely with law enforcement.

Organizations like Polaris and Operation Underground Railroad are primarily led by white people and yet perversely named themselves after the social movements that guided enslaved Black people to freedom. Like many individuals and organizations that represent the mainstream anti-trafficking movement, they refer to themselves as "abolitionists" and the sex industry as "modern day slavery" while advancing carceral responses that grow the prison industrial complex (PIC). Central to this approach, the key US federal anti-trafficking law, the TVPA, relies heavily on increased criminal penalties as the primary response to this phenomenon. Despite including young people in the definition of trafficking victims, the TVPA does not protect sex-trading youth from criminalization. While some states have passed additional laws to correct TVPA's sweeping overcriminalization, many more are reluctant to end the practice of criminalizing young people who trade sex, because, as they observe, youth are often working on their own. One federally funded study found that 85 percent of youth working in the sex industry don't have a trafficker or third-party exploiter. Meanwhile, the majority of young people working in the sex trades are Black, and to be Black is to be marked criminal within racial capitalism.

By claiming to address sex trafficking through criminalization, these groups show little curiosity about the conditions that lead people to enter the sex trades and the needs expressed by people who trade sex.

Most of us were not snatched from an IKEA parking lot by masked men in a white van and forced to enter the sex industry, the way trafficking is portrayed in thousands of viral social media posts. The vast majority of us were harmed and exploited by people we trusted, people we relied on, people we may have even loved. We ran away from homes where we were abused. We were kicked out from homes where our queer and trans identities were rejected. Many of us were even abducted from our homes by the state—kidnapped by the cops known as Child Protective Services workers who decided that we had inadequate food or housing or supervision, and so displaced us into strangers' homes instead of ensuring that we had all the resources we needed.

We entered the sex industry because it helped us to survive the impossible circumstances constructed by racial capitalism.

Black queer and trans survivors are not the perfect poster children for this movement to "abolish modern-day slavery" because most of us don't see the sex industry as a form of slavery. Instead, we understand ourselves to be living in what Saidiya Hartman in *Scenes of Subjection* calls "the afterlife of slavery": a context of anti-Black racism upheld through prisons and policing, where Black people are criminalized for everyday acts of survival.[1] For us, the term "abolition" centers Black liberation and recognizes the prison industrial complex—not the sex industry—as the historical successor of US slavery.

The historical connection from slavery to prisons and policing can be traced in part through the 13th Amendment of the US Constitution. The 13th Amendment carved out an exception to the abolition of slavery, permitting the practices of incarceration and forced labor, or enslavement, as "punishment for a crime." As Black Panther and long-time organizer for political prisoners Safiya Bukhari once wrote, "Who has the power determines what is a crime."[2] While shut out from economic opportunities, Black people faced criminalization under newly minted status offenses that policed them for a refusal or inability to participate in the systems oppressing them. In her 2019 book *Wayward Lives, Beautiful Experiments: Intimate Histories of Social Upheaval*, Hartman writes:

> In the south, vagrancy laws became a surrogate for slavery, forcing ex-slaves to remain on the plantation and radically restricting their movement. In the north, vagrancy statutes were intended to compel the labor of the idle, and, more importantly, to control the propertyless, by denying them the right to subsist and elude the contract.[3]

Through laws against vagrancy, loitering, and other so-called status offenses, Black people were policed and criminalized for occupying public spaces, being without work, and just surviving. Criminalization of status offenses was central to building the racist order of the post-Emancipation US, and continues to be used to criminalize people who work in the sex industry today, especially Black, queer, and trans people shut out of economic opportunities and experiencing homelessness.

The practice of family policing, or the surveillance and removal of children from their families and networks of care by state agencies tasked with "child protection," can also be traced back to family separation practices that were intrinsic to the institution of US slavery. In her 2022 book *Torn Apart*, Dr. Dorothy Roberts wrote about the ways that, during slavery, family separation through the sale of an enslaved mother's children was used as a tactic of control to prevent escapes or rebellion. "Slaveholders could threaten enslaved women who were rebellious with the sale of their children to make them more compliant."[4] In the immediate aftermath of slavery, many formerly enslaved Black parents worked to reunite with their children through newspaper ads, petitions, lawsuits, and purchasing their freedom. But laws passed during the Reconstruction Era after the Civil War forced Black people into new forms of slavery. From 1865 to 1866, Black Codes "place[d] Black children in the care and service of white people if they found the parents to be unfit, unmarried, or unemployed and if they deemed the displacement 'better for the habits and comfort of the child'" through a system of apprenticeship. Parents, and particularly Black parents, deemed "unfit" to care for their children continue to be targets of family policing.

For prison industrial complex abolitionists, the state is the primary organizer of all violence—recognizing prisons, policing, and borders as inherently violent and the state as upholding oppressive systems like cisheteropatriarchy reinforced in structures like the patriarchal nuclear family. Abolition is a practice, a vision, and a way of life that seeks to eradicate all forms of prison, policing, and punishment. The movement for abolition that I work toward seeks to radically restructure society so that everyone can get their needs met. Without borders around family or nation-state that strictly define who is a legitimate beneficiary of care, whole communities become responsible for collective care.

So, if we're the real abolitionists, then where did this other abolition movement originate?

The popular narrative of sex trafficking has its historical roots in the late 19th century. As the transatlantic slave trade was outlawed globally, the enslavement of Africans and their descendants began to take on new forms through mass incarceration and family policing. Erasing the realities of white men's routine sexual violence against Black women and girls, Black men were frequently criminalized and even lynched over false accusations of sexual aggression against white women. Building onto this myth, moral panic about the "White Slave Trade" took hold, first in Europe and later in the United States. Criminalization and policing became the primary response to rescue white women and girls from this imagined fate.

The narrative that white women were being forced into the sex industry enabled anti-Blackness in the forms of increased criminalization and tightened border security.

In the US, the first law regulating the sex industry was an anti-immigration law: the Page Act of 1875 restricted the immigration of Chinese women, painting them as sex workers who would contaminate the population. In 1910, the Mann Act, also known as the White Slave Traffic Act, set out to criminalize the transportation of "any woman or girl for the purpose of prostitution or debauchery, or for any other immoral purpose." Although its proponents claimed to be targeting the commercial sex industry, the broad definitions in the law including "debauchery" and "immoral purposes" had the effect of criminalizing all stigmatized relationships, and especially interracial relationships between Black men and white women. The Mann Act was most notably used to condemn and criminalize Black professional boxer Jack Johnson for his marriage to a white woman. When traveling with his wife in 1913, Johnson was charged for "transporting a white prostitute." The Mann Act further codified certain assumptions about sex and race into law: Blackness as criminality, whiteness as innocence, and trafficking as a phenomenon where strangers abduct helpless victims for the purposes of sexual exploitation.

This historical context is important to understand the imagery, language, and approach used by predominantly white anti-trafficking organizations today: a form of Blackface that legitimizes their work while actively erasing and disregarding the nuanced experiences of Black, queer, and trans people surviving in the sex industry.

Relying on the conflations of Blackness with criminality and strangers with danger, overly broad legal and social definitions of "trafficking" can encompass people who defy gender norms, engage in mutual aid, or exist in multiracial families or networks of care. Beyond the harm caused to those actually working in the sex industry, the stigma against the industry is and has historically been far-reaching. As Saidiya Hartman wrote in *Wayward Lives, Beautiful Experiments*, "Being too loud or loitering in the hallway of your building or on the front stoop was a violation of the law; making a date with someone you met at the club, or arranging a casual hook up, or running the streets was prostitution." Anti-sex work stigma is inextricably intertwined with social norms upholding the gender binary and the normative nuclear family. For those engaged in the exchange of sex for resources, every third party faces risk of being criminalized for trafficking, whether a roommate, someone who drives a worker to a date, or someone who helps a worker with their hair. People can be criminalized for working together, living together, and engaging in the peer support and mutual aid strategies that sex workers rely upon to survive. Under this regime, bystanders are encouraged and empowered to report any person they find "suspicious." In 2019, news broke that Cindy McCain, prominent anti-trafficking advocate and wife of former US Senator John McCain, reported a trafficking tip to police when she spotted an adult at an airport with a child of a different complexion. Urging others to follow her lead in reporting suspicious activity, McCain shared to her social media followers that day, "And, by God, she was trafficking that kid." Local police later contradicted her posts, stating that a welfare check had been conducted on the child and there was "no evidence of criminal misconduct or endangerment."[5] And yet, deeply embedded in white supremacy are ideas about who and what constitutes an appropriate nuclear family—ideas used to enable family policing.

The Family, in its normative nuclear form, serves as a border demarcating who is a legitimate beneficiary of care, mirroring the borders around the nation-state that enclose the national family and shut others out. Those willing or able to conform to the norms and expectations of this structure are able to access its benefits, while everyone outside of these borders is a stranger representing danger to the system, needing to be locked up or removed. These borders are reinforced by the popular myth of "stranger danger"—the idea that those outside of the borders of the nuclear family or the nation-state are both a burden and a threat to be feared. This myth acts as a pillar of criminalization and border violence, while debilitating the collectivism needed to promote true care and safety. For those who perceive themselves as abolitionists while upholding racial capitalism, the border is a necessary tool; for the abolitionists seeking to dismantle these intersecting systems of oppression, borders around both family and nation-state have been sites of violence.

The vast majority of attacks on women and girls are perpetrated by people we know, and for many of us, the violence starts at home. According to Generation FIVE, up to 90 percent of people under the age of 18 who experience sexual abuse know the person who abused them.[6] Roughly one third of those who abused were family members, and nearly 60 percent were acquaintances. About 7 percent were strangers. It is usually not strangers who sexually exploit children; it is so often their own families.

Families and a family policing system that seek to uphold cisheteropatriarchal norms make youth vulnerable to trafficking and exploitation. Up to 40 percent of youth experiencing homelessness in the US are queer and trans, and most became homeless due to family rejection of their sexualities and gender identities. On a state level, more laws are being passed to uphold gender norms. In places like Texas, families who support and affirm the gender of their trans kids are, according to the state, abusing their children, making them targets of family separation policies. The state also puts children at greater risk: about half of homeless youth and about 60 percent of youth whose experiences are legally defined as trafficking have been in the foster system. Although research shows that affirming the gender identity and sexual orientation of the children and youth in our care promotes their safety and well-being, both the state and the nuclear family model are more focused on enforcing conformity to gender norms than promoting safety and wellness.

As those who are most targeted by policing at the borders of the family and nation-state, Black people, and especially Black, queer, and trans people, have found ways to survive and build networks of care outside of the patriarchal nuclear family norm and access to state support. While the "stranger danger" myth continues to fuel criminalization and hyperindividualism, people who trade sex tend to rely on each other as sources of support in the absence of any other resources. At the margins, mutuality is a necessity.

If we center the perspectives and experiences of Black, queer, and trans youth surviving in the sex industry, the infrastructure of racial capitalism explodes—from the patriarchal nuclear family to the prison industrial complex.

For those invested in Black liberation, abolition means eradicating the prison industrial complex—defined by Critical Resistance as "the overlapping interests of government and industry that use surveillance, policing, and imprisonment as solutions to economic, social, and political problems."[7] Our movement for abolition is a movement toward abolishing the afterlife of slavery that has taken the form of criminalization of status offenses and family policing. In New York, on the Decrim NY campaign working to decriminalize, decarcerate, and destigmatize the sex industry, we specifically targeted and successfully worked to overturn the law against loitering for the purposes of prostitution, which we referred to as the "Walking

While Trans" ban. In 2018, 49 percent of people arrested in New York for loitering for the purposes of prostitution were Black, 42 percent were Latine, and more than 80 percent were cis and trans women. Often, Black and Latine trans women were targeted for wearing a skirt, hailing a cab, or just existing in public space. Similarly in DC, on the DecrimNow DC campaign, we recognized that many of the same people were being charged under different laws, like loitering, fare evasion, and even "nuisance" laws that allowed landlords to evict tenants considered a "nuisance" for their activity within criminalized industries like the sex trades. We mobilized in a coalition to end the criminalization of fare evasion and resist the expansion of "nuisance" laws, chipping away at some of the infrastructure that criminalizes Black people for surviving.

Repealing these laws were small actions, but the reality is that Black, queer, and trans people at the margins will always be targeted, surveilled, policed, and criminalized for as long as prisons and policing exists. The whole carceral apparatus needs to be dismantled, and we need to rebuild our society through values that challenge the underlying assumptions that have enabled slavery and its afterlives to exist in the US. In its place, the values of collectivism and interdependence can support us in creating a radically different kind of society. To promote the safety and well-being of young people, survivors, and all of us, we need whole communities involved in building networks of care.

Exploitation Is to Sex Work as Overdose Is to Drug Use

JUSTICE RIVERA

HUMAN TRAFFICKING AWARENESS MONTH IS MORE THAN JUST POSTERS and commercials—it is a month where we can take a critical look at our approaches and ask how these interventions are growing and evolving. This month, the anti-trafficking movement can learn from other movements for health and justice including the harm reduction movement. Using a harm reduction approach to drug use means trying to limit the potential negative consequences of drug use. While this can mean access to clean needles to prevent HIV and Hepatitis C transmission, it also takes seriously the social dynamics that influence drug use itself.[1] Just like overdose is one potential harm of drug use, trafficking is one potential harm of labor. By considering a broad understanding of harm and broader interventions to reduce trafficking, anti-trafficking advocates can learn a lot from anti-overdose advocates.

In 2009, when opioid overdoses surpassed car crashes as the top accidental fatality in the country,[2] drug users and people who loved and worked with drug users began changing laws to increase access to naloxone, a drug that reverses opioid overdose. Naloxone is an overdose intervention that saves lives. It has few to no side effects. Outside of communities directly impacted by overdose, the common misconception of naloxone and other harm reduction approaches to drug use was that it enabled people to continue using. The escalation of America's opioid crisis and success of naloxone as an overdose intervention have swayed many people's belief about how to approach overdose. Even treatment and criminal legal professionals now know that not all drug use leads to overdose and that when overdose occurs,

Originally published on Reframe Health and Justice (January 14, 2020,
https://reframehealthandjustice.medium.com/xploitation-is-to-sex-work
-as-overdose-is-to-drug-use-c1cc16cd67fa.). Reprinted with permission.

the person should be given immediate care and the option of a longer-term support strategy, which can include anything from health care to treatment to housing.

This is the public health approach to overdose—where overdose is seen as one potential negative consequence of drug use, and interventions are put into place to prevent and reverse this harm. The harm-reduction view of drug use does not stop at overdose. Harm reduction means taking these interventions one step further to recognize that overdose is one potential negative consequence of the War on Drugs. To seriously address the rise in overdose deaths, we need to consider and address ineffective policies and social conditions such as poverty and racism. These sociopolitical factors perpetuate harm and are best tackled through community-level interventions and broader social change.

Drug war tactics like policing and surveillance also push drug use underground. This exacerbates the overdose crisis by reducing people's knowledge of how or where to use safely. People are constantly put in a position where they can either use publicly and face arrest or use privately and risk fatal overdose. Community-level interventions reduce overdose by creating safe places for people to use and providing information on safety. Incite, a Safe Consumption Space in Vancouver, is an example of such a space.

Incite offers harm reduction supplies such as sterile syringes, as well as HIV/HCV testing, micro-counseling, and linkage to mental health support and housing. The facility has nurses on site to treat bacterial infections and respond to overdose, reversing it immediately. The top floor of the facility provides substance use treatment. After opening, city-wide overdoses were reduced.[3] By providing people access to safe use, rather than decreasing access to safe use like the War on Drugs does, Safe Consumption Sites create the best long-term health and wellness outcomes for people who use drugs. Movement is currently underway to open Safe Consumption Spaces in several US cities including Philadelphia, Seattle, Denver, and San Francisco.

Just as not all drug use leads to overdose, not all sex work begins or ends with exploitation. Exploitation within the sex trade is a harm that can be prevented. A harm-reduction approach to the sex trade means examining, preventing, and addressing all forms of possible harm that can occur in someone's work. Since the degree of choice someone has is often determined by that person's access to resources, applying a harm reduction lens to sex trafficking means increasing a person's access to resources, like stable housing and transportation, providing opportunities to choose things that feel good to them.

The war on trafficking, like the War on Drugs, takes prohibitionist measures to end the sex trade, but instead results in pushing it out of sight. Inflated drug charges such as the crack vs cocaine disparity,[4] mandatory minimum prison sentences, and discriminatory policing[5] mean that people who use drugs exist in a violent underground market, use adulterated products, and don't have access to safe drug use supplies. Comparably, the war on sex trafficking uses inflated charges such as pandering charges,[6] zoning restrictions,[7] and abusive policing[8] that force many sex workers to work in isolation where they have a hard time accessing safety information, community, and income. These vulnerabilities are easily exploitable. One study illuminates that prohibitionist anti-trafficking measures often create less-safe environments for the people existing in them without providing additional resources.[9]

Viewing exploitation like overdose helps shift the focus from the work itself to safety. Like promoting safe drug use, promoting safe sex work means increasing access to comprehensive sex education and addressing occupational safety concerns. It means leveraging community-based interventions like bad date lists and Pros Networks.[10] It also means promoting access to safe space. In her essay, "The Paradox of Policing as Protection: A Harm Reduction Approach to Prostitution Using Safe Injection Sites as a Guide," Emani Walks discusses the benefits of applying Safe Consumption Space models to the sex trade to create Safe Sex Work Spaces. The idea is that these community-run programs would offer sex workers rooms for reservation within a sterile, protected environment. Safe Sex Work Spaces could reduce violence and exploitation by providing free, safe, and clean places for sex workers to take dates, as well as resources, referrals, and safe sex supplies. In exchange for advancing sex worker health and safety, Safe Sex Worker Spaces would be given limited immunity from prostitution and pandering charges and unnecessary police surveillance. Programs like this that are run for and by sex workers prioritize health over capitalistic gain, thereby reducing exploitation.

It is these sorts of innovative interventions that should be discussed during anti-trafficking awareness month as people who are working to prevent trafficking grapple with what that means and looks like. When exploitation is treated like overdose, people's lives and bodily autonomy are centered over public safety. Attention is shifted from the privileged public to the most marginalized in recognition that policing and prisons negatively impact people of color[11] and people experiencing poverty the greatest. Just like drug harm reduction is a strategy for reducing overdose and racialized drug enforcement, sex work harm reduction is an anti-trafficking strategy that considers and addresses racial inequalities. It is time for it to be recognized and utilized as such.

Stimulant Stigma: Without Simple Solutions, Punishment and Inequity Persist

JUSTICE RIVERA

OPIOIDS: SIMPLE BUT NOT EASY

We all have opiate receptors in our brains that help us feel and manage pain. Opioids[1] such as heroin, Oxycodone, Percocet, and Vicodin flood the brain with these neurotransmitters, reducing physical and emotional pain and creating a "high." The opiate neuropathways, however, build up tolerance to the presence of an opioid in a person's body, requiring more and more of the drug to feel the same effects as before. The plasticity of opiate receptors is also why medication assisted treatment (MAT) such as Methadone and Buprenorphine are so effective for treating opioid dependency—they create a new baseline for people with opioid dependency.[2]

Advancements in science have produced a medication that, upon opioid overdose, isolates the opiate neuropathway. Naloxone rejects the opioid and allows the overdosing person's brain time to catch up to the amount of drug in their system, thereby reversing overdose. These magical harm reduction and treatment tools, combined with a widespread recognition of who is using opioids, have spearheaded the call for a kinder and gentler approach to handling the modern opioid epidemic.

As opposed to the crack epidemic of the 1980s, the modern opioid epidemic has increasingly been associated with white users.[3] White families who have lost a loved one to prescription painkillers have access to medical and political stakeholders who are passing policies such as Twenty First Century CURES and the Comprehensive Addiction Recovery Act[4] to support people seeking recovery and their families who the War on Drugs wasn't designed to kill and incarcerate. Headlines suggest that white people are now using opiates at higher rates than non-white people,[5] and the fact is that the only drug people of color consume and have consumed more than white people is marijuana.[6] Even then, the legalization of marijuana benefits white people more due to barriers within regulatory codes surrounding grower employment, as well as access to wealth and the small-business market.[7] Similarly, opioid MAT is more readily available to white people, despite Black overdose deaths continuing to rise.[8]

SHIFTING ENFORCEMENT

Today, politicians are playing a game of drug whack-a-mole. Increased investment in opioid drug enforcement has not only led to the widespread production and sale of more dangerous opioids that are chemically manipulated to get past security and make money, but has also caused a shift in drug demand and supply.[9] The West Coast and Midwest have historically seen high rates of stimulant use, especially methamphetamine, but now former opioid users across the country are transitioning to stimulants for easier access and to avoid overdosing from adulterated opioids. Opioid overdoses have remained steady or increased in many places, and now methamphetamine-related hospitalizations are skyrocketing.[10]

Nonetheless, harsh policies and stigma towards stimulant use and users persist—maybe it is because stimulant use complications such as overamping (stimulant overdose) and bacterial infections[11] are rarely immediately fatal, or maybe it is because harm reduction and treatment alternatives for opioid use disorders are more widely known and effective than those for stimulant use disorders. The fact remains that in the US, crack is still criminalized at a rate 18 times higher than coke (a sentencing disparity that doesn't exist in other drugs), and methamphetamine users aren't prescribed licit stimulants or narcolepsy drugs as MAT (which is widely practiced in Europe and Australia.)[12] A nasty cycle of stimulant stigma, lack of investment in stimulant treatment and harm reduction approaches, and stubborn reliance on cracking down on illicit stimulants continues to gain momentum. The impact of this acceleration is seen in jails and prisons, hospitals, and homelessness service programs across the country.

STIMULANT 101

Stimulants are a category of substances that stimulate or activate the central nervous system and are commonly referred to as uppers.[13] When swallowed, snorted, smoked, injected, or booty bumped (anally inserted), these drugs increase heart rate (blood pressure, body temperature) and brain activity, leading to increased alertness, decreased fatigue, prolonged physical activity, improved mood, and increased self-confidence. Stimulants' effects vary depending on the type of stimulant and a person's own physiological makeup. For example, I like to say I am wired backwards—coke and meth slow me down. Every time I shot cocaine, I fell asleep soon afterwards. Prescription stimulants are often prescribed to counter Attention Deficit Hyperactivity Disorder (ADHD) but many people use them and other stimulants because these drugs help speed them up.

In 2015, almost 4.3 million Americans over the age of 12 had used a stimulant drug illegally in the previous month. Cocaine was the most commonly used, followed by the non-medical use of prescription stimulants. An estimated two million of these individuals met criteria for a stimulant use disorder in the past year. Globally, there are 35 million people who used stimulant drugs in the past year, with amphetamines (including methamphetamine) being the most commonly used.[14] Crack—a combination of water, coke, and baking soda that is boiled into a solid and broken into pieces to smoke—and meth are arguably the most highly criminalized and stigmatized stimulants in the US.

In general, stimulants are widely embraced and taxed within the US economy. Licit stimulants include narcolepsy treatment pills, diet products, amphetamine salts within mental health medications, attention producing drugs such as Adderall, and stimulants given to soldiers and athletes to enhance their physical performance. Institutional rationale for why crack and meth are "bad" includes the belief that crack and meth are the most addictive stimulants. Dr. Carl Hart, an addiction neurobiologist and Columbia University professor, debunks this thinking. In his book *High Price*, Dr. Hart explains that the molecular makeup of methamphetamine and dextroamphetamine (Adderall) are only one methyl group apart. The difference is not the drug itself but, rather, how people use the drug, and drug behavior is often determined by a person's level of access to drug education.[15]

LEGAL MEANS LESS RISKY

Let's use Adderall and meth as examples. Adderall is a licit prescription drug. When someone is prescribed Adderall by a doctor, the doctor suggests a dose and advises the patient to monitor their sleep and eating schedules.

Licit vs. Illicit Amphetamines

Dextroamphetamine
(Licit - also known as dexedrine, DextroStat etc.)

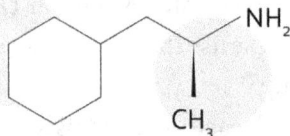

Methamphetamine
(Illicit - also known as meth)

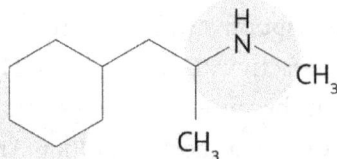

Use of large amounts can lead to anxiety, restlessness, paranoia, and erratic behavior. Withdrawal symptoms include cravings for more of the drug, nervousness, depression, nausea, fatigue, and muscle pain. Should the person have trouble sleeping or eating, the doctor will adjust the dose accordingly. In addition to receiving education on how to use the drug, Adderall users are informed of the risks associated with it. This way, people who choose to use Adderall recreationally have baseline drug information.

Juxtapose the above experience with that of accessing and using meth. Meth is not legal or safely available. A consumer never knows what product they are receiving, even if they use the same dealer consistently. Cuts and adulterates (such as laxatives, caffeine, boric acid, and laundry detergent) can cause stomach ulcers, nose sores, abscesses, and more.[16] There is little comprehensive drug education in this country, meaning that people aren't aware of the impacts of sleep deprivation, dehydration, and malnutrition, which are often side effects of meth use. Instead, users must figure it out as they go, risking their health and well-being along the way.

Hart argues that poor emotional control, disorganization, and many of the negative behaviors often associated with illicit stimulant use are actually a result of people's propensity to push their bodies to the limit while on these drugs. Someone who stays up for three days straight without giving their body many nutrients or much water is going to be highly sensitive and irrational, period. Sleep deprivation, malnutrition, and dehydration are more culpable than the stimulants for causing these behaviors. Therefore, comprehensive drug education and harm reduction that address people's behavior should be the nation's drug priorities, rather than scare campaigns and increased enforcement that punish people's behavior.[17] A compassionate approach to working with people using meth includes helping them figure out how to use meth in a way that has more long-term health benefits and fewer negative consequences, combined with addressing the comprehensive needs of that individual.[18]

ANTI-STIMULANT SENTIMENTS

Anti-crack and anti-meth media propaganda perpetuate racist, classist, and whorephobic stereotypes and foster anti-drug hysteria. The ad below by the Montana Meth Project attempts to paint a sad story surrounding meth by placing it in proximity to sex work. This ad isn't based on scientific evidence but is paid for by government drug prevention funding, as well as faith-based dollars.[19] The reality is that some people do trade sex acts for $15 out of desperation, and restrictions in the market have led more people to do so lately.

Before the passage of SESTA/FOSTA in 2018, the street price for a blowjob on the track in Seattle was $40 to $60.[20] After Backpage.com was shut down and many workers hit the streets to make ends meet, increasing supply for street buyers, street prices plummeted to $20 to $40. Older workers, transgender workers, and workers who use drugs are sometimes seen as less desirable and have to offer even lower rates to gain competitive advantage. An evidence-based ad might read "15 bucks for sex isn't normal, but under prohibition, I had to smoke meth to stay awake and sell sex to make money."

The American public is constantly consuming anti-drug messages that associate different marginalized populations with different drugs. The government's intentional pairing of crack with Black neighborhoods was a driving factor behind police racial profiling and the mass incarceration epidemic facing America today.[21] In 1986, Congress passed the Anti-Drug Abuse Act establishing mandatory minimums for crack possession and distribution (which is associated with Black and poor people) and penalizing it 100 times greater than cocaine (which is associated with white and affluent people because of its comparatively high cost). In doing so, Congress ignored the recommendations of its own Sentencing Commission and findings by medical experts that indicate that the pharmacological effects of crack cocaine are no more or less harmful than those of powder cocaine. "Compounding the problem is that whites are considerably less likely to be prosecuted for drug offenses in the first place; when prosecuted, are more likely to be acquitted; and even if convicted, are much less likely to be sent to prison."[22]

The Anti-Drug Abuse Act is one of the primary pieces of legislation driving drug war policies. By 2000, there were more Black men in jails and prison than in higher education, and racism across the prison industrial complex had created a low-cost workforce that continues the legacy of slavery in the American South. Twenty-two years after its passage, President Obama signed into law the Fair Sentencing Act that eliminated mandatory minimums for crack possession and decreased the crack/cocaine sentencing disparity from 100:1 to 18:1. Although much improved, this legislation has yet to live up to its name. Today, Black people still experience higher rates of police surveillance, police brutality, incarceration, and state supervision than any other race in the US.[23]

Systemic violence against women of color is especially alarming. A 2019 Prison Policy Initiative report expounds that women's incarceration has grown at twice the rate of men's, with more women being held in jails than prisons, many on prostitution and drug charges—and often just long enough to lose their parental rights, housing, benefits, and jobs.[24] Eighty percent of women in jails are mothers. Mothers who use stimulants are seen as the ultimate offenders since the mere presence of drugs in a mother's system or space is a risk factor for a child negligence claim in many states.[25]

Often, the only pathway towards regaining parental rights after a charge of use or possession is proof of complete abstinence. However, mothers who use opiates might have additional pathways towards recovery and regaining parental rights because opioid MAT is Food and Drug Administration (FDA) approved as such. Finally, formerly incarcerated women are more likely to be homeless than men due to gender-based employment discrimination and other barriers to employment, further complicating compliance with recovery programs.[26]

In the late '80s, the media mechanism focused anti-stimulant attention towards women and the idea of the "crack baby." Hysteria surrounding "crack babies" comes from a study done in the '80s that looked at just 23 infants with no way of studying long-term effects. The study claimed that crack damaged fetuses and stunted the development of children exposed in the womb. Furthermore, it claimed that crack destroyed maternal instincts and led to child abandonment. These claims were among the primary drivers of the Anti-Drug Abuse Act and subsequent rise in mass incarceration.[27] In 2002, Dr. Ira Chasnoff testified before the Congressional Sentencing Commission explaining that the effects of crack and cocaine are identical on fetal development and that "a child's home environment is the single most influential factor in determining whether a child will be healthy."[28] Larger subsequent research also points to poverty and the impacts of poverty as the main cause of children's issues, whether or not they have been exposed to crack.

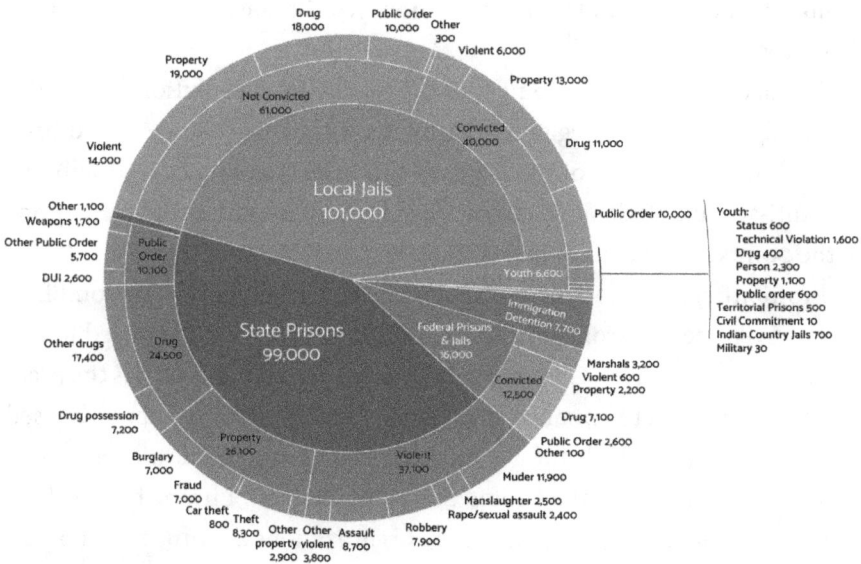

Drug 18,000
Public Order 10,000
Other 300
Violent 6,000
Property 19,000
Property 13,000
Not Convicted 61,000
Convicted 40,000
Drug 11,000
Violent 14,000
Local Jails 101,000
Public Order 10,000
Youth:
Status 600
Technical Violation 1,600
Drug 400
Person 2,300
Property 1,100
Public order 600
Territorial Prisons 500
Civil Commitment 10
Indian Country Jails 700
Military 30
Other 1,100
Weapons 1,700
Other Public Order 5,700
DUI 2,600
Public Order 10,100
Youth 6,600
Immigration Detention 7,700
Other drugs 17,400
Drug 24,500
State Prisons 99,000
Federal Prisons & Jails 16,000
Marshals 3,200
Violent 600
Property 2,200
Convicted 12,500
Drug possession 7,200
Property 26,100
Violent 37,100
Drug 7,100
Public Order 2,600
Other 100
Burglary 7,000
Muder 11,900
Fraud 7,000
Manslaughter 2,500
Rape/sexual assault 2,400
Car theft 800
Theft 8,300
Other property 2,900
Other violent 3,800
Assault 8,700
Robbery 7,900

The United States is one of the top incarcerators of women in the world. Changing that will require knowing where 231,000 incarcerated women fall within our decentralized and overlapping systems of mass incarceration.

In the mid-2000s, as a swell of evidence amassed discrediting anti-crack hysteria, media attention turned to methamphetamine as the new ultimate evil. Dr. Hart emphasized a *New York Times* headline, "Drug Scourge Creates Its Own Form of Orphan," which quoted "a police captain who said methamphetamine 'makes crack look like child's play, both in terms of what it does to the body and how hard it is to get off.' The paper also claimed: 'Because users are so highly sexualized, the children are often exposed to pornography or sexual abuse, or watch their mothers prostitute themselves.'"[29]

WHERE SEX AND DRUGS MEET, STIGMA INCREASES

Stimulants do have a profound effect on some people's libido, leading to increased arousal and pleasure during sex.[30] For people with social and sexual anxiety, stimulants are one class of drugs that can help them connect intimately. For others whose sexual practices are socially taboo, including gay men and people in the kink community, stimulants can help overcome shame so people can have the sex they want to. People who sell sex might use stimulants to improve job performance, allowing workers to stay up or inhibit their appetite and make more money, or because clients want to use drugs together.

Terence McKenna, a harbinger of the psychedelic revolution, points out that the pairing of sex-negative sentiments with drugs can be traced back to the Christian notion of the original sin.[31] The coupling of whorephobia and anti-stimulant ideology is a modern form of moral misogyny and one of the points where church meets state.

Prohibitionist attitudes toward sex and drugs, especially in combination, prevent people from getting the health information they need to live happy and healthy lives. Chemsex, also known as Party and Play, is the practice of using drugs to enhance sexual experiences. Meth is popularly used within chemsex, but little information can be found about how to engage in chemsex responsibly in the United States. In contrast, Europe has a robust chemsex harm-reduction scene, where organizations are funded to do outreach to MSM, sex worker, and kink communities to provide information and harm reduction materials that prevent the transmission of STIs, overdose, and violence within communities that commonly engage in chemsex.

Mainline is one such community-based chemsex harm-reduction model out of Berlin.[32]

This program's success is apparent in the data: the HIV epidemic in the United States has claimed 23 times more lives than Germany's, for only having four times greater population size.[33] The United States' reliance on a criminal legal approach and downright refusal to accept public health approaches to drug use and sex work has sent a clear message that gay people, sex workers, and drug users are better off dead or incarcerated than alive and well. The graphics below show the pervasive nature of intersectional[34] oppression.[35]

LGBT People of Color Are Overrepresented in the System

1 in **3**

Adults are people of color

3.8% of all adults indeitfy as LGBT

2 in **3**

Adults in prison & jail are people of color

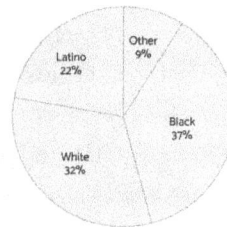

Other 9%
Latino 22%
Black 37%
White 32%

7.9% of adults in prison & jail identify as LGBT

PUNISHING POVERTY

A 2012 documentary, *The House I Live In*, examines how the War on Drugs is a war on poor people.[36] From the expansion of anti-crack laws of the '80s that targeted poor Black people to the increased use of illicit amphetamines and the targeting of users today, we have seen increased incarceration and state supervision of all poor people. The funnel continues to be placed in impoverished neighborhoods where people don't have money for or access to licit amphetamines.

Methamphetamine can be made from a few common household products, making it more widely available to people who can't afford to see a psychiatrist, who don't live near a doctor, or who are turned away from the medical establishment. Scare campaigns such as the Montana Meth Project have been applauded by the White House and used as ammunition to criminalize possession of and restrict access to many of the formerly over-the-counter cold medicines that can be used in meth production, attaching mandatory minimum prison sentences to convictions for having too much cold medicine.[37]

Some commonly held myths surrounding methamphetamine are that using it, even once, will cause the user to be addicted and then begin a rapid physical decay. Dr. Carl Hart sheds light on these beliefs by comparing the physical appearance of licit versus illicit amphetamine users. Meth mouth, sensationalized rapid tooth decay, is said to occur in methamphetamine users despite the drug's nearly identical chemical composition to Adderall, a drug that is not associated with tooth decay as a potential side effect. Both drugs restrict saliva flow, which can lead to dry mouth and tooth decay.

Therefore, meth mouth is more likely less a result of the drug than a lack of good hygiene and wellness practices of the user.[38] Someone using meth might stay up for days, losing track of time and neglecting self-care. The same approach of encouraging good sleep, healthcare, and hygiene practices can be taken with meth users as is currently taken with Adderall users and will likely have better results than pasting images of meth mouth on billboards with the caption "Meth: not even once."[39]

EVIDENCE-BASED INTERVENTIONS

Statistics show that 20 million people in the United States are in recovery from a substance use disorder, but 12 step membership is around 2 million.[40] This means that most people in recovery practice other forms of recovery including non-abstinence-based recovery. Natural recovery refers to people who have a period of problematic use but are able to correct their own course through a variety of life changes including therapy, moving, childbirth, changing jobs, leaving an abusive relationship, or experiencing significant loss related to their use. Fewer than 15 percent of those who have ever used meth will become addicted, and most people who experience a period of problematic drug use find natural recovery.[41]

Narratives surrounding both crack and meth claim that these stimulants cause violence in users. However, homicide data analysis from New

York City reveals that less than 10 percent of homicide cases are associated with stimulants and that in nearly half of the cases that are, the stimulant user was the victim.[42] Furthermore, most stimulant-related violence is less directly related to the drug itself than the environment of the underground market, which, by nature of being unregulated, relies on the use of violence to attain power and command obedience.

Cocaine and meth overdoses, called overamping, most commonly result in dizziness, overheating, inability to walk and talk, and blurred vision. Overamping is caused by a person's heart and central nervous system speeding up to the point where the body can't keep up. A fatal overamping incident is a heart attack or brain aneurysm. Although far less frequently fatal than opioid overdose, overamping doesn't have an antidote. Naloxone attacks opioid receptors and stops issues within a person's respiratory system, reversing opioid overdoses—and only opioid overdoses. We do not yet have a way to stop overamping-induced heart attacks, so fatal overamping incidents are always fatal.[43]

It is easy to pour faith and resources into interventions that are nearly 100 percent effective such as opioid MAT. But what if an intervention is only 50 percent effective, or 30 percent effective? This still means that one out of every two or three people receiving the intervention will experience relief. Limited research suggests that stimulant MAT including dextroamphetamine, Modafinil, and combinations like Wellbutrin and Naltrexone work well for some stimulant-dependent people, especially for those with attention-deficit issues, and for use in reducing chaotic use or as a taper off meth or coke.[44]

The reason opioid MAT is so much more effective than stimulant MAT goes back to the conversation about opioid receptors and tolerance. Dopamine receptors, the primary neural pathway impacted by stimulants, don't always create tolerance. Sometimes, they create sensitization, meaning that prolonged use can trigger undesirable side effects over time.[45] A perfect example of this is coffee: some people can drink coffee any time of the day and still sleep well at night without experiencing increased anxiety or stomach issues. Others need to restrict their coffee consumption to morning hours or one cup per day.

Sensitization is why stimulant MAT only works for less than half of the people who need it. Some people's brain tolerates the pharmacological compound reducing withdrawal symptoms and cravings and supporting their recovery, while others' brains become sensitized to certain chemicals complicating their bodily and mental functions. Nonetheless, several developed countries in the world approve the clinical use of stimulant MAT. The United States does not, partly because of the pervasive belief that physical withdrawal is worse than psychological withdrawal.

Author and researcher Maia Salavitz points to this belief as contributing to advancements in opioid treatment, stressing that "kicking dope" is just the first part of an opioid user's recovery. Psychological symptoms such as depression, anxiety, moodiness, and drug cravings persist for three to six months after physical symptoms subside and these symptoms are most commonly what cause people to relapse even after physically kicking the substance. Meth withdrawal also includes extreme lethargy and fatigue, lack of motivation, and extreme hunger—symptoms that half of people seeking recovery could avoid if stimulant MAT was approved in America. Beyond MAT, treatment admission data shows that discrepancies exist among what type of user gets treatment, right down to which drug someone is abusing, with opioid users receiving the most treatment.[46]

Percent of all non-medical users who got Specialty Treatment for addiction in 2012

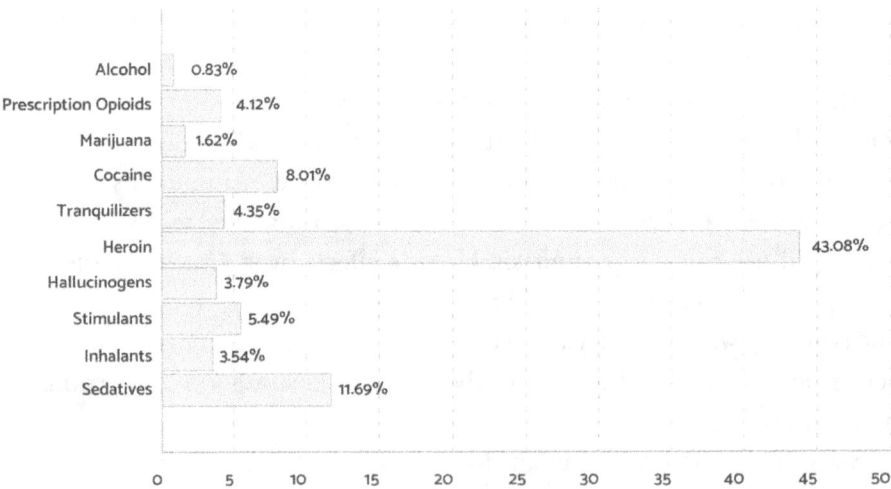

Drug	Percent
Alcohol	0.83%
Prescription Opioids	4.12%
Marijuana	1.62%
Cocaine	8.01%
Tranquilizers	4.35%
Heroin	43.08%
Hallucinogens	3.79%
Stimulants	5.49%
Inhalants	3.54%
Sedatives	11.69%

It is time for the United States to embrace the tools currently available across the drug use continuum: prevention, harm reduction, and treatment. Dextroamphetamine and Methylphenidate are attention deficit drugs that can be used (even off-label) to support people tapering off methamphetamine.[47] Topiramate, an anticonvulsant medication, shows promise as a cocaine taper. "Studies show that [Topiramate] is associated with reduced rates of relapse and longer periods of alcohol and cocaine abstinence, which have been associated with improved HIV treatment outcomes."[48]

Current rates of treatment admissions and retention for stimulant use disorder are low. People struggling with stimulant use might be hesitant to seek treatment due to feelings of embarrassment and stigma, privacy concerns, lack of insurance coverage or ability to pay, and different cultural approaches to managing issues. Furthermore, psychological interventions such as Cognitive Behavioral Therapy (CBT) show empirical improvement in treating stimulant use disorder but aren't as attractive to people seeking treatment as the possibility of receiving psychological interventions in combination with medication management.

The United Nations Office on Drugs and Crime states that the goal of treatment is to "maintain long-term and stable remission of symptoms to prevent future harm"[49] and the Substance Abuse and Mental Health Services Administration (SAMHSA) define recovery as "a process of change through which individuals improve their health and wellness, live a self-directed life, and strive to reach their full potential."[50] With this in mind, it is the United States' duty to invest in stimulant MAT evaluation and regulation.

The science supports a shift away from the current sociopolitical response to stimulants and stimulant use. Criminalization and scare campaigns only serve to perpetuate institutional, interpersonal, and internalized stigma and oppression. Compassionate and comprehensive approaches are needed instead, beginning with a shift away from police and prisons. Increased investment is needed in stimulant treatment research. Work can be done within medical schools and facilities to encourage off-label prescribing of attention deficit drugs, anti-seizure medications and narcolepsy regimens that support stimulant use recovery, non-abstinence-based approaches to recovery, and increased investment in harm reduction approaches to drug use.

SECTION THREE

Harm-Reduction Toolkits

This section offers practical tools and ideas in true harm reduction fashion: to aid in the thoughtful planning of delivering life-saving services to people pushed to the margins of society. We are reminded that harm reduction is a practice rooted in survival and compassion, and that drug users and sex workers have been taking care of each other (since long before "harm reduction" was a coined term) by sharing information and practices not yet vetted by any government oversight entity, but by necessity. When we look beyond survival, there is a place where we can play and laugh and heal, and we can get there together.

Overview of Harm Reduction in the Sex Trade

JUSTICE RIVERA WITH DEVELOPING

CONTRIBUTION FROM SHAAN LASHUN

A BRIEF HISTORY

For as long as we can remember, queer and trans communities, communities of color, and our sex working and drug using ancestors have been mitigating the harmful consequences of slavery, colonialism, and imperialism. Harm reduction practices are ancient and remembered, but the harm reduction movement began as a public health and social justice movement in the late 1970s in response to a critical need to reduce HIV transmission.[1] The community response was condoms and syringes. The government's response was sodomy laws and the War on Drugs—fearful measures that sought to eradicate communities in which supremacists' hate was already manifesting.

Drug users and sex workers created care strategies to help insulate each other from harm and the outside world. Sex workers practiced harm reduction to prevent HIV transmission by passing out and using condoms with clients. Transgender sex workers of color began underground information networks alerting each other of the extreme violence their communities continue to endure. For injection drug users, harm reduction offered a middle pathway between abstinence and chaotic or uninformed behavior. Instead of being handed a death sentence, they could simply be handed sterile syringes. To this day, syringe access[2] is one of the most successful HIV prevention interventions.[3] Meanwhile, the War on Drugs has been unsuccessful at reducing harmful consequences of drug use. It and similar ideological crusades have decimated communities of marginalized sex workers and drug users.

Over the last 50 years, the concept of harm reduction has grown from a set of practical, non-punitive survival practices to a philosophy and framework applied to a range of public health and safety issues, including domestic violence and the COVID-19 pandemic.[4] At its core is the understanding that shame is not a productive agent of change, and robbing people of resources only decreases their chances of survival. "Just say no" isn't as effective as "What do you need to be OK?"

Harm reduction confronts reality: people have varying safety and wellness needs, some of which may be stigmatized. It is important to offer people accurate sex and drug information and materials to reduce the risk of disease and violence. By giving people access to the resources they need to make their own decisions, we not only support these individuals, but also the health of their communities.[5] Harm reduction, then, must be a pillar of our approach to complex public health and safety issues (along with prevention, treatment, and exit).[6]

Harm reduction approaches, both in philosophy and practice, are excellent examples of non-carceral approaches to substance use and the sex trade that center safety and well-being. Unfortunately, despite empirical evidence that harm reduction is public health best practice, these strategies are still highly stigmatized. Potentially transmitting HIV is a felony in most states, owning drug use supplies such as a pipe may induce jail time, and condom possession can carry a prostitution charge. Money is poured into drug prevention and treatment and anti-sex work trafficking prevention and rescue/exit programs, and overwhelmingly given to law enforcement. Comparatively little funding is allocated on federal, state, and local levels to harm reduction approaches.

By remaining community driven, harm reduction helps curtail the consequences of institutionalized racism, sexism, cissexism, homophobia, ableism, and xenophobia. Today, communities of sex workers and those working with people in the sex trade use harm reduction to address violence, exploitation, disease transmission, self-harm, and state violence. Harm reduction helps mitigate consequences of police contact and a militarized state and creates a platform to speak on occupational health and safety concerns. Harm reduction is safety supplies, safety planning, self-care, connection to community, community accountability, and self-actualization. It is a blueprint for survival and the belief in something beyond survival.

ANATOMY OF HARM REDUCTION[7]

Values of compassion, self-agency, and social justice guide harm reduction practices and policies. The following principles represent the anatomy of harm reduction.

Principles of Harm Reduction Applied to Sex Work

1. Views trading sex for money and resources as neither inherently harmful or degrading, or inherently stabilizing or empowering.

2. Focuses on who people are rather than what they do and sees people as whole people.

3. Recognizes the myriad of reasons why people engage in the sex trade and seeks to help people meet goals as defined for themselves in non-judgmental and compassionate manners and atmospheres.

4. Recognizes the potential infectious disease and physical safety consequences associated with sex work and seeks to help people mitigate these factors.

5. Seeks to provide holistic support rather than isolated interventions.

6. Highlights the impact that the criminal justice response to sex work has on people in the sex trade, and seeks to eliminate sociopolitical barriers to care, safety, and general well-being.

7. Believes that incorporating a diverse range of sex workers into public health policies and discussions can be a gateway into community health. Understands that one individual's experience does not equal that of all individuals in the sex trade.

HARM REDUCTION STRATEGY #1: REDUCING VIOLENCE AND EXPLOITATION

Preventing and addressing violence is the primary occupational concern of many sex workers, because violence is the leading cause of death for people involved in the trade.

- In 2019, 220 sex workers died violent deaths.[8] Many were trans women of color claimed by transphobia and whorephobia. Others were killed by their partners or took their own lives rather than continue to experience compounded violence, stigma, and discrimination.

- A systemic review of violence against sex workers across the globe found that sex workers have a 45 to 75 percent chance of experiencing sexual violence at some point in their careers and a 32 to 55 percent chance of experiencing sexual violence in a given year.[9]

- Research from New York accounts that 46 percent of indoor sex workers disclosed being forced to do something by a client that they did not want to do.[10]

- A report produced by young women in the sex trade in Chicago explains that only a portion of violence they experienced comes from clients.[11] Other sources of violence are intimate partners, family members, police, social service providers, pimps, and community members.

- The closer in proximity a sex worker gets to poverty, the higher the chances are of experiencing violence and exploitation.

- Over 80 percent of street-based sex workers report experiencing violence.[12] Many don't live to talk about it.

Systemic Barriers

Overwhelmingly, people in the sex trade cannot use state-provided safety mechanisms due to the criminalization of sex work. Adult sex workers are arrested for prostitution, clients are arrested for solicitation, and minors in the sex trade are forced into the child welfare system.

Sex workers also aren't taken seriously when they report sexual assault. Most state-sanctioned victim's support mechanisms explicitly bar people who have been victimized in the sex trade from receiving victim's assistance.[13] Traditional social service mechanisms often replicate the institutional oppression of the prison industrial complex.

The presence of security in a building and absence of sex worker–inclusive information are a few determining factors in how much someone will disclose about themselves when receiving assistance.

Sex workers might fear disclosing their work or victimization to case managers, nurses, or therapists to avoid stigma, pressure to exit or report, or child protective service involvement. Withholding this information often increases chances of receiving resources.

One example of a police officer's response to a sex worker who was trying to stop a serial rapist was: "So, how's it OK on Monday, Tuesday, and Wednesday, but not Thursday?"[14] Comments like this show the institutional prevalence of whorephobia and the idea that sex workers can't be raped.

Individual-Level Interventions

1. *Screening* is a common practice used by sex workers to assess potential clients. Screening practices differ widely across platforms and communities but might include gathering information about clients (this gives the sex worker leverage should anything happen), asking for references from other sex workers a client has seen previously, or doing an initial assessment of the client's motives. Though these can all provide a greater degree of safety, they can never ensure it.

2. *Knowledge* is power and the more someone knows about working within the trade, the safer and healthier they can be while working. Information is shared across peer and professional networks—the more connected the community is, the more power that community has to prevent and respond to harm. For example, sex workers can let each other know when they are going on dates and alert clients that someone will know if they go missing.

3. *Leaving a cycle of violence* can be a slow and repetitive process, but many people in the sex trade have broken free from abuse on their own or with the help of close family and friends. While screening and industry-specific education might weed out harmful clients and abusive management, it doesn't address violence that might be happening at home. It is not rare for abusive partners or management to weaponize a sex worker's criminalized job against them. People in the sex trade might find it hard to leave an abusive or exploitative situation when safe houses have curfews and don't allow sex work. Often, people experiencing abuse need to keep working to gain the resources to flee violent partnerships.

Community-Level Interventions

1. *Community-based responses* to violence are hard and messy work, but they are often the only viable option. For intimate partner violence and exploitative situations, this includes transformative justice processes, housing collectives, pros networks, and mutual aid funds.[15]

2. *Bad date lists* started among trans sex workers of color in urban cities who began writing down details about violent and fraudulent encounters with clients and distributing them to others on the track. This way, someone who sees the list knows not to accept a date from someone who meets certain criteria. Today, sex workers and sex worker–sensitive service providers in a handful of cities take and distribute bad date lists among street-based sex workers. Online workers have several reporting mechanisms at their disposal. Some are run by community members and others are databases that cost money. Inputting a potential client's name through a reporting site or cross-referencing a bad date list before accepting the date is a great screening practice. Bad date lists are a low-cost intervention and one that affords leadership to sex workers. The bad date list example in the next chapter is from a Boston-based sex worker collective.

3. *Pros networks* are collectives of service providers trained to be sex worker sensitive and marketed as such. This might include social service agencies, therapists, and doctors. Many times, people in the sex trade have a bad or stigmatizing experience with a service professional and never seek assistance again. Other times, people are wary of reaching out in the first place. The presence of a local pros network better assures that sex workers can get the compassionate, high-quality care they deserve. Chicago's pros network is a good model of a successful network.[16]

Policy-Level Interventions

1. *End the carceral approach to sex trafficking and the criminalization of sex work.* At a minimum, new harmful policies need to be stopped and the impacts of recent and current policies must be examined. Other policy interventions are truly implementing harm reduction to address the damage of the dominant criminal legal approach to sex work and exploitation within the sex trade.

2. *Immunity policies* that eliminate prostitution-related charges can encourage sex workers to report violence experienced while on the job to law enforcement.[17] Much like a Good Samaritan overdose protection law provides limited immunity from arrest for drug possession when 911 is called during an overdose, reporting immunity protections allow sex workers to report violent encounters in certain cases without fearing a prostitution charge. These protections are a good step in the right

direction but can never provide the blanket immunity that is needed within the context of criminalization. People with outstanding warrants and sex workers who haven't experienced direct violence themselves are examples of people who aren't extended immunity from arrest or prosecution under these provisions.

3. *Regulatory policy reform* is another piece of the anti-violence and anti-exploitation puzzle because it offers the potential of removing administrative barriers to care, which must go in tandem with legislative reform.[18] Two examples of regulatory policy reform in this context are removing the anti-prostitution pledge within anti-trafficking funding streams and updating VOWA guidelines to be trauma and healing informed.

HARM REDUCTION STRATEGY #2: REDUCING DISEASE AND OVERDOSE

HIV

The Centers for Disease Control (CDC) doesn't consider sex workers a distinct high-risk population in need of tailored health services. Instead, sex workers receive sexual and reproductive health care through the lens of MSM health, transgender health, drug user health, or (my favorite *eye roll*) high-risk heterosexual.[19]

- Globally, a sex worker's risk of contracting HIV is 12 times higher than the general population. In the US, transgender sex workers are six times more likely to be living with HIV.[20]

- Compounding risk factors such as poverty and injection drug use mean that 20 to 40 percent of low-income femmes in the sex trade could contract HIV within their lifetime.[21]

- PrEP, the HIV prevention pill, could be widely prescribed to sex workers of all genders and orientations who might have unprotected sex.[22]

STIs, HCV, and COVID

Comprehensively addressing sex worker health means examining and tackling economic disparities along with providing robust healthcare and tools.

Individual and community-level interventions can be scaled up to support the health and well-being of people in the sex trade.

- Sex workers' risk of contracting an STI is 5 to 40 percent higher, depending on which STI.[23]

- Sex workers specializing in kink or anything that involves blood-play and sex workers who inject drugs should take special precautions to prevent Hepatitis C (HCV). Those who are living with HCV should be considered for treatment.[24] Sex workers who use drugs face compounding stigma and overlapping risks. In a 30-year study of 1,969 street-based sex workers in the United States, violence and drug use were the predominant causes of death.[25] At a minimum, free naloxone and overdose prevention education needs to be widely available and accessible for this group of people.

- COVID has been especially hard on sex workers. A plethora of articles highlight the risk many sex workers must take while continuing to see clients and survive, or the hardship on those who can't survive when clients are quarantining and can't see them.[26]

Systemic Barriers

Without tailoring services specifically to sex workers, many people in the sex trade are not receiving services through this lens. Stigma persists and turns into shame. As a result, sex workers are afraid to disclose the work they are doing and work-related challenges. Most frightening is that sex workers often don't have access to work-specific health and safety information.

- Simply handing out Bad Date Lists at a clinic or drop-in center is insufficient. This can feel like a false start to people in the industry who grab the list, disclose their work, and then are shamed for sexual practices during a health screening. Every institution that might serve someone in the sex trades needs comprehensive training on sex-worker sensitivity and an ongoing contact to ensure quality care.[27]

- Current and former sex workers should be paid to provide this training as staff members and brought in as partners in community-health planning.

Individual-Level Interventions

For sex workers, job stability means practicing safe sex and substance use. The most important thing is that everyone has safety supplies and the option to use them. Each sex worker chooses their own level of risk, and sometimes that changes encounter to encounter. This means:

1. *Accessing and having the option to use sexual barriers, PrEP, and lube* in sexual encounters. Some supplies such as insertive condoms and non-latex condoms are costly and hard to obtain.
2. *Accessing and knowing how to use safe drug supplies* such as sterile injection equipment, smoking equipment, and naloxone. Additionally, alcohol harm-reduction knowledge is important for sex workers as they might be expected to drink with clients or customers while needing to maintain professional boundaries and practices.[28]

Community-Level Interventions

1. *Sex worker and drug user health information* must be accessible and community informed. Sex worker health and rights groups often hold skill shares to discuss safety tips and tricks for navigating the sex trade and taking care of themselves. Partnerships with local harm reduction and social service agencies help spread this information to people who are trading sex but might not identify as sex workers. Health information pamphlets and zines are other great methods of distributing information.
2. *Community-wide supply distribution* helps increase health outcomes for people in the sex trade. This means a variety of different types of condoms and lube, latex gloves or finger cots, wet wipes, syringes and supplies for drug injection, naloxone, syringes for hormone injection, pipes for safer smoking, and water.
3. Low-cost sex worker–sensitive STI treatment, substance use treatment, and reproductive health care are valuable interventions with positive results. Health-care institutions that make violence prevention as much a priority as HIV and overdose prevention can best serve people in the sex trade.

Policy-Level Interventions

Two local and state-level policies that directly decrease health outcomes for people in the sex trade are HIV criminalization statutes and administrative allowance of condoms as evidence of prostitution.[29] HIV criminalization refers to a policy which exists in over 40 states that assigns a possible felony to living with HIV. Transmission does not need to occur for a felony to be triggered, and this antiquated law is disproportionately used against sex workers.[30] "Condoms as evidence" refers to a set of discriminatory law enforcement policies and practices that warrant possession of a certain number of condoms or more as reasonable suspicion or probable cause to make a prostitution arrest.

1. *HIV criminalization statues can be modernized or repealed.*
2. *Cities and states can pass "no condoms as evidence" laws.*
3. *Statutes that provide limited immunity to people who use drugs can be updated* to include people in the sex trade. SWOP's Good Samaritan Law Expansion Toolkit describes common issues with sex workers calling 911 to respond to an overdose.[31] The sex worker might be protected against arrest for drug possession in this instance through a Good Samaritan overdose law, but not from prostitution arrest. The toolkit includes step-by-step advocacy recommendations for expanding Good Samaritan protections.
4. *Challenge appropriations bans.* On the federal level, one of the greatest impediments to sex worker health is the Anti-Prostitution Pledge (APP) that exists in anti-trafficking and foreign AIDS relief funding streams.[32] Like the Hyde Amendment bars comprehensive reproductive health services[33] and the ban on syringe access funding blocks robust HIV prevention among people who use drugs,[34] the APP provides government funding to anti-sex and anti-sex worker programs that promote abstinence-only agendas. The largest recipient of anti-trafficking funding in the US until the mid-2000s was a religious organization that actively resisted distributing condoms to participants. The APP means that organizations serving sex workers are left without access to government funding that equals 80 percent of health and human services funding in the US.

HARM REDUCTION STRATEGY #3: REDUCING POLICE HARASSMENT AND INCARCERATION

Police harassment and abuse of sex workers takes many forms:[35]

- Police brutality has been documented to include the use of force during raids. Additionally, it appears as sexually humiliating sex workers through degrading and excessive derogatory remarks and actions such as ordering femmes to strip to their underwear, handcuffing their hands behind their backs, and then making them stand on the side of the road for everyone to see.[36]

- Police misconduct includes coercing sex workers to exchange sex for their freedom. Sometimes, officers promise to let a sex worker go after first receiving a sex act but then arrest them afterwards anyway.[37]

- Police corruption includes civil asset forfeiture where police take sex workers' money; entrapment, which is the basis of prostitution stings; and undercover operations where an allowance for receiving certain sex acts is written into undercover agents' contracts.[38]

Traumatic experiences of arrest are just the tip of the iceberg.

- Sex workers must sit in jail cells awaiting arraignment where they are forced to take a HIV test. A positive result triggers a separate felony charge.

- Those who can't make bail stay in jail days to weeks, awaiting sentencing. Those sentenced to prostitution must spend weeks to months in jail and then months to years on probation. Those sentenced with a sex-trafficking felony must spend months to years in prison and/or on probation.

- Many are not allowed to vote while incarcerated or while on community supervision. Many are ripped away from their families. Many have little to return to when they re-enter society.

Systemic Barriers

The collateral consequences of a prostitution charge include:

Requirements to participate in overly restrictive and punitive diversion program;[39]

Difficulty finding formal economy employment because of the arrest record and charge;

Difficulty finding housing because of the prostitution record, and a requirement to stay out of certain areas of town.

Sex workers who are hit with sex-trafficking charges experience all of these issues along with barriers and exclusions specific to sex offenses. A trafficking charge means these sex workers can't participate in some re-entry or community-based programs; they can't gain a job or housing even where ban-the-box provisions are in place; and child protective services involvement is triggered.

Individual-Level Interventions

The reality is that the criminalization of sex work puts sex workers in a position where they must either prioritize avoiding violence from the state or violence from clients. Prioritizing avoiding violence from clients means utilizing safety strategies that could get them arrested, including working together and carrying condoms. Prioritizing avoiding violence from cops means their chances of experiencing violence from clients increase exponentially.[40] This is because sex workers must decrease their visibility to avoid police interactions and doing so isolates them, thereby making them vulnerable to other sources of violence. The extent to which state violence and client violence go hand in hand is augmented for sex workers using drugs.

1. *Screening* can help to some degree. Sex workers can try and verify a potential client's employment or follow their gut. Unfortunately, a person's presence on a track or current adult advertisement online can be enough to get them arrested.[41] Femmes of color, trans folx, queer folx, undocumented people, and people with disabilities who trade sex can feel powerless under the unchecked power of the state.

2. *Safety planning* is an individual level intervention that can help sex

workers feel more in control of their life and circumstances. When planning for the event of an arrest, people should think about who to call in case of this specific emergency, who can care for their dependents while they are gone, how to cover expenses while they are gone, and how to gain access to necessary medication while incarcerated. A sample safety planning sheet created and distributed by Reframe Health and Justice is available on page 147.

Community-Level Interventions

1. *Bail-relief funds* exist for sex workers, people of color, and undocumented people who need help mitigating the costs of arrest and incarceration. Additional funding is needed for those that exist. (Donate today.)[42] The presence of additional local sex worker bail funds ensures that people in your city and region have greater access to bail relief and support.

2. *Low-cost, sex worker–sensitive legal aid* and lawyers who can help people gain their freedom and keep their rights are in demand. Sex worker-informed community efforts and local sex worker rights groups appreciate and utilize these connections.

Policy-Level Intervention

Bold budgetary reform is crucial for ending state violence against sex workers. This means divestment from law enforcement budgets and investment in community-based social and harm-reduction services.

1. *Divest/Invest* seeks to reduce police power to be proportionate with other systems. It then allows mental health and social service providers to respond to mental health crises and poverty instead of the police, centering expertise instead of authority. Marbre Stahly-Butts with Black Lives Matters explains Divest/Invest as "a key intervention in addressing not just the symptoms that need to be faced but the root causes of them. It is the idea that as we're pushing policy changes and overseeing shifts in practice, that we pay special attention to how money is being spent, and we demand a divestment from the systems that harm our communities like the criminal legal system, policing regimes, and the court system. We demand that money that's currently being spent—that's being poured into those systems with no accountability—be moved instead

to community-based alternative systems that support our people, that feed our people, that ensure we have jobs, and housing—the things we need to take care of ourselves and our communities."[43]

HARM REDUCTION STRATEGY #4: REDUCING SELF-HARM AND ISOLATION

Data surrounding the sex trade can be hard to come by due to the criminalized nature of the work and how vast an industry it is. Often, research sample sizes are very small and only indicative of one socioeconomic stratum. What we can say assuredly is that the closer someone is to poverty, the lower their health outcomes might be. This includes mental health outcomes.

Research suggests that sex workers experience mental health disorders at a rate twice as high as formal-economy or non-criminalized or stigmatized professions.[44] The need to navigate a potentially dangerous profession combined with the need to navigate criminalization, stigma, compounding oppression, previous or current trauma, and dual identities might manifest as anxiety, depression, PTSD, or suicidality.[45]

Systemic Barriers

One of the most prominent barriers to mental healthcare for people in the sex trade is economic instability. Maslow's Hierarchy of Needs shows us that people are ill equipped to care for their psychological needs when they can't meet their basic needs.[46] The Affordable Care Act extended the possibility of care to many low-income sex workers—it is a crucial pathway to care for many people, but simply isn't good enough in its current form. Much of the US South and Midwest have begrudgingly instituted the leanest Medicaid programs possible and then placed limits on who can access what and for how long.[47]

- Sex workers who live above the poverty line must either go without insurance or file as a shell business to gain access to the insurance marketplace (placing them at risk for tax felonies).

- The formal economy sex trade such as strip clubs and cam sites treat workers as contractors leaving them without healthcare coverage or benefits.

- Low-cost mental health care is hard to come by and, where it does exist, requires transportation, language fluency, and time-off to access.

Individual-Level Interventions

Trading sex can be an isolating experience, but it doesn't have to be.

1. *Connection to other sex workers* socially or politically increases mental health outcomes[48] by increasing self-esteem and reducing mental disease. Social networks can help connect individuals to self-directed care strategies, as well as sex worker–sensitive mental health services or treatment modalities.
2. *Self-care* takes many forms, and people who are already outcast by social systems can explore healing outside of traditional health care settings including intentional sexual healing practices like kink[49] and intentional substance use like microdosing psilocybin.[50]

Community-Level Interventions

1. *Reduce stigma,* reduce stigma, reduce stigma—I can't say it enough. Examine the places within yourself where there might be bias, challenge whorephobia when it presents in interpersonal interactions, and encourage institutional policies and training that synthesize sex worker–sensitivity.
2. *Telehealth services* can reach marginalized sex workers. A national Institute of Health study found that telemedicine is particularly advantageous for isolated communities.[51]
3. *Entheogenic treatment* pilots can prioritize current or former sex workers who are survivors of violence and trafficking. A pilot program in Montreal found that entheogenic therapy reduced suicidality among female sex workers by 60 percent.[52]

Policy-Level Interventions

Universal health care is vital to increase US health outcomes. In its current iteration, expansion of the Affordable Care Act offers the potential for leadership opportunities to people from communities with health disparities.

1. *Delivery System Reform Incentive Payment (DSRIP)* waivers, which are a type of state Medicaid applications to show cost savings for innovations in care, are an ideal mechanism through which to do this, and drug user health pilots are already showing promise.[53]
2. *Eliminate discriminatory healthcare guidelines* and regulatory rules that prohibit people with criminal records from working in helping professions including nursing and counseling.
3. *Decriminalize entheogenic substances* so they can be available for therapeutic use inside and outside of the medical industrial complex.

IT JUST MAKES SENSE

> "Be kinder than necessary, for everyone you meet is fighting some kind of battle."[54]

Harm reduction is crucial for people in the sex trade. Harm reduction approaches are evolutionary, revolutionary, and evidence based. On an individual level, people need information on how to stay protected and resources to do so. On a community level, sex workers need broad and affordable access to sex-worker sensitive services. On a policy level, we have a responsibility to create mechanisms that provide resources and expedite access to those services. We must dismantle mechanisms that run counter to this: those that diminish access to resources and services and those that decrease health outcomes for marginalized communities. On an ideological level, offering compassion to others means we are creating a world that can return it to us in abundance. Disconnection got us here—to the opioid epidemic, rampant gender-based violence, and inner cities filled with homeless encampments. Let's see what connection can do instead.

Bad Date List

Content warning: descriptive violence

WHO IS THIS SHEET FOR?

Anyone involved in trading sex or sexual stuff (like sensual massage or dancing) for money, gifts, drugs, or survival needs.

Last Updated: January 2018

Bad Date: Someone who offers to pay for sex but is abusive or violent when you are with them. This includes:

Boston Bad Date Sheet

- Beating, kidnapping, or robbing
- Being verbally disrespectful or abusive
- Refusing to wear a condom
- Refusing to pay
- Forcing any sex acts not agreed to
- Rape or other acts of violence

DATE	LOCATION	BAD DATE	VEHICLE	DETAILS
January 21, 2018 around noon *new report	Bradston Street by the methadone clinic	White male, 50-60 years old, medium height, and medium-beefy build, balding blond hair, no facial scars	Four door sedan, new, champagne colored	*sexual harassment assault* Two women walking down Bradston Street when the man tried to get their attention several times, he followed them to the bus stop in front of BMC, where he pulled over and got out with no pants on. Women started to scream to get attention, but man was undeterred and unafraid. Eventually man left and women walked away unharmed.

January 23, 2015 *new report	McDonalds in Newmarket Sq. Roxbury/ South End	White male, mid to late 30s, medium-chubby build, short brown hair, no facial hair	Gold car, described as "clean"	Date smoked crack but started bugging out right after the first hit. First thing he said was "Do you know…Do you do dates?" and asked where he could get crack. Date dragged her body down the street while she was hanging out the car door with him holding her by the hair after trying to rob her for the 20 rock of crack she had gotten him.
December 25th, 2017 *new report	Roxbury/ South End	Black male, 23-25 yrs old, 5' 5" with shoulder length dreads/ locks, medium build. Wore cologne, smoked weed, wore black hoodie	Date occurred in home, not in a vehicle— but was driving maroon van	Did not follow through with deal after sex; had promised weed as payment but said he "left it in his car," and when reporter slipped and fell on ice, he sped away. Later came back to retrieve his iPhone, which he left at the reporter's home, he called the police. Was very disrespectful and dishonest.
November 24, 2017	Boston/ Mass + Cass	White male, mid-40s, medium-sized, muscular, thick "southie" accent, short brown hair, no facial hair	White truck, yellow rooftop fog-lights (some reports say mattress in back)	Drove date to Waitham to park in a parking lot. Pulled gun on the date, but paid for the date. Sometimes puts on a white mask + calls this "role play"

Aug. 2017	Blue Hill Ave, Boston	Dark-skinned Black male w/ long braided hair/locks	Silver SUV, possibly Nissan Path-finder	Forces unprotected anal sex then oral sex, and refuses to pay
Aug 7, 2017	Dorchester Ave	Puerto Rican man in his mid-30s. Has lip ring.	Black sedan	Picked up a date and badly beat her, then threw her out of the moving vehicle
Aug 30, 2017	Bost, Melnea Cass	Middle-aged white guy, scraggly beard (but may have shaved)	White 2-door pick-up truck	Picks up women between Roundhouse and Sunoco, has taken women behind AutoZone on Mass Ave and raped them. Uses a gun to threaten.
Around 2015	New Bedford, Worcester, Boston	Latino man in his mid-30s. Long, dark hair. Beauty mark on his cheek.		Asked for $$ back after oral sex. Stabbed woman in thigh. Went to prison but was recently released.

Emergency Planning Worksheet in Case of Arrest

- Keep this and all other material/information in a safe place
- Make sure one of your emergency contact people has a copy of any necessary keys.

Attorney: _____

Phone: _____ Email: _____

Please call the following individuals upon arrest:

Name_____ Relation_____ Number_____

What to tell them:

Name_____ Relation_____ Number_____

What to tell them:

This is who you SHOULD NOT CALL:

Name_____ Relation_____ Reason_____

Name_____ Relation_____ Reason_____

Who to call for money:

Name_____ Relation_____ Number_____

Name_____ Relation_____ Number_____

Legal name:

Birthdate:

Sex marker on ID:

Gender Identity:

Allergies:

Dietary restrictions:

Passwords to know (computer/phone/email):

Medications (Name/Dose/Frequency):

Caregiving Obligations (include children, dependents, pets, plants):

Name	Sun	Mon	Tues	Weds	Thurs	Fri	Sat

Monthly Bills:

Name	Minimim payment	Date due	How to pay

Do you want court support? What does that look like?

What you will want to do first upon release:

Additional instructions:

Date filled out:

Compassion, Not Criminalization: Alternatives to Criminalization That Reduce Harm in the Sex Trade

An Interview with Melodie Garcia, Tamika Spellman, Wit López, and Leila Raven

SASANKA JINADASA

THE CRIMINALIZATION OF THE SEX TRADE IN THE UNITED STATES—AND globally—has been cloaked in a mass marketing campaign, painting people trading sex as victims and people buying sex or supporting people trading sex as a violent "pimp and john lobby." While large, carceral anti-trafficking organizations claim that their criminalization approach allows them to root out exploitation and coercion in the sex trade, sex workers note that this approach has severe material consequences for both victims of trafficking and people currently selling sex. Increased exposure to policing can lead to the accumulation of a criminal record—ranging from prostitution charges to other survival-crime charges like loitering, trespassing, or drug possession—as well as interruptions in income and financial stability and mental stress. Furthermore, some studies have illustrated that ongoing police violence against sex workers correlates with increased levels of client-initiated violence.[1] It is time for a non-carceral approach—a charge for a world without prisons, policing, and detention—to meaningfully and sustainably reduce harm in the sex trade.

Prohibition, moralization, and policing have reduced sex workers' abilities to address both the root causes and the immediate harm of exploitation. In this regard, advocates, organizers, and builders have challenged lawmakers, service providers, and their communities to create non-punitive approaches to addressing harm that occurs in the sex trade. "The system itself is based on carceral responses instead of people-powered responses that are stabilizing and not punitive," notes Tamika Spellman, the Policy and Advocacy Director at HIPS,[2] an organization that provides holistic services to people trading sex and/or using drugs in Washington, DC. Without ignoring the violence that people face, it's critical that all interventions center what survivors want. For Tamika, a combination of peer-led services with movements to decarcerate sex workers, defund the police, and decriminalize the sex trade is necessary to challenge the existing structures of harm.

zara raven, an advocate who has worked in grassroots advocacy in both DC and New York, contextualizes the challenges of organizing under criminalization. "We wanted it to be peer-led, and the reality was often that when people were experiencing housing instability and being directly targeted by police, even showing up can be really difficult," z points out. "I remember at one action for International Whores' Day, my colleague at the time who was a Black trans sex worker was stopped, harassed, and fined by the police over fare evasion." In the context of these challenges, success was often defined by intimate, personal interactions: How many people showed up to canvas and build public support for ending criminalization of the sex trade? How did it feel to change someone's mind about the harm people face everyday?

In some liberal cities like Seattle, the majority of available services are led by carceral organizations[3] that force people in the sex trade to specifically identify as survivors of prostitution—rather than survivors of violence and harm within the trade—in order to receive services. Peer advocates like Melodie Garcia work and participate in several initiatives to reduce potential harm. One of those initiatives is Law Enforcement Assisted Diversion (LEAD).[4] As LEAD Project Manager, Melodie shares, "We look at the economy surrounding drug use, the sex trade, and poverty from a public safety standpoint, and say, 'How can we divert people experiencing these situations into a non-carceral path?'" She goes on to ask: "'What does it take to keep these folks out of the criminal-legal system, and how can we show players in the economy (prosecutors, cops, elected officials) that incarceration actually exacerbates existing problems and at times pushes people to do more crime?'" As a peer and sex worker herself, Melodie sees working within the system as crucial to creating small shifts in philosophy and practice among state actors who hold a significant amount of power over sex workers' lives.

Philanthropy also plays a vital role in affecting how sex workers receive services; many of the existing providers for legal and social services, including housing, are explicitly pro-criminalization and anti-sex trade. Some even require pledges asking sex workers to commit to not trade sex while receiving services,[5] which can be impossible for people who have financial obligations with barriers to other types of employment. This is true for people who are trading sex regardless of choice, coercion, or circumstance. These philanthropists also fund advocacy and policy that increases criminalization, allocating more funding to police to run raids and stings. Wit López, a member of the Sex Worker Giving Circle, spoke about the necessity of resourcing sex worker–led organizations and collectives, commenting that the distribution of funds is determined by people with personal experience in the sex trade. "Paying sex workers to create grants for grassroots programs that support sex workers is a success," Wit shares. "To me, even the process of coaching a team of sex workers—the fellows—on how to engage in radical philanthropic practices is a success . . . this type of transformative grantmaking is possible."

Under the current criminal-legal landscape, it can seem difficult to imagine alternatives to involving the police and prisons in solutions to harm. However, it is imperative that we both develop alternative practices and build a network of safety for those who can't or won't seek help in the models that are currently available. With more than one third of femmes[6] experiencing gender-based violence in their lifetimes, along with the growing mass incarceration and police brutality across the United States, the need for compassionate alternatives to the criminal-legal response to the sex trade is too great.

In what follows, we share interviews with four advocates working to end exploitation and violence experienced by those in the sex trade. We explore how policy change, service provision, and philanthropy can play a crucial role in shifting towards non-carceral and anti-carceral interventions to harm.

MELODIE GARCIA, PROJECT MANAGER, LEAD (SHE/HER/HERS PRONOUNS)

I am a harm redution advocate and sex workers' rights organizer in the greater Seattle area. I work in the areas of addiction, poverty, and behavioral health at the intersection of criminal-legal intervention for a program called Law Enforcement Assisted Diversion (LEAD).[7] I myself identify as a peer in many of these capacities and also as a sex worker—so this work is vitally and demonstrably personal.

In 2019, I helped launch a harm reduction outreach organization called the Greenlight Project through a SWOP-sponsored 501(c)(3) (POCSWOP) in Seattle. I currently sit on the King County Community Advisory Council for Law Enforcement Oversight (CACLEO) and participate in research around human trafficking and consensual sex work.

Sasanka Jinadasa: How have you and your organization created non-carceral, or anti-carceral, practices with people experiencing harm in the sex trade?

Melodie Garcia: LEAD intentionally partners with law enforcement and prosecutors who ultimately decide whether and how these folks are penalized by the legal system. We look at the economy surrounding drug use, the sex trade, and poverty from a public safety standpoint, and say, "How can we divert people experiencing these situations onto a non-carceral path (e.g., Permanent Supportive Housing, Medication Assisted Treatment)? What does it take to keep these folks out of the criminal-legal system, and how can we show players in the economy (prosecutors, cops, elected officials) that incarceration actually exacerbates existing problems and at times pushes people to do more crime?"

SJ: What do you and/or your programs consider a successful outcome?

MG: Successful outcomes are hard to measure for several reasons, including changes in funding for jail beds, hospitalization, police departments, and case management resources. However, we track personal accounts of our clients; we see them interacting with law enforcement in a different way on the street; we see prosecutors willing to divert and drop charges from mainstream court, and then advocate to other community partners about the felt successes of the program. We consider any of these (seemingly small) changes in practice, philosophy, or relationship as successful outcomes.

SJ: What's been the main challenge to implementing these practices?

MG: The main challenges in implementing these practices are the politics. The police departments want different things than the prosecutors, the mayor wants something different than city council, and the public doesn't quite understand why we are advocating for diversions for VUCSA (Violation of the Uniform Controlled Substance Act) and prostitution-related charges when the sex trade and drug market is highly visible and "poses a threat" to individual safety. There are also big players in the service provision world that are "rescue based," meaning their intent is to get folks to stop engaging in prostitution—which is counterintuitive to LEAD's theory of change. This narrative is rather dominant in the Seattle area, which leads to poor public policy and coercive enforcement tactics that hurt this population.

There's a lot of community education and systems harm reduction that goes into implementation, which is part of the LEAD theory of change. That is to say, our oppressive systems are actively at work to disempower our folks—so in this exact moment, there are things we can do to change how a prosecutor prosecutes or how a police officer chooses to enforce.

TAMIKA SPELLMAN, POLICY AND ADVOCACY DIRECTOR, HIPS (SHE/HER/HERS PRONOUNS)

I began working with HIPS[8] in June 2017. I started volunteering with mobile services, then as a peer educator, then with the secondary syringe exchange program. Afterwards, I moved into a role as Policy and Advocacy Associate and I am now the Policy and Advocacy Director. I've been dedicated to helping and working to create positive policies and laws to help those engaging in sex work and drug use. I've testified on behalf of HIPS at DC city council hearings and have spoken on several harm reduction panels, and I am currently managing SWAC (DECRIMNOW). I am also an advisor to the Sex Worker Giving Circle, the Chosen Few, No Justice No Pride, a member of the Urban Survivors Union, and a board member for the Church of Safe Injection–Bangor Maine. I have been featured in op-eds in *The Root* and *Medium*, and am the recipient of an award from the Legal Society of Washington, DC, for my work on the fare evasion bill. I've had the pleasure to advise congressional members Ro Khanna and Ayanna Pressely on proposed legislation. I am extremely honored to serve as Policy and Advocacy Director for HIPS.

Sasanka Jinadasa: How have you and your organization created non-carceral, or anti-carceral, practices with people experiencing harm in the sex trade?

Tamika Spellman: HIPS has pioneered and championed for rights and protections for sex workers since 1993, where I first encountered the organization as a street sex worker. Coming from being a client to being the Director of Policy and Advocacy, I aim to continue the work from the foundation sex workers have solidly laid before me such as stopping the practice of arresting people for having more than three condoms and eliminating prostitution-free zones to the current work we undertake in advocating to decriminalize sex work as a way to stop negative policing habits and to focus efforts on trafficked victims/survivors and not just sex workers. We also work on coalitions to decarcerate the system; defund/reform the police; reform the criminal codes, the judicial system, and the probation/parole system; and to demand no new jails/prisons. We liaise on the behalf of community members, law enforcement, and the judicial system.

SJ: What do you and/or your programs consider a successful outcome?
TS: When those we serve are happy and thriving, we know that's success. We are a full-service center today, with clinical service for LGBTQ folks on hormone therapy, MAT (Medication Assisted Treatment), Suboxone, and treatment for HEP C. We have a comfortable drop-in center where people just hang out; we offer breakfast and lunch Monday through Friday, laundry service, showers, a clothing closet, a food distribution program, non-medical case management, treatment adherence, housing case management, group therapy sessions, HIV and HCV testing, condoms and safer sex supplies, and syringe exchange and safer injection supplies. We also offer mobile MAT and HIV testing Monday through Friday, as well as delivery of condom/safer sex supplies and syringe/injection supplies by appointment or through site visits across DC. On Thurday through Sunday nights, we offer overnight services where we visit sex work strips and encampments to distribute safer sex supplies and safer injection supplies.

SJ: What has been the main challenge to implementing these practices?
TS: Funding is a big challenge. The system itself is based on carceral responses instead of people-powered responses that are stabilizing and not punitive. Gaining city leadership's support is key to the implementation and functionality of harm reduction. That means removing power from police for policing people for situations and circumstances related to autonomy

and agency of self and refocusing on the health and safety of the whole city, including the most marginalized who take precedence over the majority. Shifting the focus from "arresting away an issue" to freeing people from oppressive systems is the biggest challenge. These are human lives we are talking about, and that's where we have the problem. We as a society will protect an animal before we protect human life; we will advocate for them to be free to roam but want to strip people of that same right. Not on my watch. As long as I have breath, I will speak to freedom, liberty, and the pursuit of happiness, which is the promise of America.

WIT LÓPEZ, MEMBER, SEX WORKER GIVING CIRCLE (THEY/THEM/ELLE [IN SPANISH] PRONOUNS)

For the past three years I have been a part of the Sex Worker Giving Circle (SWGC), a radical philanthropic initiative of Third Wave Fund.[9] The Sex Worker Giving Circle was established in response to the harm that SESTA and FOSTA pose to our communities. The SWGC is the first, and currently the only, fund led by sex workers at a foundation in this country.

The experience of being a fellow and an advisor in the SWGC is like no other. It was the first time I felt that I could bring my whole self into a space without having to navigate judgment and shaming.

Sasanka Jinadasa: How have you and your organization created non-carceral, or anti-carceral, practices with people experiencing harm in the sex trade?

Wit López: As a fellow of the Sex Worker Giving Circle, I feel that its creation of anti-carceral practices is multilayered. The first layer is the practice of engaging current and former sex workers to form the selection committee. Speaking from a personal place, when SESTA and FOSTA happened, I was afraid of being arrested for soliciting clientele, so I stopped cold turkey. Being paid to be a fellow of the giving circle actually helped to replace some of the income that I lost. On top of the stipends, we also received Metrocards and funds for traveling to and from in-person meetings. This measure puts some of us at less risk for unjust punishment for fare evasion in subway stations. Feeding us, paying us for our labor as fellows, and providing us with transportation is anti-carceral justice work at its core.

The second layer is the funding that is distributed to the sex worker–led organizations and collectives. Several of the groups that have been funded are actively working to decriminalize sex work in their region through policy change, while other groups are working directly with incarcerated sex workers who are doing anti-carceral organizing work inside of prisons. There are also sex worker collectives working with undocumented people to keep them as safe as possible in a system that views their citizenship status as a reason for incarceration, in addition to their status as sex workers. These grants help to support work that not only supports decriminalizing sex work, but also supports the work of humanizing people who are criminalized for the way their identity as a sex worker intersects with other aspects of their humanity: race, gender, disability, age, citizenship status, etc.

At its root, the Sex Worker Giving Circle is liberation work, abolition work. It's fundamentally anti-carceral.

SJ: What do you and/or your programs consider a successful outcome?
WL: I can't speak for Third Wave Fund staff or other fellows from the SWGC, but much like the way the anti-carceral work is multilayered, so are the measures of success. The fact that the Sex Worker Giving Circle even exists as a foundation in the United States is a minor success on the part of the people who envisioned it. Paying sex workers to create grants for grassroots programs that support sex workers is a success. To me, even the process of coaching a team of sex workers—the fellows—on how to engage in radical philanthropic practices is a success. While some of us came in with community grantmaking knowledge, that isn't a truth for everyone. What is a truth is that we leave there having learned that this type of transformative grantmaking is possible. Lastly, we get the chance to witness successful outcomes with the groups that receive funding.

One of my favorite stories that I consider a successful outcome is the work being done by Ceyenne Doroshow, the founder and executive director of G.L.I.T.S.[10] She received her first organizational grant from the Sex Worker Giving Circle, which launched her into being able to raise $2 million. Those millions went toward buying a multi-unit apartment building for the community. To me, that is a success story beyond my wildest dreams. Knowing that the work of the SWGC fellows made this possible truly warms my heart.

SJ: What has been the main challenge to implementing these practices?

WL: From my perspective as a fellow, the biggest challenge to these practices recently has been COVID-19. It has added more challenges to the work that was already being done. Trying to do anti-carceral work while comrades in the movement are being arrested for speaking up against housing insecurity and evictions, police brutality, medical racism, and more has been a challenge for many of us.

ZARA RAVEN, ANTI-VIOLENCE ADVOCATE (Z PRONOUNS)

I'm the former director of Collective Action for Safe Spaces (CASS),[11] a DC-based grassroots organization building safety without policing. From 2016 through 2020, I organized with DecrimNow DC and DecrimNY—two campaigns working to end the criminalization of sex workers while increasing sex workers' and survivors' access to resources.

Sasanka Jinadasa: How have you and your organization created non-carceral, or anti-carceral, practices with people experiencing harm in the sex trade?
zara raven: We had to start by recognizing the factors that made people in the sex trades vulnerable to violence in the first place: criminalization, housing instability, and lack of access to resources. To address those root causes, we needed a multi-pronged approach that involved policy advocacy, political education, and resource redistribution. We wanted those who were most impacted by the criminalization of sex work to be on the frontlines of the advocacy, and to make that possible, we had to pay folks and make sure their needs were met. CASS was able to dedicate funding to provide stipends to Black trans and queer sex workers to create opportunities for folks to learn from us and from each other about some of the laws enabling police violence against Black sex-working communities. We also engaged folks in canvassing communities and meeting with legislators to build public and political support to repeal the laws that criminalized sex workers, but the most important work that we did was give money directly to Black trans and queer sex workers.

We also knew that laws criminalizing buying and selling sex were not the only ways that Black and housing-insecure sex workers were being targeted by police. In DC, CASS partnered with organizations like ACLU-DC and Black Youth Project 100 (BYP100) to end the criminalization of folks accessing public transit without being able to pay the fare. Previously, people could be put in jail and fined for fare evasion, but through our canvassing and advocacy efforts, our coalition was able to change the law to reduce the fine and eliminate jail time. CASS also partnered with the People for Fairness Coalition to increase access to public restrooms and the National Coalition for the Homeless to end discrimination against people experiencing homelessness, who were often turned away from accessing even the few public restrooms that are available in DC.

In New York, Decrim NY similarly worked to provide stipends to Black trans and queer sex workers to canvass our communities and build political and public support for policies that support sex working communities, and particularly the Stop Violence in the Sex Trades Act (SVSTA), which seeks to end the criminalization of buying sex, selling sex, "loitering" for the purposes of trading sex, and various other laws that are used to target Black, trans, queer, housing-insecure, and sex-working people.

SJ: What do you and/or your programs consider a successful outcome?

zr: Since changes in policy and cultural norms take time, we celebrate the tiny victories: How many sex workers joined us to canvas? How much money were we able to give directly to sex workers? We also found joy in anecdotes: How did it make folks feel to be on the frontlines of advocacy? What were they hearing from folks on the street who changed their minds? Often, people that we canvassed weren't opposed to decriminalizing sex work; many folks had just never considered it before. When we engage in dialogue, people generally recognize that our communities need resources, not policing.

SJ: What has been the main challenge to implementing these practices?

zr: There were many challenges in maintaining the work. We wanted it to be peer led, and the reality was often that when people were experiencing housing instability and being directly targeted by police, even showing up can be really difficult. I remember at one action for International Whores' Day, my colleague at the time who was a Black trans sex worker was stopped, harassed, and fined by the police over fare evasion. Also, when the weather got cold or rainy, canvassing wasn't really an option, and we'd have to adjust our plans. Sometimes that meant making phone calls instead, and other times that just meant canceling or postponing an event. In Washington,

DC, traveling to the Wilson Building to approach legislators only took an hour or two of folks' time, but in New York, when we needed to travel up to Albany to lobby our legislators, we were asking folks who were already marginalized to give up a full day of work to take a long bus ride with us in exchange for a stipend. The distance and the time commitment made it difficult for many people to participate.

Most of all, I learned that, in order to be sustainable, we had to be flexible and do our best to accommodate the many barriers that Black, housing-insecure, street-based workers were facing.

Rematriating Drugs: Decolonial Perspectives of Substance Use, Health Care, and Recovery

An Interview with Andrea Medley, Shirley Cain, and Frederick Cortés Díaz

JUSTICE RIVERA

I WRITE THIS INTRODUCTION JUST WEEKS AFTER REMATRIATING TO Puerto Rico. The Taínos, my Indigenous ancestors, called this island Boriken, translated to mean "Land of the Brave Lord." That name holds true for me as I've needed copious amounts of courage to make the spiritual and physical journey to my beautiful motherland, burdened by colonization. To me, this land signifies safety from white supremacy and a reconnection to who I am through identity, family, and place, but the oppression is inescapable. I pay $300 per month to a US company to provide me with electrical power, but I don't consistently have it. Groceries and meals are also significantly more expensive than they should be due to a US law that requires that all goods going to its colonies come from the States. However, it is hard to get things shipped here from US companies because they think we are international. Through her chronicles on her website, Rematriating Boriken, Yasmin Hernandez further explains,

> As a continued colony of the United States, Puerto Rico does not control its own laws nor have its own citizenship to provide incentives for its own Diaspora. Nor does the local government demonstrate any interest in luring and incentivizing Puerto Ricans returning to Puerto Rico. Paradoxically, it does provide incentives and tax-breaks to wealthy North Americans setting up shop here. Despite the fact that the infamous "exodus" out of Puerto Rico post-Hurricane Maria actually began back with the fiscal crisis of 2008, there are no local government incentives to retain Puerto Rico's population, nor are there efforts to

incentivize the return of its residents who have left or returning children of the Diaspora. If you ask a Diasporican of their interest to live here, most will respond that it is not a viable option financially. Puerto Rico is a fabulous place to visit, but as a place to live it seems to be more attractive to non-Puerto Ricans than to Puerto Ricans themselves. We see the fulfilling of Pedro Albizu Campos's prophecy of the US wanting the cage but not the bird.[1] Many birds have flown the coop, to the colonizer oddly enough.

Rematriation is a term used among Indigenous people of Turtle Island. With repatriation also speaking to the return of Indigenous ancestral remains and sacred objects stolen by settlers and colonizers from their original homes, the term "rematriation" speaks to rejecting the continued conquest of lands and legacies, a return to mother earth and the sacred ways of the ancestors.

When applied to substances, the concept of rematriation asks us to consider the environmental consequences of mass consumption, the War on Drugs, the Indigenous communities who've been stewards of plant medicine, and what a return to sacredness and earth-connectedness means to us and in practice. Rematriation demands conscious drug consumerism.[2] Rematriation recognizes criminalization as a tool of colonization and seeks to decriminalize and destigmatize substance use. Rematriating drugs advocates for a return to intentional substance use while holding the harsh reality that many people need to get well first.

Rematriation is one way to decolonize. According to Andrea Medley (Jaad ahl' Kiiganga), a Johns Hopkins School of Public Health Research Associate from the Haida Nation, "Decolonization is about taking back the power, the resources, the beliefs, the agency that were attempted to be taken away from us as Indigenous people through the tools of colonization. It's about examining the systems that continue to oppress and harm us, and working together to create new ways of connecting." Decolonizing drugs and drug use, then, requires a careful examination of how each system in which people who use drugs perpetuates colonial ideologies and control. This includes the prison industrial complex and the medical industrial complex from police and prisons to Big Pharma, healthcare professionals, and drug treatment facilities.

Rematriating drugs demands health equity. Across the United States and its territories, Indigenous and tribal communities experience poor health outcomes and quality of life. Among other health and social conditions, these communities experience disproportionate rates of HIV, disproportionate fatal substance overdoses, and disproportionate rates of femicide and gender-based violence. Shirley Cain, an Elder and lawyer from the Red Lake Nation, states:

> Upon the arrival of non-Indigenous ways of knowing, Indigenous people changed a lot of our ways, including but not limited to how women were treated by their partners, families, clans, and communities. In pre-colonial times, it was unheard of that Native women were missing, unjustly mistreated, or unjustly harmed. In this modern colonized era, we have some of the highest numbers of family members who are missing, mistreated, abused, victimized, stalked, and murdered . . . The effect of colonization is also reflected in the substance use arena. For example, in both 2020 and 2021, drug overdose rates were highest for American Indian or Alaska Native (AIAN) people (42.5 per 100,000 and 56.6, respectively).[3] This is the highest rate of any ethnic or racial group in the United States. The data reflects inequities in the systems that house treatment programs and detox centers and other similar behavioral health systems. Therefore, the colonized mindset, policies, and procedures often directly affect American Indians and Alaskan Natives who utilize drugs . . .

Modern American social services and healthcare systems are often ill equipped to comprehensively support Native and Latine people and to reduce disparities among Indigenous and colonized communities. Frederick Cortés Díaz, a social worker and syringe service program (SSP) provider in northeastern Puerto Rico, drives this home:

> Colonization poses a huge challenge for those of us who are fighting for justice in public health and social services: it sees social problems as being individual, private affairs, where it is the role of service providers to "fix" the people they serve so

they can retain a minimum level of functionality for the social, political and economic structure. This ensures that the colonial establishment can keep on working "business as usual." What happens is that this individualized focus strips away our ability and capacity to find social solutions that can go beyond just patching up personal problems and achieving functionality in a dysfunctional structure for the person. In this sense, policies and regulations often discourage group interventions or don't provide any space at all for collective engagement, organization, and teamwork in finding solutions to our most urgent social needs. Colonization attempts to keep the colonized subjects powerless, convert them to objects. This is where our most important job lies, making sure to defeat that intent and build ever stronger social ties between oppressed and colonized peoples to build a new way of life.

In what follows, we share interviews with three advocates working at the intersection of decolonization and harm reduction to advance the well-being of their communities, repair harm to their homelands, and rematriate drugs. They explore the impacts of colonization on their communities, work within social service and healthcare settings, and their visions for decolonization.

ANDREA MEDLEY, RESEARCH ASSOCIATE, CENTER FOR INDIGENOUS HEALTH (she/her/hers pronouns)

Andrea Medley (MPH) (Jaad ahl' Kiigangaa) is from the Dadens Yahgu 'laanas Raven Clan, Haida Nation. She is of Haida and mixed white settler ancestry, and was fortunate to grow up in her home community of Gaw Tlagée, on Haida Gwaii. Since 2011, she has worked in public health and Indigenous health programming, policy, and education. Andrea is currently a research associate at the Johns Hopkins Center for Indigenous Health, working on projects related to substance use. She is passionate about harm reduction, community-led health initiatives, Indigenous cultural safety, and reproductive justice, and has worked with Indigenous communities across Turtle Island facilitating conversations about harm reduction, substance use, and sexual well-being. Outside of work, she enjoys live music, book clubs, and beading.

Justice Rivera: What is colonization to you?

Andrea Medley: Colonization is the intentional disruption of traditional and cultural ways of being that have supported us as Indigenous people since time immemorial. Colonization is about assimilation and exploitation, and about creating optimal environments for the colonizers. It's about disruption to Indigenous communities, through land theft, forced removal of Indigenous children from their families to the residential/boarding school systems, the imposition of the reserve system, as a few examples, and then the denial of that disruption and questioning why Indigenous communities are suffering.

JR: How do you see colonization impacting the War on Drugs?

AM: The War on Drugs is a tool of colonization, as it contributes to the intention and function of colonization: the War on Drugs is especially punitive to people of color, dislocates people from employment opportunities, and entrenches people in poverty, and increases stigma and racism against people of color who use drugs. In some contexts, colonization severs connections to traditional medicines that may have been used by Indigenous communities but are now deemed illicit drugs and therefore criminalized. As colonization calls for punitive approaches, including supporting and encouraging Indigenous communities to ban certain community members as a function of the War on Drugs, we experience a war on our traditional values of taking care of each other and managing interpersonal issues and conflict through relying on our traditional teachings.

JR: How does colonization impact the ways you can or cannot work in public health and social service systems?

AM: Colonization impacts our worldviews, for everyone, Indigenous and non-Indigenous people, and our perspectives on public health and social service systems, as it shapes what knowledge and evidence we value, as a society. Indigenous communities have ways of taking care of ourselves and our communities, and have since time immemorial, which have been disrupted by the activities of colonization. Under colonization, our ways continue to be ignored, misunderstood, and devalued. Common ideals of public health, such as "public health is neutral," the preference for quantitative rather than qualitative data, and a black-and-white versus nuanced view of health are from a colonial perspective. This is because we know that there is no neutral, that there is value in stories, and that we live in an interconnected world. Many Indigenous communities have viewed health as interconnected, and it is only more recently that these models and perspectives on health have been acknowledged and supported, largely after being validated by Western science and methods.

JR: How do you define decolonization?

AM: Decolonization is about taking back the power, the resources, the beliefs, and the agency that were attempted to be taken away from us as Indigenous people through the tools of colonization. It's about examining the systems that continue to oppress and harm us, and working together to create new ways of connecting.

JR: What are your and your communities' visions for decolonization?

AM: For me, my visioning for decolonization is about getting back into our traditional ways of governance, and for my nation, we were and are a matrilineal clan system. The more we can connect with our ways of being—that is decolonizing work. The more we can regain our traditional roles and community roles, we can build support and confidence to be our true selves and counter the systems of colonization. I also think that decolonization includes spending more time with each other to interact, to learn, and to teach. Work takes up so much of our time, and it impacts the time we have to decolonize and to learn more about our languages, ways of being, culture, and ceremonies. So decolonization is about alternatives to capitalism and finding ways to make space and time for the things that sustain us and bring us joy.

JR: What are your and your community's visions for a decolonized care system?

AM: A decolonized care system offers traditional ways of healing, cultural ways of healing, and supports practitioners in healing and cultural work so that they can sustain themselves. It's about alternatives to engaging in capitalism, and valuing trades and time as well. It's a way of life, a perspective and connection with time, and taking the time we need. Decolonized care is also about offering services at home, or as close to home as possible, rather than sending people away. It's about wrap-around services that meet our physical, emotional, and spiritual needs. When we decolonize our care system, we offer options for people for the many modes, methods, and approaches to healing that are required.

JR: How can we shift toward a paradigm where we are building with our participants rather than building for them?

AM: Providing space, time, and energy for participants to self-build and to help guide, navigate, and meaningfully contribute to our shared work are the first steps to building together. I think we (people in the helping professions) can unconsciously make assumptions about people's time or priorities, and in doing so we can unintentionally leave people out of the conversation or the process of building. Such as when we assume that figuring out a part of our process is boring so we don't include someone, or we know someone is really busy so we don't invite them to a meeting. We think we are being helpful and conscientious but we may be leaving people out and hampering them from learning important steps. As I was reflecting on this question, I was thinking about learning how to smoke fish with my mom. Some part of the process are very basic (cutting wood), tedious (cutting the fish into equal-sized pieces), or lengthy (waiting for the fish to smoke or the jars to boil), but all of the steps are important, and if I was left out of a single step then I wouldn't know how to replicate this process on my own. If we want our process and our work to be sustainable, we have to take the time to learn and the time to teach.

JR: How can you help yourself and your colleagues develop self-care?

AM: When we practice self-care, we model self-care. When we take time for self-care, especially if we are in leadership roles, we make space for self-care for the people around us. Furthermore, social service and healthcare programs can support self-care by providing time off specifically for self-care, offering self-care options through work (e.g., massage days), or extending stipends and incentives for self-care.

JR: What questions or prompts would you like to leave readers with for further thought and exploration?

AM: I would like readers to reflect on their perspectives and worldviews, and consider how there are such a variety of perspectives on this work, and ours is just one of them. I think the fact that there is no singular solution to these issues, and that we all have something to contribute to changing things for the better brings hope and meaning.

SHIRLEY CAIN

Shirley Cain, JD (she/they), is a citizen of the Red Lake Nation and avid Jingle dress dancer. She has over 30 years of experience advocating for families, children, and tribal communities affected by substance use disorder and co-occurring mental health issues in Indian Country. She provides training and technical assistance to Tribal grantees. Shirley has Juris Doctorate and Bachelor of Arts degrees. She is also a licensed attorney in the State of Minnesota, where she has served as a Tribal judge focusing on children's issues, addiction, and communication between tribal agencies. More recently, Shirley has served as a policy specialist coordinating a Native American Equity project focusing on child welfare. She has an extensive history in advancing quality services toward the advancement of Indigenous substance use reform, access to services, and development of innovative solutions supporting comprehensive care delivery for Natives. Shirley is also a fierce advocate for diversity, equity, and inclusion involving positive physical, emotional, and mental health for her Indigenous relatives. Her vision for all her Indigenous relatives is to be healthy and happy.

Justice Rivera: What is colonization to you?

Shirley Cain: Colonization is when non-Indigenous concepts arrived on Turtle Island. In precolonial times, Indigenous people lived a balanced life of health, wealth, wellness, happiness, tranquility, and peace. Upon the arrival of non-Indigenous ways of knowing, Indigenous people changed a lot of our ways, including but not limited to how women were treated by their partners, families, clans, and communities. In precolonial times, it was unheard of that Native women were missing, unjustly mistreated, or unjustly harmed. In this modern colonized era, we have some of the highest numbers of Indigenous women and Indigenous Two Spirit family members who are missing, mistreated, abused, victimized, stalked, and murdered. Due to racism and neglect by some law enforcement and other agencies, the status and location of missing Native women and Two Spirit community members are neither investigated nor searched for by any other agency or community other than by our own communities. Colonization has further resulted in Native women experiencing disproportionate violent treatment as, "more than 1.5 million have experienced violence in their lifetime." If there are about five million Native people in the United States, that is about 33 percent Native women who have experienced violence, which is a direct contribution of colonization.[4]

The effect of colonization is also reflected in the substance use arena. For example, in both 2020 and 2021, drug overdose rates were highest for American Indian or Alaska Native (AIAN) people (42.5 per 100,000 and 56.6, respectively).[5] This is the highest rate of any ethnic or racial group in the United States. The data reflects the inequities in the systems that house treatment programs and detox centers and other similar behavioral health systems. Therefore, the colonized mindset, policies, and procedures often directly affect American Indians and Alaskan Natives who utilize drugs as indicated by the above data collected by the Centers for Disease Control and Prevention (CDC).

JR: How do you see colonization impacting the War on Drugs?

SC: The War on Drugs began over 50 years ago during the Nixon era to crack down on the public enemy of drug use by communities. The War on Drugs picked up momentum in the 1980s during the Reagan Administration, which increased federal agencies' oversight and funding to punish drug users. The ultimate consequence was that Black people and other People of Color were profoundly impacted by the severe consequences of spending years in prisons due to crack use. This did not impact white communities in the same way, as cocaine was not negatively associated with crime and violence the way crack was.

Further, the War on Drugs has impacted many diverse groups of people in other ways. As stated in the *Annals of Medicine* journal, "The drug war and a punitive drug war logic impact most systems of everyday life in the US, subjecting people to surveillance, suspicion, and punishment and undermining key social determinants of health, including education, employment, housing, and access to benefits. Combined, these have resulted in poorer health outcomes for individuals, families, and communities, particularly for people who use drugs."[6]

It appears that the colonizer mindset and punitive systems that have evolved since the War on Drugs began over 50 years ago has further exacerbated an already inequitable system of treatment towards Indigenous, Black, and other marginalized groups of people.

JR: How does colonization negatively impact your communities and communities of people who use drugs?

SC: People who use drugs face a lot of inequities including lack of access to safe and affordable housing, quality health care, and good paying jobs. Colonization includes the institutionally biased systems that create and implement policies and procedures which impact people who use drugs. For example, a drug user may have a criminal history involving drug usage. If they have a felony conviction, then they cannot access safe and affordable housing with a conviction on their record. Further, they may not have access to a job that pays a good enough wage to be able to afford to pay high rental costs including the damage deposit and often first and last month's rent. If the person wants to go to treatment, they need health insurance or some method to pay for treatment costs. Once they are in treatment, they are subject to random drug testing. If they fail a drug test, that could result in expulsion from treatment. The list could be endless. Thus, a drug user often feels hopeless in their quest for any semblance of sobriety or recovery from drug usage.

JR: How does colonization impact the ways you can or cannot work in public health and social service systems?

SC: These systems in public health and social services are set up in such a way that creates more barriers than avenues to be successful in these respective systems. This was made more visible during COVID times when hospitals treated marginalized people in disparate ways such as not giving access to a COVID test due to lack of payment or medical coverage, or restricting access to medication that could save lives. Also, some clinics left patients to die alone, without family being present to accompany them on their last journey to the Spirit world. The Navajo Nation did not have running water or infrastructure for their people, and many tribal members did not have clean water or plumbing in their homes. This is still occurring in many Alaskan Native Villages as well.

In social service systems, this can be observed with the high rates of out-of-home placement of Native children in foster and adoptive care. Often, Native children are removed from the homes of their parents by social workers with middle class white standards. Children are often removed due to allegations of neglect. If a parent or caretaker is using drugs, an alternative option could be to work with the parent or parents to utilize treatment and recovery strategies so the child can stay in their home. If they must leave their home to go to treatment, then a relative can come to the home to caretake the children so the children are not traumatized by being removed from their stable environment and school.

JR: How do you define decolonization?

SC: Decolonization is about dismantling the systems and inequities that have been on Turtle Island since around 1492. Many people thought that these inequitable systems would be dismantled after the Minneapolis police killed George Floyd in 2020. His death was a part of a system of brutalism by the Minneapolis police against Natives, Black people, and other marginalized groups over a period of decades.

More recently, decolonization has begun with non-profits, governmental public health systems, and socially conscious businesses starting diversity, equity, and inclusion programs. Diversity is about recognizing the various groups that are different, unique, or have special classifications. Equity is about the system itself, aiming to change the processes that our people encounter when they interact with police, judges, prosecutors, defense attorneys, teachers, social workers, doctors, nurses, treatment center staff, emergency withdrawal (detox) staff, and numerous other employees who work in those systems. If a program has a process for an expedient assessment and referral to treatment, it can save lives. The program can have Peer Support staff and a person trained in mental health to work with the person who is misusing substances. If the staff is a Native, that is another plus for the system, as Natives relate to other Natives, especially if they have gone through that system and know how to navigate it. Inclusion is about bringing Natives into a process with all their uniqueness and celebrating differences.

The social service and public health systems should recognize the uniqueness of Natives and other diverse family systems and honor them by incorporating culture into programming. Many Natives and other marginalized groups have different types of foods they eat and rituals they practice as a family. A program could incorporate that into their operations and include families in the healing process. In some treatment programs, they also have sweat lodge and pipe and smudging ceremonies available to them. For example, at Four Winds Treatment Center in Brainerd, Minnesota, they utilize a Native-centered curriculum to focus on healing for Natives. In Lino Lakes Correctional Facility in Minnesota, inmates participate in sweat lodge ceremonies and also have drumming/singing groups. In St. Paul Public School systems, the School Board enacted a policy to allow Natives to smudge with the four traditional medicines of cedar, sage, sweetgrass, and tobacco.

Admittedly, we still have a way to go before full decolonization or removing systems of biases occurs. However, we are on a journey to inclusion and wellness that has just begun and will continue if we work together in a united fashion.

JR: What are your and your communities' visions for decolonization?

SC: I would call this a "vision for belonging and inclusivity" as this is what many people need and want for themselves. Most of us want to belong to a family, clan, or community. We need and want to be needed by other people. If we do not feel a part of a family or community, then we feel isolated and left out. If we are included in conversations, meetings, dialogues, and decisions, then we feel included. If a community is going to have a vision of wellness and well-being, then they must conduct community engagement and community dialogues. In some communities, they are doing virtual Town Hall meetings on fentanyl. In Minnesota, Ramsey County Mental Health Collaborative recently conducted a Multicultural Town Hall Meeting regarding fentanyl. They had different presenters including various outreach workers to talk about what fentanyl is, how to identify it, and how to use naloxone to help save a life. They also had a youth worker discuss signs that youth may be using drugs. Then they discussed social media as an avenue that lures youth into drug use. In another community—the Yurok Tribe—they are using Wellness Coalitions to conduct meetings around opioids and other substances. They also have various projects in other parts of California that are involved in Indigenous projects addressing substance use.

JR: What are your and your community's visions for a decolonized care system?

SC: Again, I would call this a belonging and inclusive care system that treats a person like a human being. Also, if substance use is a disease, then people who are using substances should be treated like any other person with a disease. This illness can also be life threatening and complicated. It is mostly complicated by the fact that many people attach stigma to it, as they consider this to be a "behavioral" problem. They even call this "behavioral health." It could have a new label and concept called a health and wellness system that focuses on good health, happiness, balance, positive well-being, and overall good wellness. In our Native communities, we have different ways to say it. For Anishinabe, we say: Mino Bimaadiziwin (living a good life).

Also, when a person goes to substance use treatment, they should have a longer period of treatment, including extended treatment for mental health issues, as some of our beautiful Natives continue to have historical and collective traumas due to colonization including loss of land, culture, and language. There could be adverse child experiences to consider as well. A decolonized care system could design wraparound services to include Indigenous language classes; good nutrition, including access to traditional foods and ways of life; physical movement such as walking, medicine gathering, medicine or traditional tobacco planting and tending; access to counselors or therapists that do nature walks with their people while engaging with them; education-type systems that challenge their minds; programs with experiential learning; and traditional teachings such as drum making followed by teaching traditional songs for use during ceremonies and other sacred events. Some could use Talking Circles and journal writing. It would be best practice and wise to include an Elder or Cultural Knowledge Bearer/ Keeper to work with clients/people in those wellness systems.

JR: What questions or prompts would you like to leave readers with for further thought and exploration?

SC: "What can we do to address substance use, mental health, emotional health, and physical health from a traditional Native methodology including Indigenous or Traditional Ways of Knowing?"

JR: How can we shift toward a paradigm where we are building with our participants rather than building for them?

SC: Community engagement, dialogue, and feedback. If we make time to include community members by giving them time to express their voices, this is optimal, as it allows them the opportunity to be truly involved with a project or event. We can also utilize Indigenous Qualitative Evaluation methods such as Talking Circles, digital storytelling, short and in-person surveys with incentives, and focus groups to gather input and feedback for continuous quality improvement. In this work, it is best practice and wise to always involve Elders and other community members to guide the work.

The American Indian Higher Education Consortium Indigenous Evaluation Framework centers their work in traditional ways of knowing. They also utilize the circle as a metaphor to show how this will work. They use the framework of Creating the Story; Building the Scaffolding; Planning, Implementing, Celebrating, and Engaging Community; and Building Capacity. This is intended to work as a guide for tribal members seeking to conduct an Indigenous Evaluation.[7] It is my understanding that they would like to see Tribal and other agencies follow this as a guide, rather than by the letter, much as you would be guided by a local resident who knows the territory, the land, and the cultural protocols.

JR: How can you help yourself and your colleagues develop self-care?

SC: Mindful meditation and deliberate time-outs for self-care during a workday, especially through and after times of grief and stress such as wakes, funerals, or hospitalization/illness of a loved one. We need to make time for conversations, venting of frustrations, and problem solving. Oftentimes, the person stressed only needs a willing listener, as they may not ask for feedback or advice. Self-care can include taking a quick walk when a person has high frustrations or anxiety. Another method for self-care is breathing techniques. There are free apps to guide or aid in meditation.[8]

FREDERICK CORTÉS DÍAZ, HARM REDUCTION PROGRAM COORDINATOR, INTERCAMBIOS PUERTO RICO
(he/him/his pronouns)

Frederick J. Cortés Díaz is a Community Social Worker based in Rio Grande, Puerto Rico. Currently working as a coordinator for a harm reduction program in the eastern region of the island, he has experience working with labor groups, decarceration ballot efforts, campaigns for the release of political prisoners in the United States, community and neighborhood organizations, mutual aid projects, youth development, and the provision of essential services to the homeless population in his native Puerto Rico. He is a political activist and harm reductionist with a passion for community organizing and bridge-building between people and movements across borders.

Justice Rivera: What is colonization to you?

Frederick Cortés Díaz: Colonization is a violent historical process through which one nation imposes its domination on another with the intention of extracting gains and resources in unilaterally beneficial terms. It is, at its core, an undemocratic project with the intention of expanding and preserving power in the hands of the owning classes at any cost. At certain points in history, this colonization presents itself as outright military intervention and occupation, while at others it presents itself in the imposition of hegemonic cultural norms and standards either through deceit (propaganda) or coercion. As such, it is not only a political phenomenon, but also an economic, psychological, and cultural beast that preys on those it identifies as being somehow weaker. This assumed "weakness" has a completely racialized bias against non-white, working peoples all over the globe in territories both inside and outside of colonizing countries themselves. Colonization manifests itself in our daily lives through the shaping of policy, distribution of public resources, educational curriculums, and other crucial aspects of our social environment.

JR: How do you see colonization impacting the War on Drugs?

FCD: The War on Drugs is closely entangled with colonialism, which can be more clearly seen in its global dissemination. The idea of an international War on Drugs was pushed by the United States and its growing pharmaceutical industry during a historical period in which its domination and assertion of control over historically colonized nations was being brought into question and active struggles were being fought by peoples all over the world to assert their collective right to national sovereignty. In this sense, the War on Drugs proved to be a counteroffensive by the ruling sectors of the American political establishment to regain its influence inside countries which could have soon abandoned its sphere of influence. The drug war policies, along with the millions of dollars of US taxpayer money that funded them, led to collaborative agreements between the United States government and countries where production of drugs of interest took place. In the case of Colombia, this meant the expansion of the US military presence in their territory, with the justification of closely monitoring and intercepting the cocaine trade associated with the region. In reality, drug production and trafficking never declined even after massive investments on surveillance technologies and military aid to the partner governments. In reality, most of these resources ended up being divested and funneled to organized crime organizations to surveil and persecute political actors who questioned or opposed the imposition of US domination over their territories. In this sense, the War on Drugs at a large scale was the reconfiguration of US colonial and imperial strategy, aiming to preserve its influence by supposedly addressing a highly contested social issue: public health.

JR: How does colonization negatively impact your communities and communities of people who use drugs?

FCD: The drug user community in Puerto Rico is adversely affected by colonization in varied ways. To start off, the whole structure of the Puerto Rican health-care system is based on the United States' model of private medical insurance companies as the main providers of health services. This model, imposed through neoliberal reforms promoted by US Congress in the 1990s, wiped out the previous public health–centered model developed on the island by Dr. Arbona in the 1950s and which served as an example for other countries until its dismantling, with the increased influence of health insurance companies into the medical services field. This meant the closing and consolidation of hospitals and facilities, the prioritization of cost-basis logics in the administration of health services, the establishment of something similar to a caste system in health-care access, as well as the massive disenfranchisement of Puerto Ricans with regards to who they could choose as their medical providers, especially if they couldn't afford private health insurance. This means that drug users usually don't have the option of obtaining life-saving services from the professionals that they choose, but have to just put up with whatever is assigned to them through their insurance company. The insurance companies become the ones who decide what will be the course of care for patients, instead of medical professionals making the decisions with their patients. As mentioned earlier, a core pillar of colonialism is the stripping away of power and participation of people in the spaces that make a difference in their daily quality of life. In this sense, the maximum extraction of profits, rather than better health outcomes, has become the guiding principle behind colonial public health.

JR: How does colonization impact the ways you can or cannot work in public health and social service systems?

FCD: Colonization poses a huge challenge for those of us who are fighting for justice in public health and social services: it sees social problems as being individual, private affairs, where it is the role of service providers to "fix" the people they serve so they can retain a minimum level of functionality for the social, political, and economic structure. This ensures that the colonial establishment can keep on working "business as usual." What happens is that this individualized focus strips away our ability and capacity to find social solutions that can go beyond just patching up personal problems and achieving functionality in a dysfunctional structure for the person. In this sense, policies and regulations often discourage group interventions or don't provide any space at all for collective engagement, organization, and teamwork in finding solutions to our most urgent social needs. Colonization attempts to keep the colonized subjects powerless, converting them to objects. This is where our most important job lies, making sure to defeat that intent and build ever stronger social ties between oppressed and colonized peoples to build a new way of life.

JR: How do you define decolonization?

FCD: Decolonization has many dimensions. I think our starting point has to be raising awareness and developing collective consciousness about how we got to the point we are at today. Why are our living conditions the way they are right now? Can we change them? How? Answering those basic questions, as part of a collective effort, leads us to seek out ways in which things can be made different. It pushes our minds to see possibilities instead of limitations; it reminds us that power lies in our will to act and that beyond being individuals, we are part of a collective where the united power of all its components can have a much bigger impact than each of us individually. This basic dimension of consciousness/awareness is a prerequisite to the development of a strategic vision for getting rid of and replacing colonial values, logics, and practices. In my view, this can only happen through organized, concerted action for structural change. Colonized subjects must come together regardless of ethnicity, religion, sex, gender, or any other category of oppression to build a strong political force that can dispute power and social influence within the social classes that defend the project of colonization and domination. In this sense, decolonization is necessarily a social process of political mobilization, of self recognition and redemption, and of visualizing and building the world that we really want to live in, where democracy, justice, and peace can truly form the basis for our daily lives.

JR: What are your and your communities' visions for decolonization?

FCD: In Puerto Rico, decolonization has many fronts. The cultural front is very important, as it brings colonization into the public consciousness and opens a conversation to question colonial history—its contemporary influence and impact on the daily lives of our people. In this sense, the Puerto Rican people have been able to pass down to newer generations a wealth of knowledge about cultural resistance to colonialism, while at the same time passing on the values and ethics of those who fought against colonialism before our arrival to this world. In addition, decolonization will require a large-scale organization and mobilization effort between diverse sectors of Puerto Rican society who share in experiencing the nefarious effects of colonial policy and domination. Political separation and reparations from the United States empire would be a necessary step to regain full sovereignty for our nation—to then have full capacity and resources to repair the damages sustained by our people and lands during the colonial period. In the process, new social institutions will need to be built to ensure our people have the basic elements needed for their sustainment and development as human beings, with mutual aid organizations being an essential piece in times of foreseen hardship through the transition process.

JR: What are your and your community's visions for a decolonized care system?

FCD: A decolonized care system would mean giving people back the power over their own bodies, their own autonomy to decide what is best for their health, to have a final say in issues relating to their medical care, to have the power to influence and change the policies that affect the care services they receive. It means greater democracy in society at large and greater community control over the institutions and services that ensure their livelihoods and quality of life.

JR: What questions or prompts would you like to leave readers with for further thought and exploration?

FCD: "In a time of social atomization and identity politics, how can we build bridges between diverse social groups and identities to promote and engage in large-scale social change that benefits all?"

"How can we promote a sense of capacity and responsibility in the members of our family and community so they become more willing to engage in efforts to better our quality of life and address important social issues?"

It is our duty as organizers of social change to design spaces of participation where not only can we bring our ideas to the table but also make it encouraging for everybody else to voice their concerns, have them taken into account, and feel that they have the space and backup of a bigger community to bring their ideas into reality. This is the essence of self-care in a colonial context. As such, the best self-care is collective care. Making sure to check in with our colleagues periodically ensures that bonds of emotional responsibility are created and sustained in our networks. Building community is one of the best ways to have access to resources for self-care, be it having someone to talk to, ask for council or advice, vent off, have a laugh, share our creativity, our experiences . . . At the same time it allows for the burden of caring to be distributed so that it doesn't all fall on one (or a few) individuals. Building relationships of trust, collaboration, and compassionate accountability is almost the antithesis to colonialism, where competition and domination are the guiding principles and values. No movement for social change can exist if our own people's well-being is not taken care of.

Principles of Healing-Centered Harm Reduction

Reframe Health and Justice with input from Monique Tula and Jessica Peñaranda

IN THE 1990S, A NASCENT HARM REDUCTION MOVEMENT PUT FORTH A SET of principles to guide movement work.[1,2] Though there is no universal definition of or formula for implementation, the National Harm Reduction Coalition (United States) holds that harm reduction:

- Accepts, for better and or worse, that licit and illicit drug use is part of our world and chooses to work to minimize its harmful effects rather than simply ignore or condemn them.

- Understands drug use as a complex, multi-faceted phenomenon that encompasses a continuum of behaviors from severe abuse to total abstinence, and acknowledges that some ways of using drugs are clearly safer than others.

- Establishes quality of individual and community life and well-being— not necessarily cessation of all drug use—as the criteria for successful interventions and policies.

- Calls for the non-judgmental, non-coercive provision of services and resources to people who use drugs and the communities in which they live in order to assist them in reducing attendant harm.

- Ensures that drug users and those with a history of drug use routinely have a real voice in the creation of programs and policies designed to serve them.

- Affirms drug users themselves as the primary agents of reducing the harms of their drug use, and seeks to empower users to share information and support each other in strategies which meet their actual conditions of use.

- Recognizes that the realities of poverty, class, racism, social isolation, past trauma, sex-based discrimination, and other social inequalities affect both people's vulnerability to and capacity for effectively dealing with drug-related harm.

- Does not attempt to minimize or ignore the real and tragic harm and danger associated with licit and illicit drug use.

The guidelines from Harm Reduction International are as follows:

- Respecting the rights of people who use drugs. Harm reduction is fundamentally grounded in principles that aim to protect human rights and improve public health. Treating people who use drugs—along with their families and communities—with compassion and dignity is integral to harm reduction. The use of drugs does not mean people forfeit their human rights—they remain entitled to the right to life, to the highest attainable standard of health, to social services, to privacy, to freedom from arbitrary detention, and to freedom from cruel, inhuman, and degrading treatment, among others.

- A commitment to evidence. Harm-reduction policies and practices are informed by a strong body of evidence that shows interventions to be practical, feasible, effective, safe, and cost effective in diverse social, cultural, and economic settings. Most harm-reduction interventions are easy to implement and inexpensive, and all have a strong positive impact on individual and community health.

- A commitment to social justice and collaborating with networks of people who use drugs. Harm reduction is rooted in a commitment to addressing discrimination and ensuring that nobody is excluded from the health and social services they may need because of their drug use, their race, their gender, their gender identity, their sexual orientation, their choice of work, or their economic status. People should be able to access services without having to overcome unnecessary barriers, including burdensome, discriminatory regulations. Further, the meaningful involvement of people who use drugs in designing, implementing and evaluating programs and policies that serve them is central to harm reduction.

- The avoidance of stigma. Harm reduction practitioners accept people who use drugs as they are and are committed to meeting them "where they are" in their lives without judgment. Terminology and language should always convey respect and avoid stigmatizing terms or divisions between "good" and "bad" drugs. Stigmatizing language perpetuates harmful stereotypes, and creates barriers to health and social services.

As these principles are increasingly adopted by public health and social service programs nationwide, Reframe Health and Justice seeks to adapt and grow the harm-reduction framework into an emergent space—one formed, led, and transformed by the healing movements of racial, gender, trans, and queer justice. In 2018, we—a collective informed by our individual experiences with harm reduction and healing justice at the personal, community, and professional levels (namely within the sex and drug trades)—released an intentionally broader version of the widely accepted harm reduction principles.[3]

These principles of healing-centered harm reduction are not meant to replace the current principles of harm reduction. Rather, they offer additional perspectives that build upon the original to include guidance on how communities of harm reductionists can support each other and themselves while enacting the principles of harm reduction. Informed by the many seismic shifts that have occurred throughout our world through the increased visibility of racist violence and a global pandemic, we are again releasing our working principles of healing-centered harm reduction. The updated principles below reflect our own shifts in perspective and praxis, developed through continuous self-reflection and communal learning.

RESPOND TO HARM

> *"My people cultivated pain. In a way that god cultivated his garden with the foresight that he could not contain or protect the life within it. Humanity was born out of pain."*
>
> —Terese Marie Mailhot, *Heart Berries*, 2018 (First Nation Nlaka'pamux Canadian author)

Healing-centered harm reduction acknowledges that harm is an inevitable part of the human experience. Responding to harm is one of the many ways we learn how to navigate the world. In a world shaped by oppression, harm that has been done lives on in the bodies and communities that have borne the brunt of systemic brutalization. We can condemn harm while also celebrating the resilient beings we have become as a result.

Harm partially shapes who we are. We cannot design to eliminate the occurrence of harm. We are currently, and always will be, responding to and healing from the sweeping harm caused by systems of oppression over the last 500+ years.

APPROACH HOLISTICALLY

> *"When we talk about harm reduction, we often reduce it to a public health framework, reducing risks. That's harm reduction with a small 'h-r.' Harm reduction is meeting people where they are but not leaving them there. But Harm Reduction with a capital 'H' and 'R'—this is about the movement that aims to shift power and resources to the people who are most vulnerable to structural violence."*

—Monique Tula, National Harm Reduction Conference, 2018
      (Executive Director, National Harm Reduction Coalition)

Healing-centered harm reduction recognizes that harm happens on both an interpersonal and an institutional/structural level, and that holistic approaches seek to reduce the harm perpetuated by both.

There are many kinds of harm. Those working at the intersections of public health, social services, and social justice must do our best to take into account all of these types of harm. Holistic approaches mean listening to, acting on, and compensating for the consultation of those most directly impacted, targeted, and/or vulnerable to systemic injustice. Harm reduction calls for organizational and community investment in developing and implementing holistic approaches (alternatives to calling 911, transformative justice circles), while simultaneously holding space for those whose current survival relies on the use of criminal legal approaches.

ALLOW FOR DIFFERENCE

"Sometimes, to become somebody else, you have to become nobody first. You have to let go of your mother and father, the crooked starving house you grew up in that wanted to devour you and digest you whole. Forget, if you can, all the promises you've made and the lies that you've told. Forget the scars you left one, two, three times on your left wrist. Forget flowers and killer bees and everyone you've ever known . . . I'm going to find the place where my shadow ends and my body begins. Close your eyes. I'll see you there."

—Kai Cheng Thom, *Fierce Femmes and Notorious Liars*

Healing-centered harm reduction recognizes that people experience the world differently. What is harmful or traumatic for one individual may be an act of resilience or joy to another. These perceptions and experiences can evolve over time.

We cannot expect that what is harmful to one person will be harmful to another. We may relate to our harm and our resilience differently as we move into different points in time/space. At the same time, we cannot forget our interconnectedness as a species and inhabitants of the universe. Healing and justice do not have a uniform definition, practice, and process.

RECOGNIZE CIRCUMSTANCES

"When you have PTSD, things repeat themselves over and over and over.

Guilt is a ghost.

Guilt is a ghost.

Guilt is a ghost."

—Myriam Gurba, *Mean*, 2017
(Chicana literary and cultural critic)

Healing-centered harm reduction stresses that harm—both experienced and perpetuated—is sometimes a result of the lengths some people must go to survive in the face of institutional trauma and violence.

People, especially those navigating survival conditions, sometimes both experience and cause harm. Institutional violence exacerbates this dual reality, limiting what is within an individual's control by restricting and regulating options and choices. Healing-Centered Harm Reduction emphasizes gaining empathy and unconditional positive regard for those around us who make decisions differently than we imagine we would have made them.

HONOR SURVIVAL

> *"And just because the healing process is hard doesn't mean that all the violence is the same, and that we need to address that violence differently. There is not a hierarchy in violence, it's just very important that everyone knows that each thing is not the same."*
>
> —Shira Hassan, *Beyond Survival*, 2020
> (transformative justice practitioner)

Healing-centered harm reduction honors the many ways that survival and healing look without condemning or glorifying how people survive and heal.

People do things to survive and we should honor that resilience—whether it's through drugs, sex, abstinence, or acts considered to be self-harm. We dare not say that one method is better than another—rather, we celebrate survival and work toward unpacking what methods we want to keep moving into new parts of our lives, and which methods we will release and transform.

PROVIDE TIME AND SPACE

> *"A breeze touches your cheek. As something should."*
>
> —Claudia Rankine

Healing-centered harm reduction values the act of holding space and time for rest, connection, learning, unlearning, elevation, and liberation. Growth and change require patience, effort, and care.

Harm reduction cannot be all about "results." It is a privilege to have time and resources to rest. People in survival conditions are rarely given time and space to collaboratively learn, heal, and commune. The process of healing is non-linear and takes time. People will be at varied levels of readiness along the way. An outcomes focus is antithetical to authentic systems change—our values must be centered in the process as much as the outcomes.

UNDERSCORE OPPRESSION'S IMPACT

> "Dehumanization, although a concrete historical fact, is not a given destiny but the result of an unjust order that engenders violence in the oppressors, which in turn dehumanizes the oppressed."
>
> —Paulo Freire, *Pedagogy of the Oppressed*, 1968
> (Brazilian educator, critical pedagogist)

Healing-centered harm reduction underscores the impact of shared, individual, and intersecting experiences of anti-Blackness and racism, colonization, imperialism, sexism, homophobia, transphobia, classism, ableism, and other oppressions.

In naming systems of oppression, we also name that we all face them differently—intersecting, alone, and as communities. A clear path forward in harm reduction recognizes that we must examine our position within movement spaces and care work, understanding how our positionality affects our capacity and resources to survive, heal, and grow.

BALANCE TRANSFORMATIVE AND PRACTICAL

> "[Transformative justice] recognizes that we must transform the conditions which help to create acts of violence or make them possible. Often this includes transforming harmful oppressive dynamics, our relationships to each other, and our communities at large."
>
> —Mia Mingus, *Leaving Evidence*, 2019
> (queer Korean disabled transracial/transnational adoptee)

Healing-centered harm reduction designs tailored approaches to restoration and reparation, as well as practical strategies to reduce harm and increase access to resources.

Healing-centered harm reduction invites us to think bigger than just practical strategies for survival. What does the continuum from surviving to thriving look like? Transformation has many contours and it is a magical act to dream. We also need practical strategies. Justice movement building operates like ecosystems where members of various ecosystems focus on complementary work to sustain survival, healing, justice, cultural production, social transformation or reorganization, resource redistribution, and land regeneration.

LEAD WITH COMMUNITY

> *"Black and Third World people are expected to educate white people as to our humanity. Women are expected to educate men. Lesbians and gay men are expected to educate the heterosexual world. The oppressors maintain their position and evade their responsibility for their own actions. There is a constant drain of energy which might be better used in redefining ourselves and devising realistic scenarios for altering the present and constructing the future."*
>
> —Audre Lorde, *Sister Outsider: Essays and Speeches*, 1984
> (Black lesbian theorist and activist)

Healing-centered harm reduction uplifts community-based, intergenerational and cultural approaches to resilience, healing, and harm reduction led by the people most impacted by the issues at hand. Harm reduction is fundamentally dependent on mutual aid and support.

People have been doing liberatory work for centuries, and much of it has gone unrecognized. Restoring balance means shifting the locus of power to those who are most impacted when developing interventions and approaches to reducing harm and healing.

DEMAND ACCOUNTABILITY

"In the practice of our politics we do not believe that the end always justifies the means. Many reactionary and destructive acts have been done in the name of achieving 'correct' political goals. As feminists we do not want to mess over people in the name of politics. We believe in collective process and a nonhierarchical distribution of power within our own group and in our vision of a revolutionary society."

—The Combahee River Collective Statement, 1977
(Black feminist collective)

We reject reliance on violent and exploitative state-sponsored systems like prisons, detention centers, and civil commitment where we recognize that our care systems are often embedded or complicit. We hold this tension and struggle together to build anti-violence into being. Holding systems of power and privilege accountable, we address power imbalances through transformative justice models that prioritize restoration over punishment.

The state, which perpetuates exploitation and violence, cannot be expected to be the arbiter of justice. Holding people and systems accountable for their violence is part of healing. Accountability and punishment are not the same. Collectively learning, developing, and practicing transformative justice will sustain our efforts toward abolishing state violence. We cannot respond to the institutionalized impunity of the state if our systems of accountability are underdeveloped or not in application.

Our principles of healing-centered harm reduction continue to ground us in our work to both vision and operationalize a more just world. Harm reduction's origins through the work and survival of people who use drugs offer many lessons in resilience, care, and health. As harm reduction and parallel movements and philosophies widen to broadly and intentionally consider survival and healing, we offer these principles to guide us toward a communal solidarity that challenges oppressive structures.

SECTION FOUR

Pleasure-Oriented Futures

This section explores the contentious topic of pleasure. Society often casts sex and drugs as deviant luxuries. Public health approaches to sex and drugs focus on their possible negative consequences. But what about feeling good? The following poems, stories, and articles move us beyond the nuts-and-bolts pursuit of social justice in our work and reorient us to what is elemental, human, and healing.

Pleasure as an Access Point

J. LEIGH OSHIRO-BRANTLY

JUST AS NONE OF YOU ARE MONOLITHS, I HOPE IT GOES WITHOUT SAYING that nothing I write is prescriptive. My words come from the time I have spent on this merry-go-round-the-sun simply living, examining, and framing these memories as best I can. Some things to follow might activate you negatively, but if they do, I hope you can find the space to be activated for pleasure, as well.

FROM HARM REDUCTION TO PLEASURE EXPANSION

Like many other social justice advocates, I do a lot of thinking. And lately, after a concentrated multi-year marathon of grieving so many deaths (in myriad ways and expressions), I have come to realize that the principles of harm reduction, found pervasively in my advocacy work, are no longer enough to sustain my personal life. It's not that I don't use harm-reduction principles. I do! And it's beautiful to see how these principles can integrate with my hybrid Goddess/Ryukyuan/Shinto/Hindu/Buddhist practices.

Let's look at a few harm reduction principles[1] and see how their concepts can work from within an emotional and/or spiritual framework.

- Harm reduction "accepts, for better or worse, that licit and illicit drug use is part of our world and chooses to work to minimize its harmful effects rather than simply ignore or condemn them." I've heard this in harm reduction circles expressed as, "We accept people as they are, but we don't leave them there." Expanding this into an emotional/spiritual place leaves me with a feeling of accepting myself and the world as they are, but not leaving us there. That means accepting my brain and body—its abilities or limitations—and working to give it nourishment in order to maintain what it has come to be or to encourage further healing. That is what I would give to others, so why shouldn't I have access to the same compassion?

- Harm reduction also understands drug use "as a complex, multi-faceted phenomenon that encompasses a continuum of behaviors from severe use to total abstinence, and acknowledges that some ways of using drugs are clearly safer than others." Part of my trauma history taught that life is about black-and-white thinking. There is "good" and "bad" and the "best" way to live is to stay away from the dark side. This binary thinking locked me in a jail cell of internalized transphobia, ableism, late-stage capitalism, and white supremacy. These days, I understand life concepts to exist more on a spectrum, with harm reduction as a baseline.

If we can use harm-reduction principles for all kinds of things, like the Buddhist idea that "all life is suffering" or that our bodies start to decay once they are born, does this mean that everything is harm reduction? And if "everything is harm reduction," what then? It begs the question: is the goal of life to "reduce harm?" That very well could be, but I'm not completely connected to that concept, so a more applicable question might be: if one is pursuing pleasure, could one still reject a binary idea of "happy" or "sad" in that pursuit? Could our experiences be mixed? Complex? Binary one time, non-binary the next? Like every great idea, harm reduction only goes so far. When we divorce ourselves from the presence of pleasure in drugs and sex, we end up with simple medicalization policies. There is public discourse that supports harm reduction but edits out pleasure or, worse, stigmatizes it. The reality is that pleasure is connected to so many of our choices, and yet we pretend it is nonexistent. What's wrong with just liking something or wanting something because it feels good? These days, I am focused on the expansion of pleasure.

PLEASURE STIGMA

Let's look at the journey to reach the possibility of pleasure, because folks, she ain't easy to get to. We have a lot of strikes against us even accessing the desire for pleasure, let alone pleasure itself. This is largely due to pleasure stigma. Happiness, joy, sexual gratification, and physiological satisfaction are some of the ways my pleasure manifests, but pleasure stigmatization is all around us. Just try smiling for no reason at all in a heavily populated area. Shit-eating grins and carefree vibes can put a target on one's back; they have definitely gotten me targeted, mugged, and attacked multiple times. Questions like, "Why are you so happy?" have taught the lesson that some people don't like my joy, and I have come to suspect this means they probably have issues with theirs.

The reality is that stigma can even be amplified and compounded when it is externally displayed. For people whose race, class, and gender are marginalized (read "stigmatized"), their external displays of pleasure can hyper-marginalize them in their daily lives. If you are a Black, trans, and femme person who likes to wear clothes that show off your personal pleasure in your body or even wave with happiness to someone you know, that display of pleasure can get you arrested or profiled as a sex worker. This is known as "Walking While Trans,"[2] where just existing (forget the display of pleasure) can also get you arrested, ticketed, or attacked. Similarly, decades of nebulous wars on various drugs have left more stigma than is reasonable or necessary on most substance use. And this lack of nuanced thinking is no surprise. After working for years in policy advocacy, I have found that policies, in general, don't leave room for spectrums.

GUILT AS A BARRIER TO DEEP PLEASURE

There is also the perspective that, in the midst of such rampant world suffering, happiness is just frivolous. It's a valid sentiment, but I fought like hell for pleasure. I clawed my way out of death and destruction, deep sadness, violence, fear, and a forced life that was deeply unhappy. So if pleasure is frivolous, so is glitter . . . and I'm keeping my glitter.

Why do we have to justify joy? We treat pleasure as if it is a resource of scarcity, something to be backstocked like toilet paper. Many earth-based, one-god religions, or cultures heavily influenced by them, tell us that pleasure is indulgent and to indulge is bad. And then, of course we go and indulge anyway, but we mix it with guilt. Or worse, we indulge but conveniently leave the pleasure behind.

Guilt—let's talk about it. I have a hypothesis that guilt as an emotion can actually be connected to a person's limitations on experiencing deep pleasure. Anyone who has done cold-water therapy can probably relate to this idea. It's like wading only partially into cold water. If you keep coming in and out of it, or if you never submerge a majority of yourself into that temperature because you have aversions to it or illogical fear of it, you can never fully surrender to the experience of pleasure itself, or what I call "deep pleasure." Your body stays in a heightened state of anxiety and tension, one foot in, one foot out, making it easier to have regret and feelings of guilt when you are not consumed by the experience of deep pleasure.

SAFETY AND PLEASURE

There are many barriers to accessing pleasure, but I, myself, was the most stubborn concrete wall of them all. In fact, I wouldn't have seen myself as a likely candidate for writing this piece, if I'm being real.

I intentionally came to engage with sex work and drugs at a later age. Sure, I was around it for most of my life in some form or another. I had family and friends deeply entrenched in survival and addiction, so standing that close to the fire didn't seem very warm—it felt like watching people I love burn alive. For instance, I had a close family member overdose on heroin when we were preteens. She has been brought back more than once after flatlining from her imbalanced relationships to various substances. She overdosed multiple times throughout her 30 years of navigating mental illness, drug addiction, extreme violence, the criminal legal system, and life on the streets. Directly walking through those experiences with her made me feel like I was "warm enough" as the designated driver. I was afraid to experiment, because it seemed so volatile, so destructive. A constant need for control over my mind, body, and environment (which PTSD told me was unsafe) didn't allow for the deep liberation of my own self I later came to desire and need.

It wasn't until my late 20s, after days of being stuck in a horrendous film-editing experience, that I first tried cannabis to help with the creative process, at my editor's suggestion. I was already frustrated and he suggested I use cannabis to "help me focus on details." Let's just say it ended up in (surprise!) a panicked feeling of dying from eating too much of the edible and a very cruel joke played by my editor as the prince of darkness there to haul me off to the underworld.

That experience was just a dip into letting go of unhealthy control. I did walk into that cold water, but I, like many, was trying to unreasonably control my experience and "use" this substance to help me edit. Although substances can be used well and many people do a better job at using them, part of my journey has been to understand that I prefer to be with substances, rather than to use them. Your journey is your own.

Being conscious of your "set, setting, and drug"[3] is one way to access that deep pleasure of drugs and sex with more safety support. These definitions focus on substances, but I think they also apply to sex.

- SET: this refers to all factors related to the individual consuming the drug. Such factors may include an individual's mental and physical state, genetic predispositions, gender, sleep, physique, nutrition, and any medications the individual is currently taking.

- SETTING: this refers to all factors related to the environment a drug is consumed in. Such factors may include the people or friends around you, the weather, presence of law enforcement, and dangerous environmental hazards.

- DRUG: this refers to all factors related to the drug consumed. Such factors may include the quantity consumed, the potency, the purity, the way the drug is taken, and whether other drugs are consumed at the same time.

After my cannabis experience, I slowly and intentionally sifted through a maze of disinformation,[4] anti-queer/Indigenous sentiment, religious abstinence-only education, and 1990s fear-mongering DARE campaigns warning American youth that our brains would be fried like an egg from cannabis and we would get HIV from toilet seats. With a young adult body but an elderly mind and a lifetime of negative memories from family who had less than pleasure-laden experiences in these collective "underground" worlds, I found my way to sex work and substance use. More importantly, I began to understand one very important adult concept: protection and liberation can coexist.

MULTIPLE STATES OF BEING: A LOVE STORY OF COEXISTENCE

The idea of "underground economies" brings up associations of the underworld. For so many, the idea of dark transgression is the enticement—enticing to the point of rejecting complexity that lightness or healing could even be present right there with the darkness. I think about Eastern Indigenous principles like yin and yang that resonate deeply within my ancestral spirit, reminders from my grandmother Sumiko: that light doesn't even exist without the juxtaposition of dark. She was an example of a poor Okinawan woman who navigated the waters of being a teenage mother and doing what she had to do to make a life for her and her family, then becoming an isolated immigrant after marrying into the very military who killed her family members. Sumiko had many barriers to accessing pleasure, and I feel the impact of those barriers constantly as I work to decolonize my mixed body, a body that is here because of sex work.

The irony is that I became an access point of pleasure for others—responsible for leading them into deep pleasure and freedom, time and time again, like so many of my sex-working peers—but still had so much to explore and understand about my own pleasure. We have done this as hookers, cammers, fetish workers, artists, spiritual guides, erotic massage and street-based workers, substance deliverers, bartenders, researchers, and advocates, just to name a few ways. Sex can be pleasurable, transactional, boring, violent, anticipated, non-volitional, hot, not hot, just for maintenance, gassy, underwhelming, overwhelming, passionate, short, long, catastrophic, otherworldly, and so much more. It's like marinated tofu in that it soaks up the flavors of those having it. I may have been that access point of pleasure for my clients and partners, but my own access points needed further expansion.

I lost a lot these past few years, perhaps like many of you reading this. We collectively lost a lot. And nobody ever told us that we were done losing. There was no international announcement that the global pandemic was actually over. So the finality of our suffering has not yet been given an ending. And we humans love endings. Some of us even need them in order to make sense of all the loss we suffered, to process the trauma and pain. We have funerals and wakes and second-line parades to ritualize death. But when we have no rituals for our loss, how then do we reconcile the experience?

The short answer is I really don't know. I have only that big question and an even bigger curiosity: how am I experiencing my own pleasure? Make no mistake, I care deeply for my sex-working communities, for decriminalizing our bodies, destigmatizing our collective lives, for my survivor siblings and all the creative ways in which we found to fucking survive. I don't really know the timing of it all—if the liberation of our lives, all the stigma, guilt, and oppression relief can be possible without governments first recognizing our humanity and rights, without their mea culpa and reparations, without generations of practiced transformative justice. But I do know this . . . if we don't free ourselves, it may not matter if the oppression stops, because we, in our brokenness, will probably just replicate it in some way. So lately, I am most interested in my own liberation.

POSSIBILITIES OF FREEDOM: SEX AND SUBSTANCES AS ACCESS POINTS TO PLEASURE

Maslow and his silly little hierarchy of needs[5] was at least mostly right in my case. Somewhere along the way of fumbling and stumbling through the midst of codependency and savior complexes, I had finally prioritized myself enough to break through the basic physiological level in those hierarchy of needs—the ones focused on securing food, water, shelter, a job, health, and sleep. I looked around and realized that there was finally some consistent, nutritious food, housing stability, and Medicaid. Finally having health insurance allowed treatment for a previously undiagnosed sleep disorder, autism, and a whole host of physical illnesses that I just thought were "normal," conditions that poverty didn't allow me to consider.

Sex work gave me much more stability and safety compared to my life before, because it was an access point to pleasure, money, partners, community, mission, liberation, self-actualization, and joy. Sex work came at a high cost of stigma, reinvention, and criminalization, but it gave me space, support, inner healing, and resources for a medical gender transition and more stable housing and food.

After leaving those first two levels of need (physiological and safety), I was able to re-engage with substances. Substances allowed further access points for pleasure and for me to let go of the control that had definitely kept me alive at one point, but which was keeping me cut off from pleasure. It was no longer serving me. Love/belonging, esteem, and self-actualization were the next three levels on the hierarchy of needs that began to open up through the integration of substances and sexuality. These are the playgrounds I am playing on today—knowing from experience that those first two levels of safety and physiological need can be right around the corner at any moment. Yes indeed, I am trying to dream differently.

The integration of drugs and intimacy has been a winding journey through uppers, downers, and psychedelics. Here are some highlights:

- Mushrooms had me propose to someone I secretly wanted to propose to but couldn't find the access point beyond my fear and ego. I also tried to mind-move a watermelon (still trying). So. Much. Laughter.

- Microdosing THC edibles at an amusement park gave access to childlike play and whimsy that the world says I'm too old for.

- When I had acid sex with several lovers for over 12 hours, I stopped counting the orgasms after 200.

- I worshiped at the church of music with fellow acolytes as we danced into body liberation with our friend Molly.

- Delta 8 took me and a fellow kinkster into the alien realms of intergalactic sex magic.

SEX WORK, SUBSTANCES, AND (DIS)ABILITY

(Dis)ability is my sex-work throughline, as the primary way I have connected to myself and to others as an adult. This has been true in both my personal and professional life. Like many other folks with disabilities, I did not actually understand that I was experiencing life through the lens of ableism (and participating in it myself) until I started to understand and question how I was being disabled by the world around me and admit that I was not OK all the time. It was specifically through sex work and substances that I finally understood my body was not typical. How I had sex, wanted sex, and offered sex was wildly expansive, and how my body responded to certain substances allowed me to actually be in my body and notice how it behaved. Like a curtain opening to a play, sex and drugs were beautifully revealing. I also realized that I had a superpower in connecting with other people with disabilities.

As a person who navigates the complexities around abilities and disabilities of this body and mind, it is my life's honor to journey with others in their pursuit of their pleasure, as we explore and share beautiful private moments of seeing and being seen. We meet (usually undefended and emotionally open) with room to let pleasure be a possibility. Sometimes we imbibe, we breathe in, we ingest, we secrete. Sometimes, we make the drugs within our bodies and sometimes we receive those made for us. We do either or both with an intention of gratitude, stewardship, and yes, deep pleasure.

Sometimes, we enter into an experience with a specific intention and get surprised by the doors which open from the simple act of walking that path. "Hedonism is one part of the bell curve, but it's not the whole thing," said a client. This client was initially there for their pleasure, not to heal, but they reflected that the session short circuited some of their baggage, and that having an access point of pleasure allowed them to do the work that no other part of the world would allow for. "It could have only happened in sex work," they said. Sex work got them past their touch aversion, their rigid gender identity, and the isolation, expectations, and invisibility that were probably killing them—which I know all too well, as those things were definitely killing me. I have said it before and I will say it again. Sex work saved my life.

So, what is an "access point?" Let's explore the definitions of "access" and "point" through some exercises below. If you are more visually inclined, here are some images that might resonate with how you have experienced sex and/or substances.

VISUAL PROMPT

How do you see these pictures as an access point for pleasure?[6,7]

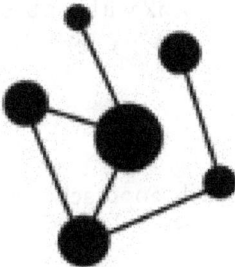

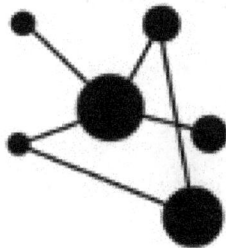

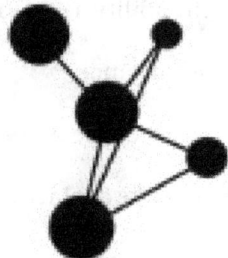

SOMATIC PROMPT

Where do you feel pleasure in your body? Can you move it? Does it have a shape, color, or form? If you are using a substance, how does this inform or give insight or new experiences to what you feel or sense?

PLEASURE AS WORD PLAY

If you're keen, let's play a game to help explore how we experience pleasure. Here are some of my favorite possibilities for us. I will choose my own adventure, if you choose yours. Pick any definition of "access" and combine it with any definition of "point." Perhaps think about how sex, drugs, or some combination of the two could connect with those mixed definitions.

Definitions of "Access"

- permission, liberty, or ability to enter, approach, or pass to and from a place, or to approach or communicate with a person or thing

- freedom or ability to obtain or make use of something

- a way or means of entering or approaching

- a fit of intense feeling

- an increase by addition

- to get at

    - to gain access to: such as

    - to be able to use, enter, or get near (something)

- to open or load (a computer file, an Internet site, etc.)

- the ability, right, or permission to approach, enter, speak with, or use

- admittance

- a way or means of approach

- to make contact with or gain access to; be able to reach, approach, enter, etc.

- computers: (of a program or system component) to retrieve (data) for use by another program or application or for transfer from one part of the system to another

- television: (of programming, time, etc.) available to the public

Definitions of "Point"

- an individual detail

- a distinguishing detail

- the most important essential in a discussion or matter

- cogency

- an end or object to be achieved

- purpose

- a geometric element that has zero dimensions and a location determinable by an ordered set of coordinates

- a narrowly localized place having a precisely indicated position

- a particular place

- locality

- an exact moment

- a time interval immediately before something indicated

- verge

- a particular step, stage, or degree in development

- a definite position in a scale

- the terminal usually sharp or narrowly rounded part of something

- a weapon or tool having such a part and used for stabbing or piercing

  - arrowhead

  - spearhead

- the contact or discharge extremity of an electric device (such as a spark plug or distributor)

- an electric outlet

- a projecting, usually tapering piece of land or a sharp prominence

- the tip of a projecting body part

- a railroad switch

- the head of the bow of a stringed instrument

- a short musical phrase

- a very small mark

- a direction indicated by a compass point

- a small detachment ahead of an advance guard or behind a rear guard

- a unit of measurement

- a unit of counting in the scoring of a game or contest

- the action in dancing of extending one leg and arching the foot so that only the tips of the toes touch the floor

- a position of a player in various games

- credit accruing from creating a good impression

- to give added force, emphasis, or piquancy to

- to scratch out the old mortar from the joints of (something, such as a brick wall) and fill in with new material

- to indicate the position or direction of especially by extending a finger

- to direct someone's attention to

- to cause to be turned in a particular direction

- to indicate the fact or probability of something specified

- to lie extended, aimed, or turned in a particular direction

- to sail close to the wind

- to indicate the presence or position of

- to direct the mind or thought in some direction

- call attention to

I was delighted to learn about the definitions of these words. Here are some of my favorite combinations:

- a fit of intense feeling to lie extended, aimed, or turned in a particular direction

- a way or means of entering or approaching an exact moment

- permission, liberty, or ability to enter, approach, or pass to and from a place or to approach or communicate with a geometric element that has zero dimensions and a location determinable by an ordered set of coordinates

- admittance to sail close to the wind

Thank you for diving in with me. May your access points be of your own making. I tend to like endings with possibilities. What are yours?

Fuck Myself into Heaven

MELODIE GARCIA

THERE IS SOMETHING INCREDIBLE THAT HAPPENS WHEN WE FUCK. MANY incredible things, actually. The big one for me is that feeling of absolute surety in the universe—that this act, this exquisite moment that takes place between bodies, is the only thing that can live and breathe outside of time, and yet forever. Sex is how I relate to other people, to the world.

I am a sex worker: a camgirl turned porn performer turned escort—a choice predicated on its ability to help me explore my complex sexuality, set my own hours, and make a shitload of cash very quickly. It's also necessary for survival, for healing, and the ease of libido.

The exploration of sex work, kink, and other deviant practices (see below) has, for me, led to some incredible healing of my own, from abuse, assault, mental illness, and ennui ... At one point in my early life, I believed heavily in the Christian God, or at least thought I did, and I sought healing in church only to realize my sense of self never felt clearer than when I was having non-marital sex! Sex made me feel like me. It was brilliant.

Kink has also offered me a platform for psychological and physical healing. In my baby hooker days, I tried all sorts of roles and activities, many of which took place at the Center for Sex Positive Culture in Seattle (formerly The Wet Spot), a members-only center for the kinky-curious.[1] Kink taught me how to set boundaries and pursue my own pleasure in the bedroom but also in my everyday life. I have learned so much about myself in these spaces. Others deserve the same.

Integrating components of kink into my practice is vital. I lean into power dynamics that challenge the assumptions of the client, thereby giving them an outlet to explore their sexuality and make mistakes—without fucking up a relationship. Being an escort is an emotionally and sexually liberating orientation and practice, but it takes a lot of work, requires a lot of (sometimes painful) honesty, and yet allows me personally

to move,

and breathe,

and thrive,

in a way that is hard to describe.

I chose my first adult industry name, Simone Débudoir (Simone Debu for short), as an homage to the feminist existentialist French philosopher Simone de Beauvoir, the lesser-known polyamorous partner of the famous philosopher Jean-Paul Sartre. De Beauvoir's writings gained popularity just before women's suffrage in the United States, and her work was seen as highly contentious at the time with its focus on the existential nature of Woman as the "other" in a male-dominated society.

The name Simone reflected my approach to sex work, centering around philosophical disassembling of societal norms and teasing out the meaning of each of our existences. Asking questions such as, "Why can't my friendship with this person move beyond the platonic?" and "What's the point of relationships if the people in them aren't sexually satisfied—and why isn't it socially acceptable to provide harm reduction (i.e., sexual services) to sexually unsatisfied people in those relationships?" If someone is unsatisfied but dedicated to a marriage, etc., it is my belief that my services as a sex worker can help mitigate the harm caused by a frustrated libido. But I digress.

I too had become frustrated with the structure forced on me by society. We all have so many walls to break, habits to learn and unlearn, and truths to dig up deep within ourselves and in the universe. As a sex worker and frequenter of the realm of psychedelics, I have been able to break down some incredible walls.

The use of psychedelics for sacred cultural practices is well documented; their use can be traced back to Olmec, Mayan, Aztec, and other North and South American Indigenous populations—so we know it's legit.[2] We also know we have built walls around these truths: laws, governments, social sanctions, etc. that keep distance between each of us as humans. So, what if we could bridge that distance? How do we even start?

Our search for the Divine (or God, the Self, Enlightenment) in churches, in deities, in societal walls, and in vices might stem from modern man's biggest obstacle: the burden of consciousness. There is a theory among evolutionary psychologists that posits what led to the development of sentience: that consciousness in humans is traceable to *Homo erectus'* consumption of psilocybin, the psychedelic compound found in magic mushrooms.[3] If you've ever taken a leap into a shroom-induced trip, you may understand the exact experience wherein your own consciousness is elevated, ripped open, and dismantled. Most people who use psychedelics report an altered perception of time and reality, insights gained about oneself, and they come out of the trip with a renewed sense of clarity.

What a drug.

As it turns out, these themes—breaking down walls, elevating Consciousness, bridging gaps between souls—are all present in both the pleasure industries and in nontraditional relationship structures such as polyamory, which was my own personal gateway into being sexually and emotionally liberated at the nexus of sex work. I tried polyamory as a way to Fuck Myself into Heaven. Being polyamorous and learning the adult industry simultaneously was a symbiotic learning experience—concepts I learned in one field easily translated to the other, from unlearning jealousy to communication and boundaries and falling in love in unexpected places. Like falling in love with a client.

Having multiple loves at once
makes you realize
That your heart can be ripped open,
Shredded to a thousand demoralized pieces
That each then multiply, and pool,
And create art inside of you.

When my friends ask about my work, "Do you really have sex with people who are ugly/you don't want to have sex with?" it's hard to tell them what I think they want to hear. I have seen through the veneers we put up and boxes we hide inside; we are one. We are a shared consciousness with a shared body, shared joys, shared tears, and shared orgasms. Pursuing polyamory and sex work has allowed me to see and celebrate the Divine in each and every living being, and as such has allowed me to find my own divinity.

Let's zoom out: if everyone on earth felt fulfilled, healed, whole . . . or at least knew how to access a platform for healing . . . the world would be a different place. It is absolutely true that people can find this through sex, kink, art, and drugs.

We can all make each other happy. I love each and every one of us. Through this love, may we all find healing.

At the center of the universe is a singularity—
One shared vision, prayer, art piece,

Our collective life force.

It shows up inside the small cracks in our facades,

In beads of sweat upon our writhing skin,

Underneath coffin-scraped fingernails,

And at the nexus of letting go.

I want to show you what I see in you and help you break down your own walls, to find the divine within yourself, and to let the rest of humanity hear of their own divinity.

I promise it's there.

Sacred Stripper: Intersections of Religion, Sex Work, Culture, and Consent

AMIRA BARAKAT AL-BALADI

GREETINGS WHORES, HEATHENS, AND VOYEURS ALIKE. I AM A DYNAMIC holistic healer here to give you an experience that you will never forget. Your worries melt away as you enter my aura and become soothed by the delicious vibes I emit. Your tension and stress ease in the comfort and softness of my presence. I ignite fires inside of you that have been dormant for far too long. Guaranteed—every experience you have with me is a healing of the highest vibration. You deserve the best in therapeutic sensual care, and I can give that to you. I'd love to.

Staying in a state of ecstasy is my religion. My spiritual practices are forbidden explorations into the lush, languid, lustful feminine divine. I love to create an environment of fun, ease, relaxation, and exploration where we can go beyond our normal human defenses and let ourselves truly love and be loved with no strings attached, just growing affection. No expectations, just gratitude for each other's presence. We all have wounds from life and walls up from previous relationships; let's heal them together in a nonjudgmental space of freedom.

Let me be your concierge of luxury and sensual healing. I will take the lead and set everything up perfectly for us, just follow me into our private den of passion and fantasy. Do as I say, and nobody gets hurt. I know what I'm doing; I do this every day. You must listen to me.

Consent, trust, openness, and willingness to connect make our interactions more sacred. The more sacred our interactions are, the more healing, high vibrational, and fun they are for us both.

That's why I ask for you to fully screen before seeing me privately, so that we can both feel comfortable and safe together with no need to fear, because we have been open with one another from the start. I need to know your name and where you work so that I can ensure that you won't try to hurt me, trick me, rob me, or fool me like so many others have tried before.

The space we create is intimate, just between us. You might speak of me to your loved ones, colleagues, and friends. You might recommend them to me; just keep the most private details between us. Treat our interactions like a secret worship of a forbidden deity. Don't tell it all if you tell it at all. That protects me and makes our experiences together more sacred and illuminating.

There is a myth that people who do the work that I do are damaged. Why else would we do this? In reality, everyone is a little bit damaged. Some of us make it look beautiful.

We find love within ourselves and others in such an unforgiving world.

Softness and beauty are not crimes. I enjoy living in an alternate reality where a little bit of wildness and toxicity is to be expected and embraced.

The healing that sex workers do takes place in murky, dreamy, liminal spaces. We orchestrate healings through our dance, our image, our touch. We receive healings from our worshippers in the form of love and money. We commune with our colleagues to influence the vibe. There is something timeless, primal, and holy about these interactions, at their best. At their worst they are deeply traumatic, confusing, raw, painful, alienating, and destabilizing. The worst part about those worst experiences is that so many people will say we deserved it.

We only see ourselves represented in the media by outsiders who seem to quite literally hate us. Where are the voices of hoes who are healers and who find divinity in stripping off our clothes and stripping the erotic energy from others in order to be cleansed? In amplifying desire in order to heal and protect entire families and communities who we don't even know? Where is the safe place for me to say, *I'm a succubus demon and I do this very well?* Only in the whispers in locker rooms and late-night meet-ups for drinks or secret smoke sessions in private spaces or Tumblr blogs in the remote reaches of the internet have I ever heard my perspective validated.

GODDESS WITHIN

Goddess worship came naturally to me because I am a Goddess. There's the knowledge I was born with and then there's the knowledge I was given. Or rather, I paid for it. It isn't just one experience but so many violations and miracles along the way to becoming a real, live prophetess. I lead others into the promised land of total mind-body-soul, emotional-sexual-spiritual freedom, through the portal of my womb and the divine healing energy I emit.

I didn't have to read about the Goddesses or study them because they showed themselves to me and they showed me where to go. They told me, "I am you. I am in you." They called upon me to make myself in their image and embody them so they may appear in the world more frequently. They told me to dance and to tell my stories. They even called me to become a teacher and empower others like me (sex workers, spiritually gifted survivors from sacred bloodlines) to become spiritual warriors and fight for our personal and collective sovereignty.

Even when so many would label me as worthless, un-rapeable, non-human, a problem—I survive and thrive.

Survival is coded in my DNA. The Goddesses my ancestors worshiped are the same ones that support me being able to thrive as a non-binary lady of luxury. Even though women in Islam were given unequal rights to men, it was still supposed to be better than before when pagan Arab tribes would commit femicide regularly. I was shocked but not surprised when I read about the Goddess worship that was prevalent in pre-Islamic Arabia. It made so much sense.

The worship of the cult of Isis and syncretized deities like Ishtar, Inanna, Al-Lat, and Al-Uzza was widespread all over North Africa, Southern Europe, Southwest Asia, and South Asia. These deities have different names but similar core values. Al-Lat, Aphrodite, and Oshun all evoke beauty and are often expressed through worship in the form of sacred sex rites and rituals to bring fertility, growth, and abundance to an entire community. Al-Uzza was one of the three main Goddesses worshiped in the region and she can be syncretized with Oya in the Yoruba pantheon or Sekhmet in ancient Egyptian. Al-Uzza was the primary deity worshiped by the tribe that Prophet Muhammed came from and, along with Al-Lat and Manat, was known as a daughter of Allah.

In the famous "Satanic verses" of the Qu'ran, Prophet Muhammed spoke of these Goddesses highly as "exalted cranes." This was pleasing to his community, especially his uncle who worshiped Al-Uzza. Later, his uncle said Muhammed was possessed by Shaytan when he said that. He took it back with an admonishment to the ways of the pagan Arabs: "How dare you ascribe daughters to Allah when you yourself bury your daughters in the desert?"

The message that modern-day Arab Muslims take from that is clear given the cultlike preservation of misogyny in our community. The idea that women could be worshiped or valued for anything other than chastity is so taboo. We are made to feel wrong our whole lives, as not enough, as less than boys and men. If you do not ascribe to rigid gender roles and a certain way of life, in many families, you're simply not welcome. It is a rare experience to witness an Arab Muslim person speak openly about sex because it is so taboo in our culture, even if you live in the diaspora. Everything that I am and all the things I like to do deviate from those norms. My whole existence is in opposition to them. This becomes a power struggle beyond the fight for my family and my people's freedom in the wider global context; beyond my desire to be accepted within my family to be part of them. It extends to a personal power struggle within myself to simply be who I am without unconsciously trying to change myself to fit in, knowing that if I don't have self-acceptance, no other type of acceptance matters.

It's life or death, because if I can't be myself, there's no point in living. While there is so much sentiment within the sex worker–rights community that this is "just a job," a "normal" job, "just like your job," for me often my work is a place to not only survive but re-create myself into my own image independent of the cult of misogyny I was born into. Like the Goddesses I embody, I lost everything in my journey through the Underworld. I accompanied all the parts of me that weren't me to their final resting places, making sure they arrived safely and with love while I was torn apart. When I began my ascent to Heaven, I looked and felt vastly different than I had before.[1]

Life isn't a straight path; it's a spiral. As we spiral deeper in and closer to our source, the repetition speeds up, events get closer together, it takes less time to move through lessons. The journey becomes like an acid, mushroom, or ayahuasca trip in that you begin to see things in a new way and make previously unseen connections between different parts of your life.

HEALING BY ANY MEANS NECESSARY

I went from assuming I could never have anything I wanted to healing myself by any means necessary. Every step of my journey is a whole paradigm shift and curse reversal for my entire bloodline. I moved out of the cult of conformity the previous generations had adopted for survival. To do this I had to deeply investigate, deprogram, and then reprogram my subconscious mind repeatedly to allow for an entirely different worldview to take shape in my brain over time.

Traumatic events change the way we think and literally the way we see. Releasing stigma and deepening our self-acceptance completely rewires our brains, reversing brain damage.

When you open yourself up to a deep inner knowing, you become vulnerable to the truth about yourself and it's much greater than anything you've ever been led to imagine. With awareness of that truth comes responsibility to act. When we heal ourselves, we heal the world.

Mental programming and deprogramming are essential. We have been born into cults of conformity, misogyny, racial bias, and discrimination and soaked in those energies for a lifetime. One of the reasons that sex workers are so feared and so dangerous is that we mingle with all levels of society and have unpredictable social mobility. We have the ability to change minds—others and our own. Our energies and images alone are influential.

When who we are is very different from who we have to pretend to be to receive love, we develop split personalities to survive. Even though it's not politically expeditious for mainstream sex worker–rights activists to highlight to correlation between sex workers and adult survivors of childhood sexual abuse, many skills learned in abusive environments are useful in sex work. Dissociation is one of them. Jungian psychology defines the shadow as either an unconscious aspect of the personality that the conscious ego does not identify in itself, or the entirety of the unconscious, i.e., everything of which a person is not fully conscious.

One of the reasons I started this journey to heal was because I kept getting drugged at work. It was one of those things that happened and I would be like, "again???" It was different than just getting really drunk or fucked up on drugs. I was completely unconscious and had no memory.

Sex workers and the work we do is glamorized as much as we are vilified and victimized. Some people look at us as sexually powerful beings who've truly cracked the code of capitalism. Within our own communities we're not encouraged to talk about our experiences of sexual abuse because it's seen as evidence of victimhood for those who would criminalize us and deny us agency to use against us. Yet sexual violence and stigma are still issues for us in a society that perpetuates rape culture and the unrape-ability of people who sell sex.

The widespread perception that sex workers "deserve" and "should expect" sexual violence on the job is a human-rights crisis. Yet what do we expect in a culture that promotes marriage that precludes consent? We are shown time and again that our bodies do not outright belong to us but that we must fight some unknown entity for ownership of them. That entity wears the face of the religious right, the status quo, old white men in government who make decisions for us, our parents, partners, religious or cultural communities, places of work, management, pimps, or simply anyone who has more power or resources than we do. We play a game in which we know the rules of every different interaction and we finesse them to our benefit for survival.

There was something so comfortable and familiar about me starting sex work. In my first year of working, I tried everything from webcam to fetish arts, non-pro to agency escorting, sensual massage, and femme domme BDSM. I even organized a lunch for radical sex workers of color at a conference for activists. It all came very naturally to me and seemed right—like it just fit. If I'm being honest, when these things were happening it felt like they were predestined to happen, and then when I learned more about the stories of the Goddesses, it all made sense. My life's mysteries began to unravel, and I could place myself and my experiences in context.

For some of us, our activism is personal, financial, spiritual, and sexual. In ancient times we were temple dancers, priestesses, and oracles. The exchange of money and goods for our services is what made it holy. Now we are strippers, porn stars, escorts, and whores. Street prostitutes and vilified angels, not fallen but forgotten from our glory of old.

I used to say I was being possessed when I was at work, dancing on stage, writhing like a snake and having no memory of it later. I was high and drunk, intoxicated, smiling, laughing, of my body but not in my body. Dancing in Atlanta was so fun until it wasn't. I was always high and drunk as a baseline. Xanax bars were my drug of choice and it felt like I could just go somewhere else, completely release my inhibitions, and go with the flow. I felt pulled along by a strange energy stronger than me, yet one that kept me paid for some reason. But it was only just enough to barely survive. My mental health was a constant struggle. I had traumatic experiences at the club, but I kept going back and didn't see better options.

Everything changed when I turned to Islam. I began fasting and reading the Qu'ran every day. I meditated, communed with nature, and ate a detox diet that included traditional Mediterranean staple foods. After 22 days I went right back to my toxic lifestyle and all hell broke loose. But I took the chaos I was experiencing and alchemized it into a beautiful life transition. I began working as a sensual masseuse, makeup artist, and spa therapist. I only went to the club when I wanted to, and I had all the money I needed for whatever I wanted. That was when I began to harness my sexual energy, and my manifestations sped up and became more consistent.[2]

Making more money meant more time to heal and more resources to spend on my healing. Deep time in meditation, communing with crystals, and doing yoga led me to uncover the "why?" behind my biggest traumas. What shocked me the most was digging deep underneath the layers of trauma from club owners, management, customers, clients, internet stalkers, and even some lurkers who I never met but whose energy I felt and finding all the trauma underneath from past relationships, early childhood, and even past lives and ancestral memory. I started to realize there was more to these seemingly random life experiences of mine than I had initially realized. I started to realize I had been taking on a lot of other people's shame and when I decided to consciously release that burden back to them, I became free. I wasn't just a bad bitch getting money—I was holy divinity, I was a portal to self-actualization. So many people had already been healed and activated in my presence. This inner knowledge flew in stark contrast to the inner shadows of shame and guilt I felt for doing and being something that my cultural conditioning told me was wrong. From the inside out I started to relax.

Before I ever consciously heeded to calling on the Goddess and allowing myself to follow the healing path, I had to make myself and my mental health a priority. I began to take time to worship me and listen to my needs, which I had never really had the space or ability to do before. I started to realize I wasn't happy. This led to me deciding to stop working in the adult industry so that I could heal both from what happened to me on the job and the stigma I experienced outside of work from family, friends, partners, and associates.

WE'VE ALWAYS BEEN SACRED

I was not out as a sex worker, and many used my shame and my secret against me in my weakest moments. I felt very split between my sex work persona and the vanilla persona I showed. I didn't feel whole. I needed a format to express all these aspects of myself personally and professionally, to integrate them and bring wholeness to myself. I came out to my friends and family as a sex worker and I started posting on Instagram as "Sacred Stripper," bringing spiritual healing and mental health advocacy to the sex workers in my audience.

That seems like another lifetime ago. The changes that have occurred in the wider consciousness since 2017 have reduced the stigma around being a sex worker. It was secret and shameful before so many of us did the advocacy work to shift this paradigm. Many are choosing an online sex work career as a response to pandemic instability and poverty, illustrating what we've known all along: that this work gives us autonomy. For very few of us this is just about having fun. For most of us it's about getting funds, but why shouldn't that be fun?

Why should sexual violence be an expectation in our work? From violent language to physical violence, our needs are the central needs of the antiviolence movement and we are so often left out of the conversation. There is so much messaging that tells us we are not important, and yet look at what we have done for ourselves just by being open and vocal. We have transformed the stigma against us to the point that everyone wants to be one of us now.

We are a reminder to so many that they aren't as accepting or understanding as they tell themselves they are. Because so many people can "tolerate" only so much. When it comes to us, we are way too free, and that scares people who still live within the constraints of so-called normal society. So we must put extra effort into looking normal in order to fight for our rights, loudly stating that this is just a job and we deserve the same rights as other workers.

But some of us . . . aren't workers. We're Goddesses, and everywhere we go we're Goddesses, and we don't necessarily belong in offices or in the fight for workers' rights. Sex work is just as valid as any other lifestyle or employment path, and it can be spiritual and a form of activism.

Respectability politics in the fight for sex worker rights leaves a lot of people out and it diminishes the very real, world-changing impact of the ways we live our everyday lives. Even just developing wealth for ourselves is a political act, granting us the space to rest and heal which we might not have if we lived according to others' standards. If we worked a more stressful job with a bigger time commitment or had a relationship in which we had to devote a lot of time to cooking and cleaning for someone else, we would have less time to devote to our own spiritual development and self-actualization. We get to make choices for the betterment of ourselves and our future through the enhanced resources sex work provides us.

That is why we are considered so dangerous. It's fine if we're feeding the machine of greed trapped in environments where we're stewed in abuse and our negative feelings about ourselves, our guilt, our rage, our shame, our denial of our own lovability, but when we embrace and accept all parts of ourselves and use our energy to purely channel our vibrational frequency of love into the things we wish to create, now we are truly dangerous.

Me being me and being happy being me is considered a problem—can you imagine?

Sex work isn't the problem; stigma is. Each person's experience of stigma and the internalized whorephobia it brings is reflective of the social, cultural, and religious background they come from. Yet religion and spirituality are places where we can find immense healing. We don't leave these parts of ourselves out when we're doing sex work, or when we're simply existing as Goddesses embodying Heaven on Earth and being spoiled by the Universe. It's always a part of us.

We've always been sacred.

Drug Policy for Breaking Intergenerational Curses: An Eco-Futurist Prayer, Analysis, and Reflection on Psychoactive Substances and Their Intentional Use

ISMAIL LOURIDO ALI AND PAULA GRACIELA AVILA KAHN

I. PRAYER IN PREPARATION: BEFORE DOSING, CONSUMING, OR SHARING SUBSTANCES

Dear ancestors of the multiverse,
from void to stardust and everything in between,

We who have explored consciousness for time immemorial,
through evolutions of organic and crystalline molecular metastructures,
generations of experimental play, intentional ceremony and remedies of relief,
pray for healing of the past, present, and future.

We pray for the youth drawn to states of altered consciousness
Seeking pleasure and escape,
Creating rites of passage,
We pray for the children within us seeking emancipation, witnessing, love, and belonging.
We pray for a revolution of love,
 real-izations of collective awakening,
a radical honesty and repaired collective memory,
holistic and wholly-embodied, in all our senses.

We pray for grounded and guided initiations
and interspecies awakenings
that recondition fixations on domination, punishment, and profit,
A mass transition where rituals of reckoning and ceremonies for repair
halt cycles of harm and spark cycles of healing.

We prepare our bodies, hearts, minds, and souls
to humbly request a smooth entrance to the portal of eternal creation
We embrace the inner wisdoms you ignite within us
to build orbs of eco-systemic safety and care for each other.

We sense & embrace the company of our shadow,
and the guidance of light on our sacred journeys home.

We gratefully delight in your everlasting truths of love and freedom,
delivered through doses of terrestrial medicines,
measured with care and precision,
in the mystical name of awe.

We respect the messages you deliver, ecstatic abundance and climactic warnings included.

May your magic open portals of love, truth, and creation . . .
For maximum favorable phenomena <3

May we weave the learnings from this experience
Into reverence for the essential elements that sustain life.

II. ACKNOWLEDGMENT AND INTERVENTION

Interrupt Collective Historical Amnesia by Bearing Witness

The global drug control scheme we have been born into has exhaustively criminalized ways people seek and experience community, culture, mysticism, pleasure, and healing. Learning and understanding the historical relationship between empire building and behaviors historically characterized as "addictive" is a promising public health strategy to facilitate awareness, empowerment, self-determination, and healing for people who use drugs and those affected by the global War on Drugs. While historic memory has not been valued as an essential public health practice, cultivating and maintaining collective memory is one of the tactics through which we can disarm and dismantle the War on Drugs while addressing the opioid overdose epidemic. The terminology in the *Diagnostic and Statistical*

Manual of Mental Disorders (DSM) used to describe individuals' complex relationships with psychoactive substances has evolved with each edition. The third edition, which was published in 1980, introduced the term *substance use disorder* (SUD), which prevailed as a humanizing and dynamic alternative for "addiction." SUD offers a "unified category" for classifying negative consequences of use, where severity is measured through a continuous scale from mild (2–3 symptoms), moderate (4–5 symptoms), to severe (6+ symptoms), out of a total of 11 symptoms. It is crucial to consider the limitations of a DSM framework and to explore culturally relevant research on the causal pathways into SUDs. Situating evolving discourse on SUDs within a nexus of historic mass atrocities, racialized stereotypes, observations of gene-environment interactions, and community-based harm reduction initiatives is necessary. Discourses on genetic predisposition to SUD and racialized stereotypes around substance use should be studied dynamically, within a historical context, to uncover how the forces of genocide have shaped oppressed populations' relationships to psychoactive substances at the individual, community, and population levels. Epigenetics is the study of heritable (transmissible to offspring) changes in gene expression based on environmental conditions. We can build our understanding of "genetic predisposition" by taking into account the epigenetic landscape of colonialism and industrialization in the modern era. Through witch hunts, the colonization and settlement of Indigenous territories, and the Transatlantic trade of enslaved African people, patriarchal European empires re-contextualized land stewardship, labor, food systems, communal relationships, and spiritual and health practices, including the use of psychoactive substances.

Enhancing collective memory and promoting cultural resilience can equip people who use drugs (PWUD) to become historically conscious agents and would strengthen public health responses to the increase of problematic drug use and overdose deaths. There is a gap in public health that needs to be filled. We need educational interventions that disrupt the normalization of colonial, imperialist moralities that have weaponized sacred plants, altered states, and psychoactive substances to justify and perpetuate territorial dispossession, state violence, mass incarceration, deportation, and disposability of poor, Indigenous, Black, Brown, and immigrant peoples.

Historic processes of European colonization around the planet sought to exterminate or manipulate psychoactive practices reserved for ceremony, worship, communing, and pleasure. Medicine was appropriated to serve the whims of empire. This transformation of paradigms was accomplished through repeated violent acts of extermination: genocide (race/tribe), ethnocide (culture), feminicide (women), infanticide (infants), ecocide (environment), and epistemicide (knowledge). The world we've inherited was created through this systematization of totalitarian violence and calculated destruction of knowledge and culture. Despite attempts to colonize memory through acts of extermination, to maintain the status quo created by this violence, researchers, somatic practitioners, healers, and artists continue to investigate how multigenerational memories live in our bodies and how our genetic code carries our ancestors' experiences.

This epigenetic inquiry resists normalization of the status quo of ongoing violence. Normalization can be defined as a process in which coercive and subliminal ideological, behavioral, and embodied conditioning transform a community or population's relationship with a previous deviation to a commonly accepted or unquestioned norm in a society. The normalization of ongoing violence has sustained the status quo through the weaponization of everyday social goods, such as health care, employment, public safety, education, food systems, and media communications, all to perpetuate a sinister narrative that poor, often racialized, "drug-using" people are undeserving of innate human rights. Breaking the curse of normalization is therefore inherently multisensory. Through oral storytelling, music, chant, dance, ritual, prayer, protest, community building, study, altered states of consciousness, and other multimodal strategies, we dispel the normalization of extermination and awaken our collective remembering, resensitization, and embodiment.

Remember: Sugar and Spice

The characterization of synthesized sugar as an essential food ingredient instead of a drug has normalized its covert infusion into nearly everything humans eat and drink. Sugar production is a defining and overlooked feature of our modern global economy, food, and health systems; sugar was actually one of the first colonial industries to develop in the Canary Islands, Brazil, and the West Indies during early European colonization. The sowing of sugar in Brazil was initially a military-agro-economic strategy by the Portuguese to carve out a stake in the "new world" in the early 16th century, and can be traced to the colonization of the Madeira and Canary Islands at the end of the 15th century, which the Portuguese used as a laboratory for 16th century sowing and labor exploitation in the colonization of present-day Brazil.[1] The products extracted from the sugar cane are molasses and cane juice, which can then be refined into sugar or fermented into rum. Both of these items became central commodities and currencies in the transatlantic slave trade.

The Portuguese, Dutch, French, and English pursued empire building through sugar production, expanding production into the West Indies. This led to the price of sugar dropping in the 17th and 18th centuries, gradually replacing locally sourced honey in European recipes and consumption, increasing demand and calling for mass production. The sugar trade further unleashed economic competition between colonial powers to establish dominance in the so-called new world. In short, large scale sugar production was driven by addiction to economic domination since its inception, at the expense of peoples' lives.

The colonial production of global addiction and disease by way of the sugar empire offers an analogy for patterns of human behaviors with other psychoactive substances—from their historical production, to their trade routes, to their consumption and physiological effects. Like sugar, caffeine, tobacco, alcohol, heroin, and cocaine are derived from plants that were converted to cash crops. Their consumption is associated with physiological responses and behaviors that when considered together may be interpreted as dysfunction: craving, binging, gratification, crash, withdrawal, sensitization, tolerance—all signals of a "drug addiction."

High rates of obesity, diabetes, lung cancer, and alcohol-related accidents indicate our society has been conditioned into dependencies. Compounded by the imperialism of Coca-Cola, water privatization, and food deserts, impoverished rural communities and communities of color have more direct access to refined sugar than to essential nutrition. Despite the annual $600 to $750 million spent on the ineffective Drug Abuse Resistance Education (D.A.R.E.) program in the 1980s and 1990s,[2] nobody told us that sugar has its own gateway effect,[3] or that the amount of people who develop addiction-like symptoms to sugar is the same as those who develop similar relationships to heroin or cocaine.[4] **The point here is not to stigmatize sugar or shame people for their consumption of it—rather, it is to draw attention to the inconsistencies of our present paradox, where one substance is subsidized and ubiquitous while the others are suppressed to the underground.** This history asks us to reckon with the reality that our relationship to everyday household items such as sugar, coffee, alcohol, tobacco, spices, and the economic infrastructure built with and around their consumption, were shaped by early market globalization activities.[5]

The colonial expansion of European empire produced a paradigm in the "West" that erased popular reverence for universal and ancient traditions rooted in earth-based spiritualities and value for the wisdom of children. Consequently, contemporary early childhood education occurs in ahistorical ways, preventing ancestral, embodied knowledge from being meaningfully transmitted across generations. Many of our elders were unable to transmit ancestral knowledge because they too were affected by cultural loss and disharmonious relationships to substances (like sugar and alcohol). Capitalism and colonization further exacerbate subconscious consumption patterns by divorcing modern use from knowledge of traditional use.

We can disarm the demonizing, punitive, and psychiatric rhetoric of addiction by learning the ethnobotanical, historical, and chemical genealogies of psychoactive substances. We can build (collective) consciousness around a substance and its contemporary uses by tracing its uses over time and space:

- What is the composition of the substance?

- Where does it grow and/or where is it produced?

- How has it historically been used?

- If it is consumed, how do you sense it and how do you relate to it, given its historically, geographically, and culturally contextualized uses?

- Does it serve sacred, social, pharmacological, or economic purposes?

Ritualizing our consumption of substances like sugar may seem unfamiliar and yet, it's a gentle exercise to reclaim reverence for the sacredness of a substance, transforming each use into a mindful and relational experience. Sugar cane is also a sacred plant that brings our lives energy, sweetness, silliness, and so much joy through the human senses of taste and feeling. Like molasses and sucrose, opium and heroin, coca and cocaine, substances derived from psychoactive plants are ends of spectra that can exist in one's life intentionally and consciously, marking new points on a web of experiences that are made up of sensation and memory.

Resensitize: Reframe Addiction and Prohibition

Researcher, author, and neuroscientist Dr. Carl Hart reminds us that we can and must look beyond the reductive example of addiction, or biochemical effects alone, to define dysfunction. Instead, we must analyze the larger societal context in which addiction is constructed and maintained.

In accordance with the Iron Law of Prohibition, new, more concentrated drugs continue to emerge, rekindling fears of an upended social order.[6] This is exacerbated by policy choices depriving communities of affordable housing, education, and access to comprehensive preventative health care. This social dis-investment, which Ruth Wilson Gilmore calls "organized abandonment," has cemented neglect and exposes new generations of youth to traumatizing harms and trauma-related substance use by way of systemic poverty, policing, mass criminalization, incarceration, and mass deportations. In turn, the production of poverty and criminality justifies policing, surveillance, and other militaristic industries that win lucrative contracts with cities, counties, and states to preserve social order. **The prohibition of drugs is rooted in profit over care, profit over genuine human security.**[7]

This trend can be explained in part by understanding the history of alcohol. Unlike other psychoactive substances that are scheduled by the Drug Enforcement Agency (DEA) into five categories along the parameters of medicinal, abuse, and dependency potentials, alcohol is not a scheduled substance. However, the 2019 National Survey on Drug Use and Health report revealed that 14.5 million people ages 12 and older had Alcohol Use Disorder, including 9.0 million "men" and 5.5 million "women,"[8] and about 414,000 youth between the ages of 12 and 17.[9]

Situating modern patterns of excessive alcohol use within a historical-economic analysis of the $1.47 trillion industry uncovers a legacy of colonial expansion during eras of mass harm and suffering.[10]

The production and consumption of fermented beverages has been a universal practice for millennia; the ancient production and consumption of beer, wine, and fermented beverage varieties across geographies were situated within local cosmogonies and sociocultural ecologies. For the pre-Hispanic, Yucatec Maya and the Lacandon, balché was an important ritual wine made from water, honey, and the bark of *Lonchocarpus violaceus*.[11] It was used in tandem with dance and song, associated with "the origin of the world," and recognized as a medicine but was banned under Spanish colonization. In pre-colonial Botswana, alcohol had a ceremonial value for ancestral veneration. The seasonal production and consumption of beer was tied to communing for a celebratory reward for cooperative agricultural labor, which in turn strengthened patrilineal bonds.[12] However, it was European landowners and traders that inscribed the psychoactive substance into colonization.[13] European traders weaponized alcohol by introducing distilled spirits to populations throughout Africa and Turtle Island,[14] warming them to friendly trading relations. This strategy catalyzed economic and psychoactive dependence on European traders importing distilled spirits within these communities. During the Transatlantic slave trade, alcohol was used as a currency on the ports of West Africa, at forts where Africans were trafficked. Alcohol was further appropriated to pacify enslaved African and Indigenous populations across territories in the so-called new world as an analgesic, to numb physical and psychic pain, and yield maximum raw materials and products for the emerging global economy.[15]

The cycle continued; liquor produced in the colonies of the so-called new world was utilized to pay for African people who were coerced to serve as an enslaved labor force. There, they produced alcohol itself and other cash crops, which sustained further colonial expansion.

The parallel story of cannabis is well known; as early as the 1600s, settlers began growing hemp[16] for use of its fibers. In the 1800s, the medical establishment promoted the medicinal properties of marijuana, and in the early 1900s, as alcohol prices steadily began to rise, marijuana was promoted as a recreational substance. However, after the Mexican-American War and in the wake of Mexicans dispersing north of the border during and after the Mexican Revolution, from the 1910 to the 1930s, the wave of new revolutionary immigrants sparked US state discourses and practices over citizenship, border control, state police power, and drug policy. The US government adopted anti-communist, anti-anarchist, anti–labor organizing, and anti-drug discourses in order to legitimize policing the border and prevent the revolution from spreading into the US.[17] Proponents of an increasingly militarized border found an ally in Harry Anslinger, former Commissioner of the Bureau of Narcotics (which later became the DEA), who used marijuana as a scapegoat for explicit anti-Mexican and anti-immigrant rhetoric. By the 1930s, in response to the Mexican Revolution and racist propaganda from Anslinger and others, both the United States and Mexico began to crack down on marijuana possession, use, and distribution. Nearly every state west of Mississippi passed marijuana regulation laws. In 1937, New Mexico took the lead in pressuring the federal government to initiate a national law, which was successfully achieved with the Marijuana Tax Act of 1937.

From alcohol to cannabis to heroin, the attempt to control the flow of substances, while pursuing a totalitarian prohibitionist policy that was so obviously contradictory to the actual behaviors of people, has led to a number of predictable consequences including state corruption and multinational organized crime. **Together, these conditions created the perfect public enemy for increasingly militarized state responses, conveniently sustaining two lucrative economies: the drug and global arms economies.**[18]

So although throughout the history of human civilization prohibition of drugs is the exception not the rule,[19] over the last 50 years the global drug control scheme has been characterized by a web of law enforcement offices in nation-states around the world that operate at varying levels of seriousness and sophistication, coordinated by international bodies like the United Nations Commission of Narcotic Drugs, alongside US-based entities like the Office of National Drug Control Policy and the Drug Enforcement Administration, and supported by other domestic and international institutions like the Department of Homeland Security, the FBI, and the CIA. This War on Drugs has joined forces with the War on Terror—conflict for profit, literally paving gardens and fumigating hillsides[20] into oblivion. The UN has previously stated its goal of creating a drug-free world—an impossible goal that offers exponential opportunities to the arms, private security, and surveillance industries.

Embody: The Emerging Aboveground

In 1995, Dr. Lester Grinspoon (RIP) and Rick Doblin (then a student at the

Kennedy School of Government at Harvard University) wrote to the *New England Journal of Medicine*, noting that "Evidence of the therapeutic value and limited toxicity of marijuana in the treatment of various symptoms and syndromes is rapidly accumulating" including for glaucoma, AIDS wasting syndrome, and nausea related to chemotherapy. After years of organizing and agitating by academics, activists, and advocates, including and especially HIV-positive gay men in San Francisco, California passed Proposition 215 in 1996 which permitted the use of medical marijuana in the state.

In 2016, California legalized the adult use of cannabis, following states like Colorado and Oregon, after dozens of states developed their own medical cannabis programs. Leading up to and over the course of those 20 years, patients, criminal legal reform advocates, and activists all over the world pushed the conversation about cannabis out of the morass of policy corruption and misapplication of criminal penalties. **Cannabis went from being perceived as a "gateway drug," leading to a life of crime and violence, to being recognized as an essential health product.**[21] As of January 2021, the cannabis industry in the United States—still not federally legal—had created over 320,000 new jobs, according to Leafly's annual Cannabis Jobs Report.[22]

Yet even as early as 2015, it quickly became clear that people who had been disproportionately targeted by law enforcement for drug crimes—especially Black and brown people, including many who had previously participated in the underground economy—were being left out of the "new" industry (and in some cases, weren't actually being arrested any less).[23] Many predicted an impending corporate takeover by white entrepreneurs and multinational companies, and knew that it would happen while leaving behind the millions of people whose lives had been destroyed by cannabis prohibition (many who are also patients simply seeking effective care for any number of ailments).

Thus, social equity was born—this idea that the economic and commercial benefits of the new marijuana industry could actually benefit people who were most directly impacted by the drug war.

"Social equity" quickly became a catchall for economic empowerment projects, including priority licensing for people who had been impacted by criminalization. Although utilizing social equity in this sense necessitates a level of "playing along" with the current economic paradigm, in which nonlicensed businesses still often risk criminal penalties for participating in the industry, it has emerged as a powerful force to bring access to a legal economic opportunity to some people. Many have critiqued social equity, arguing that, while welcome, it is insufficient—entire communities were decimated by the War on Drugs, and people who start cannabis businesses shouldn't be the only ones who benefit. The tension between the noble goal of economic empowerment and the continued funding for law enforcement, often also coming from cannabis tax dollars, prompted an evolution of the concepts that incorporated community reinvestment, meaning putting tax funds toward communities that had been impacted by the War on Drugs, regardless of whether they are involved in the emerging aboveground industry.

Although this is closer to what some might call tangible drug war reparations, it still dilutes the benefit of a multi-billion-dollar economy, while continuing to perpetuate zero-sum economic environments that completely prevent the legal industry from having the impact on the underground economy that purports to be part of its raison d'etre. This paradox offers an opportunity to look deeper at people just trying to make a living, or perhaps just a life, by expressing a devotion to the plant through the flawed framework of the current economy.

As we saw with many industries before it, we can anticipate the "tie dyeing" of corporate social responsibility in the psychedelic sector into "psychedelic equity and reciprocity programs" that end up being little more than corporate charity and philanthropy. It is important to acknowledge and appreciate that social equity efforts have been more resilient against co-optation, in part because the people who stand to benefit the most— including formerly incarcerated folks and their advocates—are actively part of the conversation, facilitated by dedicated advocates and the openness of the internet.

Today, psychedelic substances are poised to be a revolution in mental healthcare—and at the same time, just another product being brought to a market full of people desperately in need of mental health care. The pharmaceutical industry's revenues worldwide totaled 1.25 trillion US dollars in 2019.[24] The total estimated market size of the psychedelic industry could reach $100 billion.[25] **Naturally, entrepreneurs and venture capitalists are hungrily eyeing (and in some cases already attempting to claim** for themselves) **a rapidly emerging multi-billion dollar market, already full of the same intellectual-property monopoly moves and disputes that characterize the colonized worldview many are trying to heal from.** Companies are currently competing to develop intellectual property, unique sets of molecules that mimic the naturally occurring ones or those in popular synthesized psychedelics like ketamine (or those put into the public domain by people like Ann and Sasha Shulgin).[26]

Companies seek to patent these molecules as theirs, preventing others from lawfully replicating and distributing that same substance for profit. Some driving forces behind these patent applications may be traced to the competitive capitalist spirit within an emerging industry as well as desire for safeguards for financial security to venture capitalists funneling billions of dollars into psychedelic therapy research, who are hoping for a return.

The risk of privatization of psychedelic-assisted therapies has become the heart of dialogue and debate as a rising tide of Indigenous guardians of ancestral knowledge, policy advocates, researchers, harm reductionists, and others warn of entheogens and synthesized psychedelics becoming the next goldmine for empire maintenance.

In 2020, one of the authors of this chapter contributed to an article that was published in the *Journal of Pharmacology and Translational Science*, focusing on some of the ethical tensions that have emerged in the industry.[27] This article draws attention specifically to psilocybin and the Mazatec, one group of Indigenous people who are credited with educating the global North about the benefits of psychedelic substances through the story and exploitation of María Sabina, a 20th century Mazatec mushroom priestess, stating:

> Bioprospecting and biopiracy often cause conflicts, tensions, disconnection, poverty, and suffering in the communities from which the knowledge and tradition originate. This suffering tracks onto our understanding of how one's social and cultural environment can affect mental health. In other words, nonconsensual extractive for-profit ventures based on intellectual property regimes can cause intergenerational distress and suffering in impacted Indigenous communities in a way that could actively perpetuate mental illness, while cutting them off

from rightful benefits derived from their intangible cultural heritages. [28]

These are days for asking what kind of societal healing processes need to unfold in the sectors of psychedelic venture capital, entrepreneurship, and research, even (and especially) if the risk of reproducing global inequality is not factored into most investors' risk assessments.

The demographics of access to venture capital foreshadow the demographics' access to psychedelics themselves; even as psychedelic start-ups excitingly conduct research to identify effective treatments for a variety of mental health disorders, we wonder if these endeavors can reach their lofty objectives, even while the funding that underpins them sustains historic wealth gaps along the lines of race and gender.[29] To avoid reproducing inequities and prevent further mass harm, the circumstances that perpetuate global mental disease must be addressed at the root.

Even in the midst of such visionary possibility, we must remember that the root of the crisis our world faces today is characterized by poverty within empire, contaminated drug supplies, and a crisis of overdoses, all overshadowed by an ongoing pandemic.

It's at the center of these episodes of planetary apocalypse that healing justice movements are born out of the emergence of mutual aid, harm reduction, overdose prevention, and drug checking, often positioning community members to put themselves at legal risk to offer care by utilizing criminalized paraphernalia to keep people safe. It is the same scenes of social and economic abandonment by the state that have catalyzed today's compassionate and evidence-based efforts to support the health and rights of people who use drugs.

Today, the anthropocene (or capitalocene[30]) is an open wound from land to sky, an era bearing the sum of human extraction and consumption behavioral patterns. We face totalitarian regimes that persist in seizing control over the means of health and survival, through agricultural, medicinal, and medical monopolies across generations. Despite the ongoing epistemicides, the attempted eradications of ancestral oral and written knowledge—an affront to public memory, and therefore public health—we have enough information to wisely and responsibly respond to the repackaging of ancient, psychoactive substances for mass production and commercialization.

The unconscious mass consumption of somas in Aldous Huxley's *Brave New World* warns readers of the dystopian dangers underpinning state operated, large scale dosing of euphoric stimulants to maintain peace and social order under hierarchical capitalism.

The plot of the novel offers a moral compass for evaluating whether the legal and economic status of psychedelics advances land rematriation, demilitarization, and justice or further entrenches the human condition in colonialism and state violence.

The irony that Huxley also introduced the Western world to psychedelia through his description of mescaline in the *The Doors of Perception* is not lost on us. Indigenous people throughout the so-called new world continue to steward peyote (traditionally known as *hikuri*) through habitat loss and land theft, and as the scam of prohibition is revoked, political and cultural shifts have showered light (and dollars) toward the medicine so persistently protected over the last 500 years. We echo warnings of our Indigenous community members against endeavors seeking to expedite the mass extraction of naturally occurring medicine for profiteering. In our collective code of ethics, the risks of irreversible ecological damage must be a guiding compass. The persistent dialogue and debate over the ethics of including peyote in local city ordinances and state legislative bills is but one example of the stakes at play.

The US Food and Drug Administration has designed MDMA- and psilocybin-assisted treatments as breakthrough therapies, and the market for psychedelic health care could reach $6.8 billion by 2027.[31] This unfolding economic boom is a modern social experiment, investigating whether behaviors can be holistically treated through pharmacological-psychiatric models sterilized of tradition and historic memory. So far, psychedelic research has approached treatment for depression, anxiety, and PTSD through an individualized framework, and thus has to contend with that framework's associated baggage.

Prompts

- Which historical events are necessary to include in building historic memory around the origins of drug prohibition? How can engagement with the past shape the present and future of drug policy?

- How do we measure success in treatment, or progress in social or cultural development, if an experience allows an individual to be temporarily liberated from psychic pain and discomfort, but also fails to interrupt conscious or unconscious participation in structures that cause harm in the social and ecological fabric?

- While miraculous that colonizers lacked the worldview to understand the value of (and thus commodify) the visionary medicines 500 years ago, what obligations and considerations do people bringing them into the imperialist globalized economy have today? To say this in a more pointed way: is exploitative commodification and globalization inevitable, or are there measures that can be implemented to avoid this outcome?

- Altered states, in addition to being transformative for trauma, can also be fun, celebratory, pleasurable, meaningful, and symbolic.

- How can we weave storytelling, archetype, and play into this education and embodied awareness to invite the most ecstatic and loving outcomes?

III. REFLECTION: PSYCHEDELIC PRAXIS, RESPONSIBILITY, AND VISIONARY SOLIDARITY

In intermissions between ongoing revolutions, windows of opportunity emerge. Exactly 100 years after the 20th century's age of prohibition, and exactly 50 years after Richard Nixon called for a "War on Drugs," the decriminalization of entheogens and all drugs across territories is not only possible, but within reach. Clinical research is happening at dozens of major institutions, and policy change and cultural shifts have built momentum toward victory. While the 21st century psychedelic revolution promises a pluralist utopia, those of us driven by freedom and justice must remain vigilant and aware of how this paradigm shift is driven by the political will and economic interest of paradoxical forces: both the underground cultural and justice movements, and the financial and biomedical sectors. Each of these forces emerged from historical conditions we cannot afford to be aloof to.

Today, in the midst of these tensions, we have the opportunity to orient ourselves as bridge builders and mapmakers, between an inventory of the past and emerging liberatory futurisms.

Knowing this history brings awareness to the ongoing relationship between these substances and their full-spectrum context beyond their effects, and offers an opportunity to view production, distribution, and consumption of drugs through a more nuanced lens.

The magic of "shamanism," "curanderismo," or psychedelics has hxstorically been a vehicle for breaking the intergenerational curses of the "magic of the state." Yet in an age of emerging psychedelic monopolies, these practices risk co-optation by institutional actors in service to the superstructure; entheogenic ceremony alone won't save us from the consequences of historic harms. Only through substantive solidarity, care, and horizontal opportunities for collaboration with Indigenous stewards of ancestral knowledge will these sacred practices ever activate their true potential. So, we are tasked with reflecting about how to tilt the scales of justice (and the market) toward global healing, instead of perpetual exploitation.

Today's drug user–rights movements, increasing popular affinity for entheogens, a return to herbalism and earth-oriented spiritual practices, a returning belief in magic, and the mainstreaming of trauma-informed consciousness are all evidence of transformation.

Yet even if society is starting to agree that the War on Drugs is an abomination, the global fight against it starts fractalling into factions once the discussion of alternative approaches starts to confront what is seen as possible. Many who want to end prohibition also have concerns about how contemporary market economies manipulate and exploit people for profit. The gears of the market grind us down and are taking life on earth with it. Today one might suspect that a full audit of all the actors, patents, companies, investors, retreats, and farms behind psychedelic research, synthesis, growing, harvesting, and overall economies would point to the absorption, commodification, and repackaging of psychedelics by global capital. Others view the magic of these substances infiltrating the system to uproot archaic addictions to greed, exploitation, and punishment.

Across traditions, the essence of plant medicine is priceless. Psychoactive molecules, synthetic or not, are progeny of these plants and practices. Our generations are tasked with urgently addressing the overall laissez-faire, free-market traits of psychedelic entrepreneurship, venture capital, tourism, global trade, and consumption dynamics that cater to "first world" populations, at the expense of "third world" populations. To do so, we must interrupt the narrative that insists on patenting the synthesis of molecular doppelgängers to naturally occurring substances, or facets of the practices surrounding them.

We acknowledge that the United Nations Declaration on the Rights of Indigenous Peoples (UNDRIP)[32] falls short of addressing private interests that can and do circumvent states' obligations to Indigenous populations, and for that reason actors in psychedelic research and therapy movements must voluntarily commit to adhering to provisions articulated in the Declaration, including and especially Article 11 (about redress and restitution when intellectual property is taken), Article 19 (calling for good faith consultation and cooperation prior to implementing legal or administrative measures that impact them), Article 24 (which establishes the right to traditional medicine and health practices, including conservation, as well as the right to social and health services), and Article 25 (which establishes the right to maintain and strengthen their relationship with traditionally owned and occupied territories). We encourage anyone in the field to read UNDRIP in its entirety.

While the pendulum of psychedelic therapy research goals swings between large-scale healing and large-scale profit, the impetus for addressing Indigenous rights and people impacted by the War on Drugs is clear: **large-scale impact of any kind risks corruption and ultimately perpetuation of violence if the rights of and responsibilities to formerly colonized populations and territories are not respected and integrated into the emerging ecosystem.** The fact that many people impacted by global drug control are in fact Indigenous people further cements this obligation.

Meanwhile, educational institutions around the world have established centers dedicated to psychedelic research, and combatants responsible for acts of harm in the US and Israeli militaries are poised to be the first government-funded beneficiaries to psychedelic-assisted therapies. The humanity of combatants is intimately and complexly woven with the humanity of civilians living through armed conflict, occupation, and apartheid, and so it is incumbent on advocates working toward mainstream acceptance of psychedelics into psychiatry to ensure that those impacted by all violence—whether extrajudicial or state-sponsored—are centered as stakeholders and beneficiaries of psychedelic research and therapies.

How can we ensure protections for the plants, safety for practitioners, respect for culture, and accountability for people, without using violence or coercion?

How will the emerging psychedelic movement and industry grapple with the reality of the impact that increasing demand could have in places where the medicine naturally grows, whether it is Texas, San Luis Potosi, Huautla de Jimenez, or the Amazon Basin? What relations need repair and trust building, and what infrastructure needs to be in place to allow for healing and medicine to spread without increasing pressure on already impacted ecosystems of underground trade and without drawing predatory attention from federal or state law enforcement, or paramilitaries in other countries? A movement that wields the language and claims the cosmology of earth-based sacredness should back up that rhetoric with meaningful engagement with these dilemmas.

We land at a recognition that cognitive experience-seeking is historically complicated. The experiences accessible through today's most sought-after sacraments were eradicated and criminalized for most of American and global modern history, which forces us to recognize that the stewardship of and access to these practices has come at great human and epistemic cost. This cost ought to be recognized, honored, and viewed as an opportunity for people seeking access to sacraments to do so in reciprocity with the plants, people, and places that have held sacredness for generations, even if doing so complicates the calculus of our own consumption.

People coming into contact with the psychedelic zeitgeist are becoming aware of the legal and social constructs that currently restrict these powerful substances, and they are forming newly spiritualized and politicized communities. The legacy of harm reduction shows that there is a movement for healing, justice, and freedom which extends its compassion to include all people with various relations to plants, molecules, and other psychoactive substances. Solidarity of this kind could allow this visionary expansion to play a role in liberating our communities from the trauma cycles that characterize so many social movements, within drug policy and beyond.

It is both in integrity and practical to recognize that decriminalizing drugs and liberating our relationship with substances, including entheogenic plants, is one piece of a much larger transformation. This transformation takes us away from coercive, violent, and antisocial punishment and takes us toward holistic, evidence-based, and pro-social healthcare.

Being in alignment and solidarity with people who have been most directly impacted by the War on Drugs, the repression of entheogenic practices, and with people who have stewarded those practices for centuries, could ensure that the movement aligns with the medicine's core spirit to embody that transformation.

Prompts

- Psychocosmology is presently understood to mean a seeking of alignment between the external world as one understands it, and the inner self as one creates it.

- How do the substances you consume support you in making meaning from your experiences? How do they facilitate access to different physical, emotional, and spiritual states?

- To use substances to explore and world-build across the cosmic playgrounds of our minds is a form of magic, a form of entheogenic alchemy. What positive world-building can you do in the experiences you have with substances, and how can you bring that forward into the interpersonal and relational ecosystem in which you exist?

- How do patterns of use of different substances in your life inform your understanding of the world you believe in, or are trying to create? How do your patterns of use of different substances reflect your values and relations, both social and ecological?

IV. REIMAGINATION: LOOKING FORWARD TO FORKS IN THE ROAD

The age of COVID-19 will be remembered for its quarantine, essential labor, Black-led uprisings, mass virus fatalities, awakening class consciousness, US prison abolitionists calling for politicians to free them all, civil unrest, and accountability culture. Today the author of the 1994 Crime Bill, now the President of the United States, has included decarceration, harm reduction, and treatment (albeit coerced) in his policy agenda; these are all necessary but not sufficient steps to dismantle the system he helped create and presumably being the process of accounting for, and perhaps even repairing, past harms. Notably, his administration seems resistant to allowing people who casually use cannabis to serve.[33]

George Floyd protests in Uptown Charlotte, 5/30/2020. Clay Banks on Unsplash.

This era's crossroads are also haunted by entrepreneurs prematurely ready to sell the cure for anxiety and depression, conveniently without the fall of empire (aside from some minor disruption to the insurance markets). Through all the theory and reflection, we come back to the substances themselves. **What impact do they have on the superstructure, or the collective cultural experience, that their states contain?** People have a myriad of relationships with drugs, far more than the narrow worldview offered by prohibition can hold. Like our ancestors, we use drugs to heal, to celebrate, to process grief, to focus, to perform labor, to transform. And sometimes the conflation of communion and consumption does not apply to the context of 21st century life, and those powerful psychoactive effects can overtake, corrode, destabilize, and harm.

Beyond dismantling criminalization, we also need more imagination for the possibility of economic transformations.

The privatization of synthesized imitations of naturally occurring substances historically revered by Indigenous civilizations begs the question whether these kinds of psychedelic therapies are truly designed to free us all. While some are subject to archaic punishments for their participation in underground drug economies, others multiply legacy wealth when exercising their rights to cognitive liberty and risk taking in the playground of the free market.

Right now, legalization of a substance inherently brings it into the cynical market dynamics of the commercialized economy. **We hope that future regulatory systems permitting commercial sale of psychoactive substances specifically incorporate cooperative economics, social equity, community restoration, reparative justice, transformative justice, reciprocity, and reparations to Indigenous people and people who have been impacted by the War on Drugs in the articulation of commercial contexts.** These efforts must decriminalize all drugs and create funded, noncoercive, compassionate, public health–oriented approaches to wrap-around services, treatment, recovery, and reentry services. These efforts must simultaneously study ways to better sustain the psychoactive ecologies and the cultures that have existed and are being created around them.

One way of doing this is to reimagine and recapture the commons: we can and should paint a vivid depiction of possible futurist trajectories that depend on the collective priorities and choices of the present.[34]

Imagine gardens, farmers' markets, and safer use spaces where people can seek and find alleviating experiences with substances, without coercion, without violence, without having to succumb to the gears of the globalized market economy.

V. AN OFFERING: INSTEAD OF TRYING TO SEE THE FUTURE, LET'S FEEL INTO IT

adrienne maree brown's books *Pleasure Activism*[35] and *Emergent Strategy*,[36] Camille Barton's Ecologies of Transformation,[37] concepts of spiritual anarchy,[38] anarcho-pacifism,[39] and entheogenic alchemy all offer paths to create futures in the immediate vicinity of all kin willing and able to participate. We can integrate and actualize these futurist ways of being by following the guidance of embodied wisdom and pleasure. Orienting our sensory experiences to spiritual and material emancipation gives our inner compass a direction to follow and brings with it the duty and opportunity to help build bridges for the rest of us.

From this orientation, in the midst of perpetual change, let's breathe life into these possibilities:

- Cannabis and entheogenic communities that lift up their most harmed members—incarcerated folks, immigrants, asylum seekers, and families impacted by forced separation, communities decimated by policing—to being forces for revitalization of medicinal ecosystems and economies. We can build a world where neither migratory status nor citizenship status prevents participation in medicine ecosystems and economies, or leads to punishment through deportation.

- A psychedelic commitment to embodying the post-prohibition world through healing, art, and creative expression made accessible for all. Global psychedelic political commitments to authentic safety rooted in divestment of planetary militarization, borders, and mass incarceration and reinvestment in universal health care, basic income, housing, and climate and cultural reparations.

- A sacred, earth-based, reciprocal, reparative, and relational exchange of knowledge, care, and resources that unifies divine purpose around ecological restoration.

- A relational natural product economy of sacred, medicinal, celebratory plants and substances that are locally produced and prepared, traded through cooperatively owned, environmentally sustainable, and culturally appropriate infrastructure.

- Processes of rematriating land to Indigenous and/or collective stewardship by building trust, weaving symbiotic relationships for future generations.

- A collective will to slow down, and bring the rest of creation along with us into the future.

We'll join you along the way.

Black Trans Joy: A Love Letter to Poppy

PRESTO CRESPO

This article is dedicated to Raysa Martinez Carrera and my dear companion, Carla Scott.

ON AND OFF FOR YEARS, I HAVE REMAINED STILL AND CONTEMPLATED what my own last words will be, what my legacy will be, and all things concerning my own death.

———————

Last year, I moved out of my childhood home and into my own apartment. This was the first time I was able to actually get to know myself and begin to understand how gender dysphoria has affected my life and, at times, dictated my decisions. Most of the time I feel like and identify as a trans man or transmasculine, and there are times when I feel agender or genderless. Either way, I am far from cisheteronormative, no matter how badly I may have ever wanted to change that, and I have been this way as far back in my memories as I can recall. But before I could process all of this, I knew there was a disconnect between my body and mind, but I could not put my finger on what was causing this.

But even before I began the work of truly understanding this disconnect, I had already found something that ultimately helped turn the gender dysphoria I was experiencing into gender euphoria: consuming the poppy plant (*Papaver somniferum*) and the different medications that can be created from its seedpods.

The poppy plant has fascinated me since I was a teenager, when I noticed the plant had relevance in popular culture as well as in countercultural spaces. I saw the plant's flower, with its bright pop of color, in punk art and in fashion houses—like Kenzo's poppy print midiskirt in their Spring/Summer 2022 collection under creative director NIGO, which paid homage to the brand's founder Kenzo Takada, who was also fascinated by the poppy plant and flower.

In addition to cannabis and alcohol, the drugs that came from the poppy plant were popular in the Castle Hill area of the Bronx and Harlem where I grew up. When I was a teenager, older folks often sold their Percocet or oxycodone to friends around my age. When I first tried a Percocet, after figuring out how to offset the nausea, I decided that this was the recreational drug that agreed with my body the best and gave me the most desired effects: focus, an energy boost, instant confidence, and a profound reduction in social anxiety.

The drug connects with my body in a way that no other does, and I have tried all of them. As a transmasculine/gender-nonconforming person in a cisheteronormative society, I not only felt a disconnect between mind and body from a very young age but also had no idea what to do about that disconnect. When I became sexually active as a lesbian, I noticed that intimacy was quite difficult for me, though not for lack of interest or motivation. Since I was not particularly shy about my sexuality, what I liked, or anything else, why the anxiety around sex? Why the lack of focus during my most intimate moments with the people I loved? It was causing great distress for me, as it would for anyone. Even worse, when it finally came time for me to really embrace my gender identity, I felt heartbroken that I could not, due to this aching feeling.

During quarantine, I took the opportunity to read radical theory of all sorts, including gender theory. I had read and heard about gender dysphoria from my friends, who had talked to me about how they experience dysphoria when they have to speak out loud in a public space or when they are forced to use a bathroom that does not match the gender they identify with. Around the same time, I began to self-medicate and self-soothe my fatigue and anxiety with opioids. I had access to a safe supply of Percocet pills—that is, until the unemployment money I was receiving stopped coming in and I returned to my previous job within the nonprofit industrial complex. I was also attending college courses part time to work towards completing my bachelor's degree so, on top of dysphoria, general anxiety, and fatigue, I was stressed out when it came to school. There are so many reasons why that time of my life was difficult for me, but I was determined to not live the way I was feeling. I just had to figure out an inexpensive way to access the medication I needed.

Dr. Irwin Lucki, professor and chair of the psychology department at the Uniformed Services University of the Health Sciences, studies the different opioid receptors that are endogenous to the human body and how those receptors can either be blocked or used for the desired effects of enhanced mood,[1] sociability, and reduced stress and anxiety. For me and my comrades and siblings that face the stress and anxiety of living our everyday lives under capitalism and within the colonies of the imperial core—what is currently known as the United States—poppy and its use is one way we can rebel, resist, and oftentimes rest.

However, myself and many others believe opioids can be used to treat an even wider set of ailments. For example, the opioid agonist buprenorphine was found to be effective in treating major depressive disorder (MDD)[2] in individuals who are opioid naive.[3] This medication, also used for opioid use disorder (OUD), was effective in treating MDD in those who had been taking the drug for the purpose of treating OUD and was also found to be effective for treating acute suicidal ideation in both opioid-naive individuals and those who had been taking opioid pain medications for some time.

So I began to consider using powdered dope. I use this term because "heroin" would be inaccurate and "Fentanyl" would be somewhat dishonest. You see, there is hardly any heroin left within the underground economy being sold on the streets. It is my understanding that this is a direct result of the international War on Drugs and, within that, the eradication of the poppy plant.

The poppy is a resilient plant that can grow in varied temperatures and soils around the world. Its resiliency would prove crucial, as governments would begin targeting the plant for eradication despite its history in numerous ancient civilizations as a medicine for several kinds of pain and sleeplessness—including the Sumerians, who may have used the plant as far back as 2,100 BCE.[4] The international War on Drugs, spearheaded by the United States and emulated by other nations, has sought to eradicate poppy in places like Afghanistan, where the United States assisted with funding the Islamic Republic of Afghanistan's "counternarcotics efforts,"[5] resulting in the eradication of poppy farming throughout the nation. Destroying this plant means severing the connection the poppy has with the Indigenous populations who have used it as a source of economic prosperity and independence for millennia.

I made my decision to try dope with a friend of mine and to see how it would feel. I tried a small amount and it felt very similar to the Percocets and oxycodone I had tried before, but this time it felt much warmer. That feeling of warmth, something like a hug at the perfect moment, overtook my whole body and went to places I had never felt connected to prior to that. The experience was deeply spiritual and I felt in touch with my emotions. After that, I began to use the time that I would indulge in the drug for journaling and expressing myself to others. At times, I would have so much stress built up from the dysphoria that it was hard for me to focus on work, and even socializing was difficult. All of that was lifted off me during these times of bliss when engaging with poppy. I respected it and kept my use under control by treating the times I was under its influence as sacred for me. I noticed that it was so much easier to talk with those I was intimate with about my issues with sex when I was under the influence of opioids, specifically heroin and Fentanyl (I prefer heroin but I know individuals who prefer the latter for recreational usage). However, I was still living with my parents at the time, so I still did not have even a slight grasp on my gender identity.

I decided that I would try having sex after having used dope as a way to explore myself in a more intimate way. Because I have rolling veins, I could never inject, so I always snorted the powder. When I snorted a line and had sex under the influence of dope for the first time, it changed the trajectory of my life. I had experienced an orgasm before this event but not in the way I did that night. For the first time while having sex, I felt whole, like the entirety of my being was involved. That included my entire body, my mind and its thoughts, as well as my spiritual self. There were no intrusive thoughts in the midst of it, my mind was not eager to find distractions during some of the more uncomfortable moments. In all honesty, there were no uncomfortable moments.

Of course, this was absolutely mind-blowing for me. I thought I would never be able to experience this sort of peace while having sex or engaging in any intimate act. What did this mean about my sexual past and what did it mean for my future? Up until this moment, I would feel excited to date, excited to tease—ready to feel and be felt—until the actual feelings came. Our clothes would come off, mine only partially . . . The excitement would turn to nervousness and anxiety, the anxiety into self-doubt. As a result, I doubted myself sexually; I doubted my ability to be the man I am, and thus to be the better man I wish to be in the future.

One time, something happened in the middle of a sexual encounter with my ex-partner that solidified my experience with opioids as not only my pursuit of pleasure but my pursuit of happiness. I believe it happened with this person and at this time because my ex-partner makes me feel very safe in my gender identity and even goes as far as reminding me who I am when I'm feeling highly dysphoric. I had a flashback of me having some internal dialogue with myself as a child. The topic of the conversation was my body, its parts, and what I was going to do about the fact that I did not like them because they felt foreign to me. I made the decision that day, as a child, that I was going to allow myself the pleasure of poppy in spite of society's stigmatized way of viewing it. I knew I was risking the loss of friendships, being judged heavily by my family members, and all of the other risks that come with using dope: arrest, hospitalization, or worse.

When I am in these moments of bliss with my drug of choice in my system, life feels worthy of living. I try to remember this every time I have to take breaks, as I must. Our current medical infrastructure does not support drug "addicts" so I must try my best to not be labeled as such, although I'm sure I am already on someone's paperwork. Meanwhile, when people seek pleasure through sex or social media or food or the latest Netflix series, it isn't usually seen as a problem. We all deserve to seek pleasure and community connection and play time, and even these common activities (television/social media as well as drinking and having sex) require balance and taking self-inventory, the same way substance use does. Yet the stigma against dope is so extreme that I find myself constantly shamed for my "hard" drug use.

When I use dope, my true self emerges—he feels full of kindness and empathy. He wants a new world for the people around him, for the ones he knows and the ones he does not know. What is the crime in getting in touch with this side of myself? From what I see, the crime is that the powers that be do not make money off of it. We have been socialized to place drugs in a hierarchy and opioids have been heavily demonized, placed toward the bottom of that hierarchy, while cannabis and psychedelics sit at the top mostly unscrutinized.

Of course, which drugs are considered "acceptable" in our society comes from the intersection of race and class—a history of colonialism and power imbalances where those who were deemed to be "other" were and still are criminalized for the same things white people are not. The drug war in the US that sparked the mass incarceration boom of the '70s and '80s began with xenophobia, alongside the complete disregard of bodily autonomy of those indigenous to what we now know as the "Americas," as well as enslaved people from Africa. During the presidencies of Roosevelt, Nixon, Reagan, and Clinton, the targeting of Black and otherwise colonized individuals for drug raids and racketeering hit all-time highs. The public associated crack and heroin use with Black urban centers like where I grew up and now live in the Bronx.

Outsiders looking into my neighborhood see our crumbling infrastructure and a desperate need for decent mental health treatment and assume we do not care about our communities. Some of my community members have even internalized this sentiment that it is the neighborhood and its inhabitants that ultimately cause the everyday harms we experience. However, none of us as individuals had the power to abandon ourselves and to leave our families and friends in oftentimes horribly austere conditions. We are left in perpetual cycles of harm from the state's abandonment. For some individuals like myself, drug use relaxes the everyday aches and pains of being Black and poor in the US. We are punished for having the audacity to reach for something different. We are criminalized as the result of our self-determination and resistance.

In community with other trans and gender nonconforming individuals, the phrase "gender euphoria" is used as a counter to the dysphoria we experience. Gender dysphoria comes from internal as well as external factors; we all have ideas in our heads about what a specific gender is supposed to look or feel like because that is how we are taught and, as a result, so many trans individuals like myself carry internalized transphobia. I would like to say that "gender euphoria" is being able to wake up every day and live as exactly who you are, and that could be a different gender and sexuality for every day of every year for the rest of your life. I imagine it as being like water, ever so fluid and shifting in form based on the environment. It would also mean that externally, one is cherished by their community for whichever form they take—not something they have chosen, as so many people like to exclaim, but simply because we just are. Gender euphoria does not require any further justification to a society that has denied us our ability to self-determine anything about ourselves. To experience euphoria in gender without the gaze of systems could be as easy as breathing air.

With the current unregulated street supply of drugs, it is possible that what has brought so much new joy and understanding into my life may also be what is responsible for my death. While heroin was formerly derived from the poppy plant itself, the current supply is mostly manufactured in labs, and stronger opioid analogs are entering the drug supply regularly. A regulated supply of drugs available for the public at cost (meaning with no profit incentive) would certainly reduce overdose numbers, as we've seen with the organization DULF (Drug User Liberation Front), which sells tested cocaine, heroin, MDMA, and methamphetamine in British Columbia at cost. No one who has ever purchased their drugs from DULF has overdosed since the group began distributing drugs they purchased off of the dark web and tested themselves for purity. Both legalization and safe supply with a harm reduction approach would address the root causes of possible "problematic" drug use like homelessness, mental illness, and trauma. Not a single individual needs to die from an overdose and I believe that can be actualized utilizing harm reduction as a philosophy and pairing it with concrete action.

Before I leave this Earth, no matter which way it occurs, I owe all of my respect to the poppy plant. Without it I may have missed out on some of the most beautiful, fun, and pleasurable experiences of my entire life, and it is very possible that there would be no me writing these words today. While trying my best to keep myself alive, I discovered that death is nowhere near the end, because the mind and the spirit can both travel much further than the physical body can. Life and death are inextricably connected. Unfortunately, the damage from demonization and stigma prevents me from accessing this medicine and its pleasurable aspects in a safe way, but a large community that includes myself is fighting for that to change. Even through the struggle, for the insight into the proximity of life and death, for a good night's sleep when my anxiety is literally paralyzing, for being able to stop and breathe when I've been crying for 20 minutes straight—I am forever grateful to the poppy.

Only through imaginative and spiritual eyes could I have ever come to these points when thinking about what kind of life I understand to be worth living. My opioid use has allowed me to imagine a world that myself and others could exist and thrive in as opposed to simply surviving. I reference community in my writing extensively because the words and thoughts

I have put together in order to explain the lengths I go to when ensuring some sense of pleasure and rest in this lifetime do not belong only to me. Those who have acted in resistance before us, before myself, laid this foundation for me and others to stand on.

These days, my thoughts of death settle on how I wish to be remembered and what I wish to leave behind. If to be Black is to be doomed, if to be Black and Trans is something even more agonizing than that—then to stand in the face of that reality and deny it as the only option is certainly gender euphoria. Black Trans Joy is the legacy I am determined to leave behind. With that joy comes autonomy, which is not given to us but must be demanded and etched out of struggle and unity.

Ancestral Healing for Liberation

RICHAEL FAITHFUL

"WHAT DO YOU DO FOR A LIVING?"

I've learned to smile when asked this inevitable question at every new social event among Washington DC's work-obsessive professional class.

"I'm a shaman," I'd answer wryly.

Then, I'd wait for the initial response, ranging from indignant to intrigued, followed by a barrage of questions.

"How does someone become a shaman, anyway?" "Do real shamans live in cities?" "What do you actually do, like, day to day?"

I smile at these questions because I understand them. My vocational calling as a shaman was unexpected. I deciphered a spiritual invitation more than two decades into my life, after committing to a career as a community civil rights lawyer. I was formally introduced to shamanism just two years before my own initiation. I did not envision this ministry either, yet here I am.

I do not fit the shaman archetype. To the degree that any vision of a shaman exists in the white US imagination, I am far from it—younger, queerer, Blacker, and often in street wear. I exist in contrast to the Indigenous elder living in isolation as a village medicine man, or even in contrast to the racist trope of the "tribal" Black male priest who performs sacrificial rituals with chickens. The fact is modern shamanic practitioners look more like me, and perhaps even like you. The spiritual world order is shifting, which means that our notions of modern shamanism need a serious update.

Most often, modern traditional healers, especially healers of the global majority, live at the intersections of real and otherworldly; secular and spiritual; city and country; refined and wild; untried and wise. We are both resisting oppressive systems to facilitate our own and others' healing, and we are alchemizing legacies of inherited trauma to transform our lives and the lives of those whom we love. This role and work is not about becoming born again, as much as it is about retelling our own origin stories.

MEDICINE THAT HAS ALWAYS BEEN HERE

Shamanism is our Indigenous integrative medicine that supports our individual and collective well-being and connection. This medicine follows our indigeneity, all over the world, within all cultures. Shamanic medicine heals spirits, bodies, minds, psyches, lands, families, and other life forces that shape our realities. Examples of common practices include divination for prophecy or deeper knowledge, herbalism/plant healing, ritual for significant events and/or ailments, music making, and dance. Most of all, shamanism is the people's medicine that honors our interrelation to all nature, earth, ancestors, spirits, and the cosmos.

The word "shamanism" itself is a newer umbrella description for these sacred medicinal folkways. According to Itzhak Beery, *shaman* is derivative of *saman*, the word of the Eastern Siberian Tungus people to describe their healers, later adopted by colonizing Russians, and has since spread worldwide.[1] Specifically shaman means "one who knows," "one who can fly," or "messenger between worlds," and a couple of other translations depending on a particular shaman's abilities. Although *Webster's* dictionary links shamanism to the Tungus people exclusively, shamanism has been adopted as a more general term to describe the practice of Indigenous medicine.

A remarkable fact about our ancestral folkways is that despite centuries of empire making, colonization, repression, and theft, shamanic practice is still present in some of our lives, particularly people of the global majority. Some visible shamanic voices include Don Miguel Ruiz, author of the Toltec Wisdom Series, including *The Four Agreements*; Martín Prechtel, educator and writer of *The Smell of Rain on Dust: Grief and Praise*; and Shaman Durek, a sixth-generation shaman who appeared on the CBS program *The Doctors*. There are many more practitioners offering sacred work who we will never hear about and whose work will never be known who are supporting our communities, quietly and routinely.

So many people, currently, rely on shamanic support, especially communities of color in the US. For instance, many people from the Latine diaspora are familiar with curanderos (or curanderas, curanderxs), a traditional healer, whom families visit alongside western allopathic doctors or for concerns that only a medicine person can address, like chronic or recurring illness. Along the same vein, some people of the African diaspora seek out babalawos, or high priests of the Yoruba tradition of Ifa, for castings only practiced by initiated and ranked healers.[2]

Modern shamanism means, in part, that healers offer their gifts in the range of places we live, and through digital connection. Some curanderas, for example, are adapting their offerings online, like Grandmother Flordemayo, a Mayan practitioner originally from Nicaraguan highlands and now based in New Mexico, who teaches webinars or holds private remote sessions. Similarly, from the Chinese wisdom tradition, Master Wu, author of *Shamanic Tiger Qigong*, also has an online presence. He shares about seasonal conditions and treatments through an email newsletter, offers qigong classes inspired by his book on Zoom, and practices Fu 符, the creation of shamanic power symbols by way of talisman calligraphy.

In this context, modern shamanism is about remembering and reclaiming our indigeneity, its medicine, and adapting them for our needs. This is the role that I play alongside many others who are reconnecting to ancestral and legacied knowledge. The vision of shamanism as an esoteric set of practices, for occasional use, performed by obscure savants who are apart from the communities they serve is slowly receding. And for good reason—not only is it time for us to decolonize our inherited wisdom, it is re-emerging to help us get free.

EVERYDAY MAGIC

Magic is another word that carries wide meaning. Yvonne Chireau, professor of religion at Swarthmore College, defines magic as "a particular approach or attitude by which humans interact with unseen powers or spiritual forces."[3] Based on this understanding of magic, our relationship with what is not visible (to most of us) and spiritual forces is emphasized over whatever we believe the "it" of magic to be. Whether we believe that magic exists or agree on what it is, we all interact with questions about phenomena under the surface of our perception or readily accessible knowledge. Every one of us deals with the transmission of reality at the edge of our common awareness.

I define magic as a force of which we understand very little. A lot of our lives can fit into this idea of magic, matters big and small. Along with our relationship with these forces that Professor Chireau defines, to me, it is significant that magic contains power that it is less knowable and, therefore, less controllable. I believe it is these aspects that compel so many in the US, conditioned by Enlightenment rationality,[4] to reject magic in theory or in public, but still accept the lesser known parts of our reality in practice and in private.

An example is prayer. In the US, over half of the population reports daily prayer with almost three thirds sharing at least weekly prayer, an outlier among wealthy countries with its high levels of prayer (and we apparently even have a Day of Prayer on my birthday).[5] However, it is hard to know the efficacy of prayer—what would we attribute its power to? For many people, prayers petition a more powerful force that can exert its volition onto our lives, even if it is mysterious how that force does so. Prayer represents some fleeting suspension of disbelief from rational laws that govern our universe or momentarily indulgence into the less knowable. Frankly, it is magic to me. And not far from the other forms of magic that have been long feared, relegated, and rejected.

Magic is a central part of a shamanic worldview. A practitioner, by definition, is communicating, relating, or otherwise working with the supernatural. Their role is to tend to the "unseen" reality as much as the material reality—bridging dimensions to help us make meaning is the vocation of a shaman. Magic is the effect that allows these relationships to exist and for us as a community to have faith, to be hopeful, and to better relate to one another. At the same time, a shaman tries to effect these forces through ritual, ceremony, and other practices. Such a sacred role is not very distinct from a priestess, raba[6], imam, or bhikkhunī.

It is also true that magic can feel extraordinary. These are the events that strain our sense of reality or disorient us completely. In my own experience, during my shamanic study, I encountered a traumatized lost soul, whose former Black body was lynched on the land. This soul needed to use my physical body and energy healing training to transition into another realm. I consider this moment my shamanic initiation that tore my reality asunder. Twelve hours later I was on a city bus to my temp job downtown. Although I had an entirely different sense of the world, I still needed to code 40 documents an hour so I could afford to eat. I do not want to completely normalize magic, because its essence is remarkable. My hope is that we can begin to see magic, from prayer to prophecy, woven into our everyday lives. We may not yet fully understand, but we know enough to know that it has meaning.

RESISTANCE IS IN OUR VEINS

Our world is powerfully brutal, so that healing is always necessary. It is even more necessary to heal—and more urgent—when we are denied opportunities as a matter of cultural design. Many of our systems in the US depend on the dissociation, toil, and hopelessness of rote survival and the unhealedness of the marginalized. The result is polyhedrons of unintended pain that reinforce their sources. Intergenerational trauma cycles are our reality in a brutal world where some of us believe that the pain can no longer be passed on. It needs to end, now.

Pain shapes us regardless of our preferences. As a healer, I routinely encounter the underside of collective heartbreak, torment, and discards. These truths are undeniable. Among the thousands I've supported in my role, most have experienced sexual assault (often as children), physical abuse, economic exploitation, institutionalization, and usually all of these traumas and others. I know from my own practice, as well as other empirical evidence, that unaddressed trauma festers into more vulnerability to violence, infliction of violence, addiction, and mental illness.

The magnitude of generational violence is beyond measure. Though I am a witness to some of the most marginalized people in my communities, their traumas are not an aberration. Rather, I'm convinced that systemic denial and erasure undergird the harms we survive, especially childhood sexual abuse, which is at epidemic proportions. To contend with generational violence is to confront a culture of secrecy so deeply embedded in our family and communal lives in the US. Once we make commitments to be more truthful about what happened to us, and to be more honest about how we reenact those traumas, we can finally interrupt cycles of violence that otherwise feel inescapable.

Part of the problem is the way in which our social and medical systems treat trauma. In many cases, these systems not only fail to end cycles of violence, they profoundly contribute to them. Three social justice frameworks—healing justice, transformative justice, and disability justice—critique the historic harm of systems and policies created to help, and point us toward other strategies. Interestingly, these other strategies have always existed alongside harmful systems, and many people still rely on these other options because they have often felt more accessible, safer, and self-determined. If the carceral state and the medical industrial complex are the master's tools, healing justice, transformative justice, and disability justice are solutions that were generated at night on the plantation, and that eventually stir the uprisings.

Healing justice, in particular, is a framework that centers collective safety and healing as integral to our political liberation. Cara Page, a cultural worker and founding member of Kindred Southern Healing Collective, has defined healing justice as rooted in the traditions and practices that sustained our collective resilience, memories, and bodies through ancestral, cultural, environmental, and spiritual contexts. Not only does healing justice disrupt interpersonal and family cycles of violence, it seeks to transform historical trauma from oppression, policing, surveillance, colonization, and attempted genocide. As an organizing strategy, healing justice reminds us that healing is part of political work, not an afterthought or outside of "the work." I describe healing justice as the work that is necessary so that we can live and stay in social justice movement, and be full beings in the process.

Here we are brought to an important pathway by which traditional medicine, intergenerational healing, and political liberation meet. If our social and medical systems have not been, nor are currently safe for so many people and communities, and if we are moved to transform these systems to help end generational cycles of harm, then accessing our traditional healing practices, tools, and technologies seem like the most evident options.

There's a clear alignment between politics of safety and the politics of care/well-being, in which we are relying on what has worked. Moreover, it's definitive. A desire follows to understand what our ancestors did to resist violent forces that sought their annihilation or oppression, and cultures that sanctioned such cruelty. And then we might ask, who am I without connections to these histories? What can I reclaim from false narratives and distortions that I inherited? Who were the people who chose risk against past versions of these forces? How can we be the ancestors that our children will remember for our moral clarity? And how can we leave evidence that we existed and continued our ancestral wisdom?

OLD MEDICINE, NEW USES

We know where we are from our pasts, and where we want to go from our lessons. Yet, so many of us in the US are grievously disconnected from eldership, ancestors, meaningful places, long-held traditions, and some-times our native tongues. A perfect storm of cultural phenomena, from assimilation and individualism to racial caste and colonial conquest, have dislocated entire communities in relatively short periods of time. It is unsurprising that more than 26 million people in the US have taken at-home ancestry tests to know more about their lineages.[7] This level of dislocation along with other indications of social isolation translates us to a people experiencing mass disorientation. Seeking connection and making meaning are some of the most essential investments many of us can make at this moment.

Some of the ways I and others are locating ourselves is by remembering, reclaiming, and reinventing ancestral healing. Although this process varies for every person, it generally offers opportunities to learn more about folks, the world in which they lived, and the forces that shaped them. Learning about them alone isn't enough either—we must make meaning through context. And once we have a deeper understanding of a fuller picture of our past, we trace this picture onto our own lives, often unearthing lies, distortions, and superficialities that were passed down to us (intentional and not). As we decolonize our histories, we know the truth about ourselves, and more vividly envision our futures.

I call this kind of work "cycle breaking." It's when a person engages in remembering, reclaiming, and reinventing, which are all healing and political pursuits, in equal measure. Even if one doesn't seek out traditional healing practices specifically, their truth seeking and telling translate into potential healing pathways—airing corrosive secrets, reframing narratives, finding positive discoveries—that disrupt harmful patterns. Their willing-ness to break the cycles is a strong enough intention to "do" the work of generations.

It is not hard to imagine from this place that many of us reconnect to old medicine along the way, whether it be spiritual teachings, herbal medicine, artistic expressions, rituals and rites-of-passage, and other troves of prac-tices and traditions. Even though lines to this medicine might have been lost, they are far from broken. Learning about old medicine, and developing the skills to create it, is the ultimate form of resistance that heals us too. A growing number of people are honing enough skills to sustain themselves and their closest kindred. Some of us have the honor of cultivating our skills to share with our broader communities and beyond. This work is service based, a vocation bestowed by our ancestors to meet the healing of our times. It is a gift for which we have tremendous responsibility and benefit if we steward it well.

As shamanism grows more popularly referenced in the United States, almost impressively, older affluent white faces are the posterchildren of shamanism by co-opting Native traditions. The late Michael Harner, an anthropologist, and Sandra Ingerman, a therapist, are examples of white professionals whom, decades ago, observed shamanic practices from cultures other than their own, and then amalgamated these distinct cultural practices into a handful of "standard" shamanic rituals, such as journeying and soul retrieval.

These whitewashed rituals allowed for a factory-line of trainings, courses, and media for mainly white "new age" consumers. And notably, this cohort of exploiters have established themselves as shamanic "experts" who are best positioned to teach because they published numerous books and propagated a couple of generations of white practitioners. Plus, they are easy to find on search engines, which matters in a digital age where many ancient traditions are passed down through oral, visual, and kinesthetic traditions.

Decolonizing shamanism starts with naming the extractive origins of this shamanic school, with rejecting these practices as gold standards (and any standardization of practices altogether), and with pressing the second and third generation of this industry to be more critical of what they've consumed as teachings. It also requires exploiters to take account of wisdom that they stole and repackaged.

There is another commercial extension of shamanism that is even more popular with increasing interest in plant-induced altered states of consciousness. A tourist industry around ayahuasca, a Peruvian/Ecuadorian ceremonial entheogenic plant, developed from white American and European demand for alternative healing. Essentially, thousands of consumers pay large sums to travel to South America, undergo plant rituals under shamanic care, seeking life insights or healing from the psychoactive experience. Reports show that the industry attracts many thousands of people to a few concentrated centers each year.[8]

This work, which I call ancestral healing, takes many different forms that depend on one's access, resources, contexts, and histories. The danger of the co-opted, white-washed modern shamanic practice I shared before is that it creates a "healing-fits-all" approach based on a diluted and arbitrary formula. This standardization removes essential nuance from practices, as well as the reasons things were done in the first place. We won't ever really know the various conditions under which traditions exploited for the US shamanic industry were employed, how these traditions were different from one another, or what was lost in translation and/or the white gaze.

For example, the concepts of "soul loss" and "soul theft" are super general descriptions of when traumas are so severe that they fragment the soul, requiring a "soul retrieval" ceremony. Such a ceremony should reflect needs dictated by the layers of a trauma pattern in this person's life, their bloodlines, and other events or conditions that reinforced that trauma or prevented healing. This complex endeavor should assume a lot of variance in a ceremony from one person to the next. Instead, the shamanic industry's answer contains a four-part ceremony that is the same for everyone. Here we have the fast-food equivalent to our most important spiritual rituals. I'd argue it's killing us too—the same way that capitalist symptoms incentivize us to ignore deeper systemic problems is much like repackaged ancient practices that promote feeling over individual and collective transformation.

The truth is ancestral healing becomes our whole lives. In my own experience, ancestral healing meant reclaiming my roots as a Southerner, learning healing arts through a meditation community, and rediscovering the folk healing tradition of conjure in my 20s. Then, for the first half of my 30s, I had to rely on a range of sources to build a conjure practice, choose to elevate conjure as partly a shamanic tradition, define my own style of conjuring, and develop skills as a sacred space-holder.

Over this 12 year period, I nurtured my childhood wounds, validated certain experiences, transmuted family grief, treated chronic conditions, removed transgenerational and continental curses, resolved community conflicts, companioned organizers and artists as they healed their traumas, and served as a doula and coach for other cycle-breakers and leaders, to name only some adventures. I don't think that I'm exceptional—rather, there is a generation of ancestral healers who are emerging for our collective liberation. We are learning that returning to our indigeneity supports all of us toward sovereignty.

ANCESTRAL HEALING FOR LIBERATION

After surviving the year 2020, the personal as political holds a stronger resonance with me than ever before. That year made manifest the need for deep healing practices to sustain us, the value of our resilience skills, and the lifeline of our web of relationships. Even more was revealed in this single year about the poor responsiveness of our institutions, lack of cultural adaptability, and limits of consumption than in my previous 35 years. As much as my endurance was tested, I was grateful to have prepared alongside so many for this moment. Our work did not make our heartbreak any less painful, or the demands any less strenuous, it just meant that we had the perspective, supports, and relationships to keep going, keep going, keep going.

Black feminists have reminded us, time and time again, that our survival is defiant. Quarantining gave me an opportunity to read a collection of Audre Lorde's posthumous essays, *Burst of Light*, chronicling her yearslong experience living with cancer. She offered these words that have stayed with me: "For me, living fully means living with maximum access to my experience and power, loving, and doing work in which I believe." Lorde's words contain a key to liberation—the more of herself she could have, or even have back, the more fulfilled her life. She wrote this passage when her life was at its most precarious state, when she circled her own bouts of denial with cancer, and yet still traveled the world to be in solidarity with other women of the diaspora, inviting us to remember that access to our power, love, and purpose offers meaning. This wisdom not only applies to her or her life, but also reflects the politics of being in a disposable world.

Ancestral healing is liberatory work. It is not self-indulgent romanticism or fantastic reminisce. It is our way back home at literal and cosmic levels. The maps for our personal and shared liberation are charted similarly. Decolonization removes the debris from legacies of destruction and distance from our deepest connections, but fails to compass us much further. Here, we must remember and reclaim what we can discover and use, and allow to make sense for us today. Learning who we are is our birthright; creating our futures is our design.

Of the many gifts of shamanism, folk healing, and conjuring is the inversion of my reality. I sense the world through intergenerational, interdependent, and infinite connection, instead of singular, nuclear, and scarce fragments. At this stage I can no longer accept myopia. If we are wise ancestors, we have to do the living, healing, and loving that our ancestors were not afforded, or wasted.

Years ago, when I entered this path, I urged myself to create as if all life depended on it. These days, through ancestral healing and collective healing, our mandate is to create as if all life flows from it.

Afterword

SINNAMON LOVE

IN 2023, I CELEBRATED MY 30TH YEAR AS SINNAMON LOVE, MY NOM DE guerre as a sex worker, writer, Black feminist pornographer, and community organizer. Early in my career, I met my "Fairy Whore Mothers," Black women who taught me that porn would not be enough to sustain me and how to diversify income streams successfully. Throughout my career, I have worked as a full-service sex worker; porn performer, director, and producer; cam model; professional Dominatrix; BDSM and fetish model; and phone sex operator and have danced in strip clubs, at bachelor parties, and after-hours clubs—often concurrently.

Before I became Sinnamon Love, I was a 16-year-old in Flint, Michigan, who was violently kicked out of my home and traded sex for food and shelter on the streets of Hollywood and the shores of Venice Beach. I became a child bride at 17, married to a man 18 years my senior, and eventually found my way into the porn industry after my divorce with two toddlers on my hip.[1]

Sex work saved my life. On my darkest nights, it offered healing and connection. It kept a roof over my head and fed my body and family. The wisdom and support I received from fellow sex workers helped me earn a living and became the guidepost in understanding the potential for self-determination and community care.

I thank my ancestors for protecting me and keeping me safe.

In the lightest moments, sex work fed my wanderlust and guided me to climb the pyramids at Teotihuacán, chase butterflies in Montezuma, and explore the back alleys of Paris, crate digging for rare vinyl records and retracing Anaïs Nin's steps, paid for by the generosity of lovers I met online who booked my time and services.

Sex workers in the formal economy, like myself, are often painted in a narrow framing of privilege that fails to acknowledge us as potential survivors of sexual violence, trafficking, exploitation, workplace injury, labor violations, and interpersonal and state violence. My solidarity comes from a place of lived experience, not charity.

Often, people who oppose sexual labor do not understand how to engage with sex work from a critical lens. Anti–sex work feminists cling to the belief that poor, immigrant, queer, trans, and disabled women are either forced to violate social norms around sexual propriety, cannot consent due to "economic coercion," or, worse, are simply making bad choices. Conflating labor with trafficking infantilizes women, moralizes sexual behavior, and upholds the belief that sex workers need to be saved from themselves, their clients, and their subscribers. Many anti–sex work crusaders do not honor "circumstance" as a legitimate entry point into the sex trade because they do not view poverty itself as a form of violence. They argue that individuals like myself, who enter the trade due to extenuating economic circumstances, aren't making authentic, autonomous choices. This bastardization of Black feminist theory's interrogation of the relationship to choice in proximity to racial capitalism lacks a nuanced understanding of race, gender, class, and caste. Moral panic scapegoats sex workers and substance users for systemic failures to continue funding the practice of forced family separation, to justify the surveillance and overpolicing of our communities, and to use racialized fearmongering to pass sweeping legislation that degrades our civil rights. As you were reading *Body Autonomy: Decolonizing Sex Work and Drug Use*, I hope you began untangling the threads between evangelical conservatism; the policing of Black and immigrant communities; and the ongoing criminalization of poverty, Indigenous healing practices, substance use, and sex work.

Domestic missionaries believe they are helping poor communities of color, sex workers, and substance users through faith-based diversion programs like "Dress for Success" and forced "Return-to-Work" initiatives that reinforce the myth of basic-needs insecurity as a personal failure while failing to address the root causes of poverty.

Respectability politics tell us that if you pull your pants up, go to school, and wear modest clothing, you will avoid harassment and arrest by law enforcement, won't have state-dependent children out of wedlock, will avoid sexual violence, will land a well-paying job, and will live happily ever after. The illusory curtain surrounding these archaic ideals of the American Dream and nuclear family continues to fall as even those who did all the "right" things struggle to participate meaningfully in capitalism.

I suppose if the ongoing lack of affordable housing in the United States and the mishandling of COVID-19 have taught us anything, it's that most of us are one missed paycheck, illness, accident, or global pandemic away from being unhoused, and no one, not even the government, is coming to save us. What's more, 1.3 million people were willing to move from taking pole classes for fitness and joking about selling feet pics to actually getting naked on the internet for money when push came to shove.

After George Floyd was brutally murdered, I watched as colleagues participated in marches around the country. I lamented with my therapist about how the necessary isolation to protect my immunocompromised grandson quelled my ability to protest in the streets. She reminded me that every movement needs people in varied capacities and asked, "What can you do from behind your computer?"

I began reposting about rallies and marches, information to keep protestors safe, and engaged in conversations about racism in the porn industry. When it seemed like adult companies were using the global Movement for Black Lives as clickbait to "listen to Black people talk about race," I invited an intersectional group of performers to compile a list of desired changes to improve working conditions in the industry. Within a month, porn agents agreed to end the racist practice of charging more money for white female performers having sex with Black men on film for the first time.

In a subsequent meeting, we prioritized fundraising to support people struggling due to the production halt caused by COVID-19. We received 380 requests for assistance in the first 90 days. We tapped into the organizing power of our community to offer free webinars to teach BIPOC sex workers how to navigate the learning curve of earning money online. Jet Setting Jasmine, a sex worker, award-winning adult film director, entertainer, master fetish trainer, and licensed psychotherapist, agreed to offer a psychoeducational support group for BIPOC sex workers navigating the isolation and uncertainty of the pandemic—free of charge.

And the Black, Indigenous, and People of Color (BIPOC) Collective was born.

Sex workers and people who use drugs are not a monolith. In BIPOC Collective's first year, we discovered that 61 percent of Black, Indigenous, Latinx, Asian, queer, and trans sex workers who sought financial assistance worked in both the formal and informal sexual economies and that many of them were using more than four third-party platforms for work without earning enough to meet their basic needs. We confirmed that sex workers can have lots of followers and simultaneously be unhoused or housing insecure.

Thanks to the generosity of donors like you, BIPOC Collective provides financial assistance, peer support, and resource referrals for community members facing eviction, escaping violence, and navigating problems in the workplace. Sex workers and people who use drugs deserve to receive culturally concordant, compassionate, survivor-led care. Too often, doctors and mental health professionals blame sexual labor for mental health issues, dismiss complaints of chronic pain as drug seeking, and make assumptions surrounding the reliability of reported patient history. Dismantling racism, sexism, classism, homophobia, transphobia, fatphobia, whorephobia, and ableism at the hands of the Medical Industrial Complex is an essential part of survivor-led patient care.

BIPOC Collective seeks to build relationships with organizations and providers who are committed to decriminalizing sex work as a harm-reduction practice and will not force individuals to exit or rehash their trauma to get help. Mental health professionals and coaches interested in serving sex-working clients should consider taking classes through Sexual Health Alliance[2] or the Equitable Care Certification, an AASECT (American Association of Sexuality Educators, Counselors and Therapists) continuing education curriculum designed by QTPOC sex-working therapists, to increase the number of qualified individuals providing non-stigmatized care.[3] Additionally, mental health, psychiatric, and affordable prescription coverage through state and private insurance must be expanded so that anyone seeking life-affirming care can receive the support they need.

Additional ways to curate safer spaces for the larger community include

- ending federal restrictions on funding organizations that support decriminalizing prostitution and syringe exchange;

- applying gender justice when referring to sex workers and survivors of sexual violence;

- increasing access to fentanyl test strips, NARCAN, safe consumption spaces, and education to reduce the risk of accidental overdose;

- advocating for medically accurate, HIV, STI, and consent-based comprehensive sex education in schools;

- ending implicit bias and occupational discrimination by making sex work a protected class;

- codifying abortion rights, universal healthcare, and housing for all. Period.

Recidivism can be reduced by increasing record expungement and putting an end to exclusion from SNAP benefits, public housing, and federal student loans for those with prior prostitution and drug convictions. Mandatory HIV testing for prostitution sting arrests where no crime was committed and the arrests of minors in the sex trades under the guise of saving them must end.

There must also be an end to the conflation of sex work and trafficking by lawmakers, media, and nonprofits. Law enforcement and border patrol cannot be allowed to use funds earmarked for rescue efforts to entrap, arrest, or deport consensual workers. It is imperative to end the expansion of the definition of trafficking, which criminalizes nonexploitive third parties, including landlords, childcare providers, family members, and others who provide housing and support for sex workers.

Body Autonomy: Decolonizing Sex Work and Drug Use helps readers deepen their commitment to healing justice so they can begin to develop an understanding of how harm reduction can keep themselves, their loved ones, and their communities safe without increased policing or prisons. Intracommunal virtue signaling lacks empathy for our most vulnerable community members and creates a culture of fear that allows people to forget that survival, healing, and success under racial capitalism look different for everyone. This is a call to action: Love one another beyond the limits of what is considered socially or morally acceptable. Love is the antidote to fear-mongering and opens the door to radical, collective liberation.

Notes

FOREWORD

1. Ashley Montagu, "They Could Not Live Without the Love," European Institute of Perinatal Mental Health, accessed January 9, 2024, https://eipmh.com/they-could-not-live-without-the-love/.
2. Alexandra Benisek, "Touch Starvation: What to Know," Web MD, September 15, 2023, accessed January 10, 2024, https://www.webmd.com/balance/touch-starvation.
3. Eva Anagnostou-Laoutides and Michael B. Charles, "Herodotus on Sacred Marriage and Sacred Prostitution at Babylon", *Kernos* 31 (2018): 9–37, https://doi.org/10.4000/kernos.2653.
4. "Questions over state-funded sex care for people with a disability in Amsterdam," *Dutch News*, Jan 21 2022, accessed Jan 10, 2024, https://www.dutchnews.nl/2022/01/questions-over-state-funded-sex-care-for-people-with-a-disability-in-amsterdam/; Marguerite Ward, "The Surprising Way the Netherlands Is Helping Its Disabled Have Sex," *Mic*, March 13, 2014, https://www.mic.com/articles/85201/the-surprising-way-the-netherlands-is-helping-its-disabled-have-sex.
5. Ronald K. Siegel, *Intoxication: Life in Pursuit of Artificial Paradise* (New York: Dutton, 1989), 100.
6. Giorgio Samorini, *Animals and Psychedelics: The Natural World and the Instinct to Alter Consciousness* (Vermont: Park Street Press, 2002), 78.
7. Samorini, 87.
8. Silvia Federici, *Beyond the Periphery of the Skin: Rethinking, Remaking, and Reclaiming the Body in Contemporary Capitalism* (Oakland: PM Press, 2020), 11–12.

INTRODUCTION

1. In her book *Revolting Prostitutes*, Juno Mac defines carceral feminism as "feminism that welcomes police power." Juno Mac and Molly Smith, *Revolting Prostitutes: The Fight for Sex Workers' Rights*. (London: Verso, 2018).
2. Critical Resistance defines the prison industrial complex (PIC) as "a term we use to describe the overlapping interests of government and industry that use surveillance, policing, and imprisonment as solutions to economic, social and political problems." See "What Is the PIC? What Is Abolition?"

Critical Resistance, accessed March 20, 2020, https://criticalresistance.org/mission-vision/not-so-common-language/.

3. Michelle Alexander, *The New Jim Crow: Mass Incarceration in the Age of Color-blindness* (New York: The New Press, 2012).

4. Jennifer S. Forsyth, "The Constitution, Designed to Change, Rarely Does," *Wall Street Journal*, December 4, 2008, https://www.wsj.com/articles/SB122835767216478251.

5. Ismail Lourido Ali and Justice Rivera, "Colonization Laid the Groundwork for the Drug War," *The Fix*, April 11, 2018, accessed March 20, 2020, https://www.thefix.com/colonization-laid-groundwork-drug-war.

6. Healing Justice is a social justice concept and framework that was coined and crafted by Cara Page in the early 2000s: "Healing Justice means we all deserve to heal on our terms, and we confront oppressive systems that get in our way. We honor the trauma and resilience of generations that came before us and use interactive, daily practices that anyone can do. Healing Justice is a reminder to social movements that the concept of action should be expanded to support the self-determination, interdependence, resilience and resistance of those most impacted by oppression. Healing Justice is revolutionary in confronting the capitalist, colonial, individualistic paradigms that tell us we are alone when we seek out healing." "Healing Justice," TransformHarm, accessed March 20, 2020, https://transformharm.org/healing-justice/.

MECHANICS OF THE SEX TRADE: AN INTRODUCTION

1. Mark Koba, "$2 Trillion Underground Economy May Be Recovery's Savior," CNBC, April 24, 2013, accessed February 17, 2020, https://www.cnbc.com/id/100668336.

2. Michelle Rindels, "Indy Explains: How Legal Prostitution Works in Nevada," *Nevada Independent*, May 27, 2018, accessed February 17, 2020, https://thenevadaindependent.com/article/the-indy-explains-how-legal-prostitution-works-in-nevada.

3. Norman E. Zinberg, *Drug, Set, and Setting: The Basis for Controlled Intoxicant Use* (New Haven: Yale University Press, 1984).

4. Yes, I know that, by law, this is considered sex trafficking; however, age remains a push factor into the sex trade for minors. For more information on the realities of the sex trade for people under the age of 18, I recommend Alexandra Lutnick's book *Domestic Minor Sex Trafficking: Beyond Victims and Villains* (New York: Columbia University Press, 2016).

5. Erin Fitzgerald, Sarah Elspeth Patterson, and Darby Hickey with Cherno Biko and Harper Jean Tobin, *Meaningful Work: Transgender Experiences in the Sex Trade*, December 2015, accessed February 17, 2020, https://transequality.org/issues/resources/meaningful-work-transgender-experiences-in-the-sex-trade.

6. Janet Mock, *Redefining Realness: My Path to Womanhood, Identity, Love and So Much More* (New York: Atria Books, 2014).

7. Meredith Dank et al, *Surviving the Streets of New York: Experiences of LGBTQ Youth, YMSM, and YWSW Engaged in Survival Sex,* Urban Institute, February 2015, accessed February 17, 2020, https://www.urban.org/sites/default/files/publication/42186/2000119-Surviving-the-Streets-of-New-York.pdf.

8. "Individuals to Remember," Sex Workers Outreach Project, December 11, 2019, accessed February 17, 2020, https://december17.swopusa.org/individuals/.

9. "Prostitution in Home Put Children at Risk Even if They Were Not Witnesses," American Bar Association, Child Law Practice Today, June 1, 2013, accessed February 17, 2020, https://www.americanbar.org/groups/public_interest/child_law/resources/child_law_practiceonline/child_law_practice/vol_32/june-2013/prostitution-in-home-put-children-at-risk-even-if-they-were-not-/.

10. Sadie Nicholas, "Why More and More Women Are Losing Custody Battles over Their Children," *Daily Mail* (UK), Femail, June 5, 2008, accessed February 17, 2020, https://www.dailymail.co.uk/femail/article-1024304/Why-more-women-losing-custody-battles-children.html.

11. Beth Avery and Han Lu, "Ban the Box: U.S. Cities, Counties, and States Adopt Fair Hiring Policies," National Employment Law Project, Toolkit, October 1, 2021, https://www.nelp.org/publication/ban-the-box-fair-chance-hiring-state-and-local-guide/.

12. These enhancements vary from place to place. When I worked at Prax(us), one of my participants was given a felony after five prostitution charges in one county. See Tim Dees, reply to "Are there a certain number of misdemeanors that equal a felony?," Quora, September 14, 2015, https://www.quora.com/Are-there-a-certain-number-of-misdemeanors-that-equal-a-felony.

13. "Five Important Facts About America's Mass Incarceration Problem," Civil Survival, News, July 16, 2018, accessed February 17, 2020, https://civilsurvival.org/five-important-facts-about-americas-mass-incarceration-problem/.

14. Monica Llorente, "Criminalizing Poverty Through Fines, Fees, and Costs," American Bar Association, October 3, 2016, accessed February 17, 2020, https://www.americanbar.org/groups/litigation/committees/childrens-rights/articles/2016/criminalizing-poverty-fines-fees-costs/.

15. Global Network of Sex Work Projects (NSWP), "Policy Brief: The Impact of Anti-trafficking Legislation and Initiatives on Sex Workers," January 29, 2019, accessed February 17, 2020, https://www.nswp.org/resource/policy-brief-the-impact-anti-trafficking-legislation-and-initiatives-sex-workers.

16. Mac and Smith, *Revolting Prostitutes.*

17. "The Prevalence of Labor Trafficking in the United States," National Institute of Justice, February 26, 2013, accessed February 17, 2020, https://nij.ojp.gov/topics/articles/prevalence-labor-trafficking-united-states.

18. The Sex Worker Advocates Coalition, "Sex Workers Need Housing, Not

Handcuffs," HIPS DC, March 6, 2019, accessed February 17, 2020, https://medium.com/@hipsdc/sex-workers-need-housing-not-handcuffs-7fc057d278a9.

19. Andrew Bloomenthal, "Can a Family Survive on the US Minimum Wage?" Investopedia, November 10, 2022, https://www.investopedia.com/articles/personal-finance/022615/can-family-survive-us-minimum-wage.asp.

20. Jamiles Lartey, "Median Wealth of Black Americans 'Will Fall to Zero by 2053', Warns New Report," *Guardian*, September 13, 2017, accessed February 17, 2020, https://www.theguardian.com/inequality/2017/sep/13/median-wealth-of-black-americans-will-fall-to-zero-by-2053-warns-new-report.

21. Jasmine Sankofa, "From Margin to Center: Sex Work Decriminalization Is a Racial Justice Issue," Amnesty International, accessed February 17, 2020, https://www.amnestyusa.org/from-margin-to-center-sex-work-decriminalization-is-a-racial-justice-issue/.

22. Eleanor Busby, "Students Are Turning to Sex Work for Extra Money but Experts Warn Universities Are Ignoring the Issue," *Independent*, December 26, 2018, accessed February 17, 2020, https://www.independent.co.uk/news/education/education-news/students-sex-work-prostitution-webcam-university-tuition-fees-education-a8614186.html.

23. Refer to the epilogue of my memoir, *Candy Coated*, to see the impacts of SESTA/FOSTA.

24. Karol Markowicz, "Congress' Awful Anti-Sex-Trafficking Law Has Only Put Sex Workers in Danger and Wasted Taxpayer Money," Insider, July 14, 2019, accessed February 17, 2020, https://www.businessinsider.com/fosta-sesta-anti-sex-trafficking-law-has-been-failure-opinion-2019-7.

25. "COYOTE-RI Impact Survey Results—2018," SWOP Seattle Organizing Meeting, accessed February 15, 2022, http://www.swop-seattle.org/wp-content/uploads/2018/11/COYOTE-Survey-Results-2018.pdf.

26. Jessica Heslam, "Survivor Fought Her Way Out," *Boston Herald*, March 13, 2017, https://www.bostonherald.com/2017/03/13/survivor-fought-her-way-out/.

27. Iris Marion Young, "Five Faces of Oppression," chapter 2 in *Justice and the Politics of Difference* (Princeton, New Jersey: Princeton University Press, 2011), 39–65, https://doi.org/10.2307/j.ctvcm4g4q.

28. For a more information on trafficking, refer to the "Realities of Trafficking" interview in the next section.

29. Trafficking Victims Protection Act of 2000 (TVPA), Pub. L. No. 106–386 (2000).

30. Brandn Green et al, "Safe Harbor Laws: Changing the Legal Response to Minors Involved in Commercial Sex: Phase 3, The Qualitative Analysis," Development Services Group, Inc., December 2018, https://www.ncjrs.gov/pdffiles1/ojjdp/grants/253244.pdf.

31. Young Women's Empowerment Project, "Girls Do What They Have to Do to Survive: Illuminating Methods Used by Girls in the Sex Trade and Street Economy to Fight Back and Heal," 2009, https://ywepchicago.files.wordpress.com/2011/06/

girls-do-what-they-have-to-do-to-survive-a-study-of-resilience-and-resistance
.pdf.

32. Referring to the movie *Taken* with Liam Neeson.

33. Sarah Fader, "What Abusers Hope We Never Learn About Traumatic Bonding," Better Help, accessed February 17, 2020, https://www.betterhelp.com/advice/trauma/what-abusers-hope-we-never-learn-about-traumatic-bonding/.

34. Lilly Yu et al, "Alternative Forms of Justice for Human Trafficking Survivors: Considering Procedural, Restorative, and Transitional Justice," Urban Institute, March 2018, https://www.urban.org/sites/default/files/publication/97341/alternative_forms_of_justice_for_human_trafficking_survivors.pdf.

35. Elizabeth Nolan Brown, "America's Newest War," *Politico* Magazine, Law and Order, June 1, 2015, https://www.politico.com/magazine/story/2015/06/justice-for-victims-of-sex-trafficking-war-on-crime-118512/.

36. Melissa Gira Grant, "Liberal Feminism Has a Sex Work Problem," the *New Republic*, October 24, 2019, https://newrepublic.com/article/155481/liberal-feminism-sex-work-problem.

37. Sex Workers Outreach Project, "Good Samaritan Law Expansion Toolkit: Strategies to Bring Immunity to Sex Workers Who Seek Help in the case of an Overdose," 2016, https://www.swopusa.org/wp-content/uploads/2016/11/Good-Samaritan-Expansion-Kit-for-Sex-Work.pdf.

38. Young Women's Empowerment Project, "Girls Do What They Have to Do to Survive."

39. "Gary Ridgway," Biography, accessed February 19, 2020, https://www.biography.com/crime-figure/gary-ridgway.

40. Zhana Vrangalova, PhD, "Do Sex Workers Have More Mental Health Problems?" *Psychology Today*, October 30, 2014, https://www.psychologytoday.com/us/blog/strictly-casual/201410/do-sex-workers-have-more-mental-health-problems.

41. Bella Chudakov et al, "The Motivation and Mental Health of Sex Workers," *Journal of Sex and Marital Therapy* 28, issue 4 (2002): 305–315, https://doi.org/10.1080/00926230290001439.

42. Find an event near you through SWOP USA's database at https://december17.swopusa.org/.

43. See "Exploitation Is to Sex Work as Overdose Is to Drug Use" in Section 2.

44. Dan Vergano, "This Was the Decade Drug Overdoses Killed Nearly Half a Million Americans," *BuzzFeed* News, December 6, 2019, https://www.buzzfeednews.com/article/danvergano/opioid-overdose-decade-war-on-drugs.

45. Jack Lamson, "New York Numbers Show a Significant Drop in Opioid Overdose Deaths," CBS 6 Albany, December 10, 2019, https://cbs6albany.com/news/local/state-numbers-show-significant-drop-in-opioid-overdose-deaths.

46. The lesson being that public health and human rights–based approaches have better outcomes than criminal justice ones. Prevention and harm reduction are useful in the sex trade, but treatment is a misnomer since sex work is not a disease,

so it is important for me to clarify that treatment is not a pillar of a human rights–based approach to the sex trade. For more information, refer to "Compassion, Not Criminalization" in Section 3.

47. Emani Walks, "The Paradox of Policing as Protection: A Harm Reduction Approach to Prostitution Using Safe Injection Sites as a Guide," *Duke Journal of Gender Law and Policy* 26, issue 157 (2019): 157–180, https://scholarship.law.duke.edu/cgi/viewcontent.cgi?referer=&httpsredir=1&article=1340&context=djglp.

48. Check out prostitution.procon.org for a list of federal and state charges—most people are charged for solicitation on city and county levels, though, so you will have to google your local laws for the most accurate information.

49. Andrea J. Ritchie and Brit Schulte, "Anti-Prostitution Ordinance Promotes Racial Profiling in Chicago," *Truthout*, July 24, 2018, https://truthout.org/articles/anti-prostitution-ordinance-promotes-racial-profiling-in-chicago/.

50. Tim Craig, "D.C. 'Prostitution-Free Zones' Probably Unconstitutional, Attorney General's Office Says," *Washington Post*, D.C. Politics, January 24, 2012, https://www.washingtonpost.com/local/dc-politics/districts-prostitution-free-zones-likely-unconstitutional-ags-office-says/2012/01/24/gIQAe3qNOQ_story.html.

51. Sara Jean Green, "Name Change for Prostitution Charge in Seattle Brings Errors in Background Checks," *Seattle Times*, June 14, 2017, https://www.seattletimes.com/seattle-news/crime/name-change-for-prostitution-charge-in-seattle-brings-errors-in-background-checks/.

52. "About Us," Demand Abolition, accessed February 19, 2020, https://www.demandabolition.org/about-us/.

53. Emi Koyama, "'End Demand' Policies Toward Prostitution *Increase* Supply: An Insight from Development Economics," Eminism.org, August 30, 2012, http://eminism.org/blog/entry/340.

54. Global Network of Sex Work Projects, "The Impact of 'End Demand' Legislation on Women Sex Workers," 2018, https://www.nswp.org/sites/nswp.org/files/pb_impact_of_end_demand_on_women_sws_nswp_-_2018.pdf.

55. Jane and I served on the board of SWOP USA together 2018–2019. She has given me permission to tell this story.

56. Fabian Luis Fernandez, "Hands Up: A Systematized Review of Policing Sex Workers in the U.S.," (master's thesis, Yale University, 2016), http://elischolar.library.yale.edu/ysphtdl/1085.

57. "Police Interactions Linked to Increased Risk of Client Violence for Female Sex Workers," Johns Hopkins School of Public Health, December 20, 2018, accessed February 19, 2020, https://www.jhsph.edu/news/news-releases/2018/police-interactions-linked-to-increased-risk-of-client-violence-for-female-sex-workers.html.

58. Elizabeth Nolan Brown, "Sex Work and Civil Asset Forfeiture Increasingly

Go Hand in Hand," *Reason*, August 28, 2015, https://reason.com/2015/08/28/asset-forfeiture-for-sex-workers/.

59. Margaret H. Wurth et al, "Condoms as evidence of prostitution in the United States and the criminalization of sex work," *Journal of the International AIDS Society* 16, 1 (2013), https://doi.org/10.7448/IAS.16.1.18626.

60. Walks, "The Paradox of Policing as Protection."

61. Unfortunately, this information isn't public.

62. Meagan Morris et al., "Prostitution and Denver's Criminal Justice System: Who Pays?" Laboratory to Combat Human Trafficking, February 2012, https://combathumantrafficking.org/our-research/who-pays/.

63. Global Health Justice Partnership of the Yale Law School and Yale School of Public Health, "Diversion from Justice: A Rights-Based Analysis of Local 'Prostitution Diversion Programs' and Their Impacts on People in the Sex Sector in the United States," September 2018, https://law.yale.edu/sites/default/files/area/center/ghjp/documents/diversion_from_justice_pdp_report_ghjp_2018rev.pdf.

64. Thomas Shevory, *Notorious H.I.V.: The Media Spectacle of Nushawn Williams* (Minneapolis: University of Minnesota Press, 2004).

65. *Victims of Crime Act Victim Compensation Grant Program*, FR Doc. 01-12256 (May 16, 2001), https://www.federalregister.gov/documents/2001/05/16/01-12256/victims-of-crime-act-victim-compensation-grant-program.

66. "Crime Victim Compensation: An Overview," National Association of Crime Victim Compensation Boards, accessed February 19, 2020, http://www.nacvcb.org/index.asp?bid=14.

67. "Rape Shield Statutes," National District Attorney's Association, March 2011, https://ndaa.org/wp-content/uploads/NCPCA-Rape-Shield-2011.pdf.

68. Walks, "The Paradox of Policing as Protection."

CASUALTIES OF WAR: THE WARS ON DRUGS AND TRAFFICKING

1. Carol S. Steiker, "Lessons from Two Failures: Sentencing for Cocaine and Child Pornography Under the Federal Sentencing Guidelines in the United States," *Law and Contemporary Problems* 76 (2013): 27–52, https://scholarship.law.duke.edu/lcp/vol76/iss1/32.

2. "Mandatory Minimums in a Nutshell," Families Against Mandatory Minimums, April 26, 2012, https://famm.org/wp-content/uploads/FS-MMs-in-a-Nutshell.pdf.

3. Melissa Gira Grant, "Trafficking from the Top Down: Why Prop 35 Passed and What It Means," Melissa Gira Grant (blog), November 7, 2012, https://melissagiragrant.com/trafficking-from-the-top-down-why-prop-35-passed-and-what-it-means/.

4. A third-party charge that is essentially assistant pimping or arranging prostitution.

5. Dara Lind, "How Police Can Take Your Stuff, Sell It, and Pay for Armored Cars

with the Money," *Vox*, March 28, 2016, https://www.vox.com/2014/10/14/6969335/civil-asset-forfeiture-what-is-how-work-equitable-sharing-police-seizure.

6. "Asset Forfeiture," Arizona State University, Watts College of Public Service and Community Solutions, accessed February 3, 2022, https://popcenter.asu.edu/content/asset-forfeiture-print-full-guide.

7. "New York State Assembly Bill S1379/A2305," Sexworkers Project, accessed February 3, 2022, https://sexworkersproject.org/campaigns/2011/new-york-condom-bill/.

8. Wurth et al., "Condoms as evidence of prostitution in the United States and the criminalization of sex work."

9. Matt Fisher, "A History of the Ban on Federal Funding for Syringe Exchange Programs," Center for Strategic and International Studies, February 7, 2012, https://www.csis.org/blogs/smart-global-health/history-ban-federal-funding-syringe-exchange-programs.

10. Hal Rogers and Daniel Raymond, "Congress Ends Ban on Funding for Needle Exchange Programs," interview by Audie Cornish, *All Things Considered*, NPR, January 8, 2016, https://www.npr.org/2016/01/08/462412631/congress-ends-ban-on-federal-funding-for-needle-exchange-programs?t=1700486108745.

11. "End the Ban: Help Us End the Ban on the Use of Federal Funds for Syringe Services Programs!" amfAR, In the Community, February 27, 2013, accessed February 3, 2022, https://www.amfar.org/articles/in-the-community/2013/end-the-ban/.

12. Kate Zen, "Lonely Little Red Umbrella: Sex Workers' Rights in the Anti-Prostitution Loyalty Pledge Hearing," *Tits and Sass*, June 20, 2013, https://titsandsass.com/lonely-little-red-umbrella-sex-workers-rights-in-the-anti-prostitution-loyalty-pledge-hearing/.

13. Alexander, *The New Jim Crow*.

14. Vicky Peláez, "The Prison Industry in the United States: Big Business or a New Form of Slavery?" *Global Research*, March 10, 2008, updated September 28, 2023, https://www.globalresearch.ca/the-prison-industry-in-the-united-states-big-business-or-a-new-form-of-slavery/8289.

15. "No Simple Solutions: State Violence and the Sex Trades," INCITE!, April 22, 2011, https://incite-national.org/2011/04/22/no-simple-solutions-state-violence-and-the-sex-trades/.

16. Jenna Diamond, "NYC Trafficking," Red Umbrella Project (blog), March 1, 2018, https://redumbrellaproject.org/advocate/nyhtic/.

17. Global Alliance Against Trafficking in Women, *Collateral Damage: The Impact of Anti-Trafficking Measures on Human Rights around the World*, December 18, 2007, https://gaatw.org/Collateral_Damage_Final/singlefile_CollateralDamage-final.pdf.

18. Caty Simon, "For Their Own Good: SWOP-Phoenix's Campaign Against Diversion Initiatives," *Tits and Sass*, November 12, 2013, https://titsandsass.com/for-their-own-good-swop-phoenixs-campaign-against-diversion-intiatives/.

19. Sunnivie Brydum, "Arizona Activist Found Guilty of 'Walking While Trans,'"

Advocate, April 15, 2014, https://www.advocate.com/politics/transgender/2014/04 /15/arizona-activist-found-guilty-walking-while-trans.

20. Morris et al., "Prostitution and Denver's Criminal Justice System: Who Pays?"

21. "How to Eliminate Demand," Demand Abolition, November 4, 2020, https:// www.demandabolition.org/end-demand-for-sexual-exploitation/how-to -eliminate-demand/.

WARS ON BODILY AUTONOMY: A TIMELINE

1. Timothy J. Gilfoyle, *City of Eros: New York City, Prostitution, and the Commercialization of Sex, 1790–1920* (New York: W. W. Norton and Company, 1992).

2. Laura McTighe and Deon Haywood, "'There Is NO Justice in Louisiana': Crimes Against Nature and the Spirit of Black Feminist Resistance," *Souls* 19, no 3 (2017): 261–285, https://doi.org/10.1080/10999949.2017.1389584.

3. "Convict Lease System," *Digital History*, ID 3179, accessed June 11, 2020, http:// www.digitalhistory.uh.edu/disp_textbook.cfm?smtid=2&psid=3179.

4. Jeffrey A. Miron and Chris Feige, "The Opium Wars, Opium Legalization, and Opium Consumption in China," National Bureau of Economic Research, NBER Working Paper Series, May 2005, https://www.nber.org/papers/w11355.pdf.

5. Diana L. Ahmad, "Opium smoking, anti-Chinese attitudes, and the American medical community, 1850–1890," *American Nineteenth Century History* 1, issue 2 (2000): 53–68, https://doi.org/10.1080/14664650008567016.

6. Kathryn Krase, "History of Forced Sterilization and Current U.S. Abuses," Our Bodies Ourselves, Politics of Women's Health, Book Excerpts, October 1, 2014, accessed August 13, 2020, https://www.ourbodiesourselves.org/book-excerpts/ health-article/forced-sterilization/.

7. Jacob Sullum, "Three Bouts of Meth Hysteria Illustrate the Politics of Panics and the Need for Speed," *Forbes*, May 8, 2014, accessed August 13, 2020, https:// www.forbes.com/sites/jacobsullum/2014/05/08/three-bouts-of-meth-hysteria-illustrate-the-politics-of-panics-and-the-need-for-speed/#21a71fb43932.

8. Amanda Sawyer, "The Reservation," *Waco History*, accessed August 13, 2020, https://wacohistory.org/items/show/93.

9. William L. Hewitt, "Wicked Traffic in Girls: Prostitution and Reform in Sioux City, 1885–1910," *The Annals of Iowa* 51, issue 2 (1991): 123–148, https://doi.org /10.17077/0003-4827.9577.

10. Bart Elmore, "What Coke's Cocaine Problem Can Tell Us About Coca-Cola Capitalism," Oxford University Press (blog), March 21, 2014, https://blog.oup .com/2014/03/coke-cocaine-coca-cola-capitalism-business-strategy/.

11. "Alaska's Old Red Light District: Ketchikan, Alaska," YMT Vacations, accessed August 13, 2020, https://www.ymtvacations.com/travel-blog/ bootleggers-and-brothels-alaskas-old-red-light-district.

12. Melissa Hope Ditmore, *Encyclopedia of Prostitution and Sex Work*, vol. 1, *A–N* (Westport, Connecticut: Greenwood, 2006).

13. Sarah Laskow, "Most American Cities Once Had Red-Light Districts," *Atlas Obscura*, March 15, 2017, https://www.atlasobscura.com/articles/red-light-districts -united-states.

14. Lisa Ko, "Unwanted Sterilization and Eugenics Programs in the United States," PBS, *Independent Lens*, January 29, 2016, accessed August 14, 2020, https:// www.pbs.org/independentlens/blog/unwanted-sterilization-and-eugenics -programs-in-the-united-states/.

15. "The Mann Act," PBS, *Unforgivable Blackness: The Rise and Fall of Jack Johnson*, accessed August 14, 2020, https://www.pbs.org/kenburns/unforgivable-blackness/ mann-act/.

16. "The Nation's First Marijuana Raid Likely Happened in Los Angeles," *LAist* 89.3, KPCC-FM, September 19, 2014, https://www.kpcc.org/programs/offramp /2014/09/19/39399/the-nation-s-first-marijuana-raid-likely-happened/.

17. "National Motor Vehicle Theft Act Law and Legal Definition," USLegal.com, https://definitions.uslegal.com/n/national-motor-vehicle-theft-act/.

18. Johnson Hur, "History of the Television," *BeBusinessed*, History, accessed August 17, 2020, https://bebusinessed.com/history/history-of-the-television/.

19. Bud Fairy, "How Marijuana Became Illegal," Ozarkia.net, accessed August 17, 2020, http://www.ozarkia.net/bill/pot/blunderof37.html.

20. Johann Hari, "Afterword: The Opposite of Addiction Is Connection," in *Chasing the Scream: The First and Last Days of the War on Drugs* (New York: Bloomsbury Publishing, 2018), 299.

21. Katherine Andrews, "The Dark History of Forced Sterilization of Latina Women," *Panoramas Scholarly Platform*, October 30, 2017, accessed August 17, 2020, https://www.panoramas.pitt.edu/health-and-society/dark -history-forced-sterilization-latina-women.

22. Johann Hari, "The Hunting of Billie Holiday," *Politico*, History Dept., January 17, 2015, https://www.politico.com/magazine/story/2015/01/drug-war-the -hunting-of-billie-holiday-114298.

23. Sofia Barrett-Ibarria, "BSDM Can Provide Profound Healing Experiences," *Vice*, Health, August 29, 2017, https://www.vice.com/en/article/nee9yg/ bsdm-can-provide-profound-healing-experiences.

24. Lukasz Kamienski, "The Drugs That Built a Super Soldier," *The Atlantic*, Health, April 8, 2016, https://www.theatlantic.com/health/archive/2016/04/ the-drugs-that-built-a-super-soldier/477183/.

25. Patrick H. Hughes et al., "The Natural History of a Heroin Epidemic," *American Journal of Public Health* 62, no 7 (July 1972): 995–1001, https://doi.org/10.2105/ AJPH.62.7.995.

26. "A Social History of America's Most Popular Drugs," PBS, *Frontline*, Drug Wars,

accessed August 18, 2020, https://www.pbs.org/wgbh/pages/frontline/shows/drugs/buyers/socialhistory.html.

27. *Robinson v. California*, 370 U.S. 660 (1962), https://supreme.justia.com/cases/federal/us/370/660/.

28. Melinda Chateauvert, *Sex Workers Unite: A History of the Movement from Stonewall to SlutWalk* (Boston: Beacon Press, 2013).

29. Neal Broverman, "Don't Let History Forget About Compton's Cafeteria Riot," *Advocate*, August 2, 2018, https://www.advocate.com/transgender/2018/8/02/dont-let-history-forget-about-comptons-cafeteria-riot.

30. Hana Muslic, "A Brief History of Nonprofit Organizations (And What We Can Learn)," *Nonprofit Hub*, October 27, 2017, https://nonprofithub.org/a-brief-history-of-nonprofit-organizations/.

31. "Thirty Years of America's Drug War," PBS, *Frontline*, Drug Wars, accessed August 20, 2020, https://www.pbs.org/wgbh/pages/frontline/shows/drugs/cron/.

32. Chateauvert, *Sex Workers Unite*.

33. "Chicago Police Torture," People's Law Office, Issues and Case Updates, accessed August 20, 2020, https://peopleslawoffice.com/issues-and-cases/chicago-police-torture/.

34. Lynn Arditi, "Behind Closed Doors: How R.I. Decriminalized Prostitution," *The Providence Journal*, Rhode Island News, May 31, 2009, accessed August 20, 2020, http://www.projo.com/news/content/PROSTITUTION_LAW31_05-31-09_NVEHGBH_v161.3e90048.html.

35. Wikipedia, s.v. "United States federal budget," accessed August 22, 2020, https://en.wikipedia.org/wiki/United_States_federal_budget#/media/File:US_Federal_Outlay_and_GDP_linear_graph.svg.

36. Elizabeth Wilson, "The Context of 'Between Pleasure and Danger': The Barnard Conference on Sexuality," *Feminist Review* 13, issue 1 (March 1983): 35–41, https://doi.org/10.1057/fr.1983.5.

37. Ronald J. Ostrow, "Meese Panel Asks Porn Crackdown: Sexually Violent Materials and Actions Connected, Commission Concludes," *Los Angeles Times*, World & Nation, July 10, 1986, accessed August 24, 2020, https://www.latimes.com/archives/la-xpm-1986-07-10-mn-22453-story.html.

38. "About Us," Drug Policy Alliance, History of DPA, accessed August 24, 2020, https://www.drugpolicy.org/about-us#history-of-dpa.

39. Wanda Fowler, "Syringe Services Programs: A Proven Public Health Strategy," The Council of State Governments, September 28, 2010, accessed August 24, 2020, https://knowledgecenter.csg.org/kc/content/syringe-services-programs-proven-public-health-strategy.

40. "Overdose Prevention," National Harm Reduction Coalition, Harm Reduction Issues, accessed August 24, 2020, https://harmreduction.org/issues/overdose-prevention/.

41. "Heidi Fleiss," *Biography*, Notorious Figures, accessed August 24, 2020, https://www.biography.com/personality/heidi-fleiss.

42. "Weekly News in Review," *DrugSense Weekly* #215, August 31, 2001, http://www.drugsense.org/dscgi/dispn.pl/2001/ds01.n215.html#sec2.

43. Uniting and Strengthening America by Providing Appropriate Tools Required to Intercept and Obstruct Terrorism (USA PATRIOT ACT) Act of 2001, Pub. L. 107-56 (2001).

44. Charlie Savage, "U.S. Transfers First Guantánamo Detainee Under Trump, Who Vowed to Fill It," *New York Times*, May 2, 2017, https://www.nytimes.com/2018/05/02/us/politics/guantanamo-detainee-transferred-trump-al-darbi.html.

45. Peter Taylor, "'Vomiting and Screaming' in Destroyed Waterboarding Tapes," *BBC News*, May 9, 2012, https://www.bbc.com/news/world-us-canada-17990955.

46. "Poll: Talk First, Fight Later," *CBS News*, CBS News Polls, January 24, 2003, accessed April 23, 2020, http://www.cbsnews.com/stories/2003/01/23/opinion/polls/main537739.shtml.

47. "CMEA (Combat Methamphetamine Epidemic Act of 2005)," US Department of Justice, Drug Enforcement Administration, Diversion Control Division, accessed April 12, 2020, https://www.deadiversion.usdoj.gov/meth/.

48. Craig, "D.C. 'Prostitution-Free Zones' Probably Unconstitutional."

49. Justice Rivera, "Weed Washing," *Reframe Health and Justice*, May 21, 2020, https://reframehealthandjustice.medium.com/weed-washing-2757d4b5ffeb.

50. Bella Robinson and Elena Shih, "The History of Sex Work Law in Rhode Island," *Uprise RI*, Civil Rights, November 20, 2019, https://upriseri.com/2019-11-20-sex-work/.

51. Derek Thompson, "Occupy the World: The '99 Percent' Movement Goes Global," *The Atlantic*, Business, October 15, 2011, https://www.theatlantic.com/business/archive/2011/10/occupy-the-world-the-99-percent-movement-goes-global/246757/.

52. "Herstory," Black Lives Matter, accessed September 1, 2020, https://blacklivesmatter.com/herstory/.

53. Eric Steuer, "The Rise and Fall of RedBook, the Site That Sex Workers Couldn't Live Without," *Wired*, Business, December 21, 2015, https://www.wired.com/2015/12/the-rise-and-fall-of-redbook/.

54. Alia Chughtai and Christian Mugarura Mafigiri, "Know Their Names: Black People Killed by the Police in the US," *Al Jazeera*, accessed September 1, 2020, https://interactive.aljazeera.com/aje/2020/know-their-names/index.html.

HUMAN TRAFFICKING: THE BIGGER PICTURE

1. Find more information online at iamwomankind.org.

2. These diversion programs conflate sex work with trafficking and mandate that

both survivors and sex workers (which they see as the same thing) complete counseling and classes to expunge prostitution records. There are 12 counties with HT intervention courts in current operation across New York State, and they are touted as a criminal justice reform intervention, but the question remains: why would people who are seen as victims have to work away records connected to their victimization? For more about diversion with people in the sex trade, see the article "GHJP Releases Reports on Prostitution 'Diversion' Programs" (Yale Law School, September 17, 2018, accessed May 6, 2020, https://law.yale.edu/yls-today/news/ghjp-releases-reports-prostitution-diversion-programs).

3. This campaign's mission is to decriminalize, decarcerate, and destigmatize the sex trades in New York City and State. For more information, visit https://linktr.ee/decrimny.

4. Freedom Network USA is the largest coalition of survivors, service providers, and law enforcement working to address trafficking in the United States. Find more online at freedomnetworkusa.org.

5. Find more about Red Canary Song online at https://www.redcanarysong.net/.

6. The Audre Lorde Project (ALP) is an organizing project for Lesbian, Gay, Bisexual, Two Spirit, Trans, and Gender Non-Conforming People of Color in the New York City area. Check them out online at alp.org.

7. For more on end-demand, see "Mechanics of the Sex Trade: An Introduction" in Section 1.

8. For more on anti-prostitution pledges, see "Mechanics of the Sex Trade: An Introduction" in Section 1.

9. For example, someone working in an exploitative massage establishment may make the decision to also offer sexual services for extra money. So even if the issue they need addressed is the fact that they were being exploited or were facing violence by their employer, law enforcement is obsessed with the fact that they were "prostituting."

10. Sam Levin, "What Does 'Defund the Police' Mean? The Rallying Cry Sweeping the US—Explained," *Guardian*, News, June 6, 2020, https://www.theguardian.com/us-news/2020/jun/05/defunding-the-police-us-what-does-it-mean.

11. "Trafficking in Persons Report," US Department of State, https://www.state.gov/trafficking-in-persons-report/.

12. There are tons of articles and reports that support this, including "The False Promise of 'End Demand' Laws" by Sebastian Kohn (The Open Society Foundations, Voices, June 2, 2017, https://www.opensocietyfoundations.org/voices/false-promise-end-demand-laws).

13. For more information on Transformative Justice, start with "Transformative Justice: A Brief Description" by Mia Mingus (TransformHarm.org, Transformative Justice, January 11, 2019, https://transformharm.org/transformative-justice-a-brief-description/).

ABOLITION MEANS NO MORE POLICING

1. Saidiya V. Hartman, *Scenes of Subjection: Terror, Slavery, and Self-Making in Nineteenth-Century America* (New York: Oxford University Press, 1997).
2. Safiya Bukhari, *The War Before: The True Life Story of Becoming a Black Panther, Keeping the Faith in Prison, and Fighting for Those Left Behind* (New York: The Feminist Press, 2010).
3. Saidiya Hartman, *Wayward Lives, Beautiful Experiments: Intimate Histories of Social Upheaval* (New York: W. W. Norton and Company, 2019).
4. Dorothy Roberts, *Torn Apart: How the Child Welfare System Destroys Black Families—And How Abolition Can Build a Safer World* (New York: Basic Books: New York, 2022).
5. Jonathan J. Cooper, "Strangers' Suspicions Rankle Parents of Mixed-Race Children," *Associated Press*, February 13, 2019, https://apnews.com/article/9e73ee4106c74188b643f91c7ed59157.
6. Generation FIVE, *Ending Child Sexual Abuse: A Transformative Justice Handbook*, Generative Somatics, Resources, Reports and Research, June 2017, https://generativesomatics.org/wp-content/uploads/2019/10/Transformative-Justice-Handbook.pdf.
7. "What Is the PIC? What Is Abolition?" Critical Resistance, accessed March 20, 2020, https://criticalresistance.org/mission-vision/not-so-common-language/.

EXPLOITATION IS TO SEX WORK AS OVERDOSE IS TO DRUG USE

1. Check out the Harm Reduction Coalition at www.harmreduction.org for more information on the origins and philosophy of harm reduction.
2. Natasha Bach, "Opioid Overdoses Kill More Each Year in the US than Auto Accidents," World Economic Forum, January 17, 2019, https://www.weforum.org/agenda/2019/01/opioid-overdoses-now-claim-more-u-s-lives-than-auto-accidents/.
3. Thomas Kerr, Sanjana Mitra, Mary Clare Kennedy, and Ryan McNeil, "Supervised Injection Facilities in Canada: Past, Present, and Future," *Harm Reduction Journal* 14, issue 1 (2017), https://doi.org/10.1186%2Fs12954-017-0154-1.
4. Deborah J. Vagins and Jesselyn McCurdy, *Cracks in the System: Twenty Years of the Unjust Federal Crack Cocaine Law*, American Civil Liberties Union, October 26, 2006, https://www.aclu.org/other/cracks-system-20-years-unjust-federal-crack-cocaine-law.
5. "Race and the Drug War: Hundreds to Gather at Columbia University in New York City for Historic Strategy Session on the Eve of the UN Special Assembly on Drugs," Drug Policy Alliance, Press Release, April 12, 2016, https://drugpolicy.org/issues/race-and-drug-war.
6. Marisa Gerber, "Crackdown on Pimps Fuels a Rise in Human Trafficking Charges

in L. A. County," *Los Angeles Times*, Local, California, November 27, 2015, https://www.latimes.com/local/california/la-me-sex-trafficking-20151127-story.html.

7. Sarah Anne Hughes, "Advocates Rally in Support of Repealing Prostitution Free Zones in D.C.," *DCist*, April 11, 2014, https://dcist.com/story/14/04/11/advocates-rally-in-support-of-repea/.

8. Emily Shugerman, "Department of Homeland Security Agents Paid to Have Sex with Alleged Sex Trafficking Victims They 'Rescued,'" *Daily Beast*, December 23, 2019, https://www.thedailybeast.com/department-of-homeland-security-agents-paid-to-have-sex-with-alleged-sex-trafficking-victims-they-rescued.

9. "COYOTE-RI Impact Survey Results—2018," SWOP Seattle Organizing Meeting.

10. Check out the chapter "Overview of Harm Reduction in the Sex Trade" in Section 3 to learn more about these interventions.

11. Ashley Nellis, PhD, "The Color of Justice: Racial and Ethnic Disparity in State Prisons," The Sentencing Project, Research, Resource Library, Reports, October 13, 2021, https://www.sentencingproject.org/publications/color-of-justice-racial-and-ethnic-disparity-in-state-prisons/.

STIMULANT STIGMA: WITHOUT SIMPLE SOLUTIONS, PUNISHMENT AND INEQUITY PERSIST

1. This is the umbrella term for anything that acts like an opiate. Opiates come from opium and are naturally occurring; however, opioids include synthetic drugs that mimic naturally occurring opiates.

2. National Institute on Drug Abuse, "Effective Treatments for Opioid Addiction," November 1, 2016, accessed November 20, 2023, https://archives.nida.nih.gov/publications/effective-treatments-opioid-addiction.

3. Taylor N. Santoro and Jonathan D. Santoro, "Racial Bias in the US Opioid Epidemic: A Review of the History of Systemic Bias and Implications for Care," *Cureus* 10, issue 12 (December 2010), https://doi.org/10.7759%2Fcureus.3733.

4. M. Lerman, "Building on CARA and 21st Century Cures," NASTAD, October 17, 2017, accessed February 21, 2020, https://www.nastad.org/resource/building-cara-and-21st-century-cures.

5. "Addiction Among Different Races," Sunrise House, accessed March 12, 2020, https://sunrisehouse.com/addiction-demographics/different-races/.

6. I have intentionally chosen to use this word to reclaim it for Mesoamerican people after the racist anti-marijuana smear campaigns of the 1930s that warned about the dangers of "Mexican devil weed."

7. Janell Ross, "Legal Marijuana Made Big Promises on Racial Equity—And Fell Short," NBC News, December 31, 2018, https://www.nbcnews.com/news/nbcblk/legal-marijuana-made-big-promises-racial-equity-fell-short-n952376.

8. Martha Bebinger, "Opioid Addiction Drug Going Mostly to Whites, Even as Black Death Rate Rises," *All Things Considered*, May 8, 2019, https://www.npr

.org/sections/health-shots/2019/05/08/721447601/addiction-medicine-mostly-prescribed-to-whites-even-as-opioid-deaths-rose-in-bla.

9. Ying Han et al., "The Rising Crisis of Illicit Fentanyl Use, Overdose, and Potential Therapeutic Strategies," *Translational Psychiatry* 9, 282 (November 11, 2019), https://doi.org/10.1038/s41398-019-0625-0.

10. "Stimulant Use: Harm Reduction, Treatment, and Future Directions," Drug Policy Alliance, Report, September 7, 2018, http://www.drugpolicy.org/resource/stimulant-use-harm-reduction-treatment-and-future-directions.

11. Infections such as abscesses and endocarditis that are the result of germs and debris that enter a person's drug supply can result in the permanent loss of a body part, bodily function, or heart failure.

12. United Nations Office on Drugs and Crime, "Treatment of Stimulant Use Disorders: Current Practices and Promising Perspectives," https://www.unodc.org/documents/drug-prevention-and-treatment/Treatment_of_PSUD_for_website_24.05.19.pdf.

13. "Stimulant Use," Drug Policy Alliance.

14. United Nations Office on Drugs and Crime, "Treatment of Stimulant Use Disorders."

15. Carl Hart, *High Price: Drugs, Neuroscience, and Discovering Myself* (London: Penguin Books, 2013).

16. "What Is Cocaine Cut With? Adulterants and Cutting Agents," American Addiction Centers, Cocaine Treatment, accessed February 21, 2020, https://americanaddictioncenters.org/cocaine-treatment/cut-with.

17. Check out Drug Policy Alliance's drug curriculum for high schoolers to be the change at home: "Safety First: Real Drug Education for Teens," accessed February 21, 2020, http://www.drugpolicy.org/resource/safety-first-real-drug-education-teens.

18. Harm Reduction Action Center, "A Harm Reduction Service Provider's Guide to Methamphetamine and Other Stimulants," What We Do, Downloadable Resources, accessed March 12, 2020, https://www.harmreductionactioncenter.org/new-page.

19. GuideStar, "The Meth Project Foundation," Candid, accessed February 21, 2020, https://www.guidestar.org/profile/20-2343265.

20. For more information, check out the chapter "Mechanics of the Sex Trade: An Introduction" or my memoir, *Trigger Warning.*

21. Frida Garza, "Nixon Advisor: We Created the War on Drugs to 'Criminalize' Black People and the Anti-War Left," *Quartz*, Economics, March 23, 2016, https://qz.com/645990/nixon-advisor-we-created-the-war-on-drugs-to-criminalize-black-people-and-the-anti-war-left/.

22. Vagins and McCurdy, *Cracks in the System.*

23. The Prison Policy Initiative has comprehensive, up-to-date data on the impact of the prison industrial complex at www.prisonpolicy.org.

24. Aleks Kajstura, "Women's Mass Incarceration: The Whole Pie 2019," Prison Policy Initiative, Reports, October 29, 2019, https://www.prisonpolicy.org/reports/pie2019women.html.

25. Child Welfare Information Gateway, *Parental Substance Use and the Child Welfare System*, October 2014, https://www.childwelfare.gov/pubPDFs/parentalsubabuse.pdf.

26. Lucius Couloute, "Nowhere to Go: Homelessness Among Formerly Incarcerated People," Prison Policy Initiative, Reports, August 2018, https://www.prisonpolicy.org/reports/housing.html.

27. German Lopez, "A Big Part of the War on Drugs Is Based on a Huge Myth," *Vox*, July 10, 2015, https://www.vox.com/2015/7/10/8928421/crack-babies-myth.

28. Vagins and McCurdy, *Cracks in the System*.

29. Carl L. Hart, Joanne Csete, and Don Habibi, "Methamphetamine: Fact vs. Fiction and Lessons from the Crack Hysteria," Open Society Foundations, .https://www.opensocietyfoundations.org/uploads/43c2d274-ab5d-4c77-b162-f29034de40a8/methamphetamine-dangers-exaggerated-20140218.pdf.

30. Mark Hay, "This Is Your Sex on Drugs," *Vice*, November 8, 2015, https://www.vice.com/en_us/article/avymd5/this-is-your-sex-on-drugs-456.

31. Terence McKenna, *Food of the Gods: The Search for the Original Tree of Knowledge: A Radical History of Plants, Drugs, and Human Evolution* (New York: Bantam Books, 1992).

32. "Chemsex," Mainline, Drugs & Health, accessed February 21, 2020, https://english.mainline.nl/posts/show/8360/chemsex.

33. Michael Hobbes, "Why Did AIDS Ravage the U.S. More than Any Other Developed Country?" *The New Republic*, May 12, 2014, https://newrepublic.com/article/117691/aids-hit-united-states-harder-other-developed-countries-why.

34. Coined by Kimberly Crenshaw in 1989, the term "intersectionality" is used to explain harm that exists when two marginalized identities overlap. Here, LGBTQ people are disproportionately incarcerated, and people of color are disproportionately incarcerated, so LGBTQ people of color experience the most harm.

35. Center for American Progress and Movement Advancement Project, *Unjust: How the Broken Criminal Justice System Fails LGBT People of Color*, August 2016, https://www.lgbtmap.org/file/lgbt-criminal-justice-poc.pdf.

36. Eugene Jarecki, *The House I Live In* (White Plains, NY: Charlotte Street Films, 2012), http://www.pbs.org/independentlens/films/house-i-live-in/.

37. Hart, Csete, and Habibi, "Methamphetamine: Fact vs. Fiction and Lessons from the Crack Hysteria."

38. Hart, *High Price*.

39. "Paint the State," The Meth Project, Take Action, accessed February 21, 2020, http://www.methproject.org/action/paintthestate.html.

40. 2017 Opioid and Heroin Treatment Summit, April 2017, Atlanta, Georgia.

41. Hart, Csete, and Habibi, "Methamphetamine: Fact vs. Fiction and Lessons from the Crack Hysteria."

42. Vagins and McCurdy, *Cracks in the System*.

43. Reframe Health and Justice is one of a handful of harm reduction agencies across the nation specializing in stimulant harm reduction capacity building assistance.

44. Maia Szalavitz, "Can Amphetamines Help Cure Cocaine Addiction?" *Time*, December 8, 2008, http://content.time.com/time/health/article /0,8599,1864767,00.html.

45. Maia Szalavitz, *Unbroken Brain: A Revolutionary New Way of Understanding Addiction* (New York: St. Martin's Press, 2016).

46. Kenneth Anderson, "Addiction Treatment: Who Gets It and Who Needs It?" *Pacific Standard*, December 5, 2014, updated June 14, 2017, accessed February 23, 2020, https://psmag.com/social-justice/addiction-treatment-gets-needs-95360.

47. Karran A. Phillips, David H. Epstein, and Kenzie L. Preston, "Psychostimulant Addiction Treatment," *Neuropharmacology* 87 (2014): 150–160, https://doi .org/10.1016/j.neuropharm.2014.04.002.

48. "ADAP Formulary Coverage of Substance Use Treatment," NASTAD, July 24, 2018, accessed February 23, 2020, https://www.nastad.org/resource/ adap-formulary-coverage-substance-use-treatment.

49. United Nations Office on Drugs and Crime, "Treatment of Stimulant Use Disorders."

50. "Recovery," Substance Abuse and Mental Health Services Administration, 2014, https://www.samhsa.gov/sites/default/files/samhsa-recovery-5-6-14.pdf.

OVERVIEW OF HARM REDUCTION IN THE SEX TRADE

1. Don C. Des Jarlais, "Harm Reduction in the USA: The Research Perspective and an Archive to David Purchase," *Harm Reduction Journal* 14, 1 (2017), abstract, https://doi.org/10.1186/s12954-017-0178-6.

2. Syringe exchange is a model in which someone exchanges a used syringe for a sterile syringe. Syringe access is a better practice that recognizes the many reasons why people might not be able to carry a used syringe around and provides sterile syringes no matter what, while still incentivizing used-syringe collection.

3. "Summary of Information on the Safety and Effectiveness of Syringe Services Programs (SSPs)," Centers for Disease Control and Prevention, Syringe Service Programs, accessed August 21, 2020, https://www.cdc.gov/ssp/syringe-services-programs-summary.html.

4. Julia Marcus, "Quarantine Fatigue Is Real," *The Atlantic*, May 11, 2020, https://www.theatlantic.com/ideas/archive/2020/05/quarantine-fatigue -real-and-shaming-people-wont-help/611482/.

5. Community Health refers to health and wellness strategies that are community

informed and directed. Public Health refers to the governmental health system that is stifled by administrative control and reliance on the criminal legal system.

6. Magalie Lerman, "Beyond the Prevention and Treatment Binary: Leveraging Harm Reduction as a Critical Component of the Drug User Service Continuum," NASTAD (blog), September 26, 2016, accessed July 30, 2020, https://www.nastad .org/blog/beyond-prevention-and-treatment-binary-leveraging-harm -reduction-critical-component-drug-user.

7. These principles of harm reduction as applied to sex work are an adaptation of the principles of harm reduction as applied to drug use put forth by the Harm Reduction Coalition. The original principles can be found at www.harmreduction.org. The principles were adapted to suit the sex trade in 2017 by Reframe Health and Justice and can be found at www.reframehealthandjustice.com.

8. "Individuals to Remember," Sex Workers Outreach Project.

9. Kathleen N. Deering et al., "A Systematic Review of the Correlates of Violence Against Sex Workers," *American Journal of Public Health* 104, 5 (2014): e42–54, https://doi.org/10.2105/ajph.2014.301909.

10. Juhu Thukral, Melissa Ditmore, and Alexandra Murphy, *Behind Closed Doors: An Analysis of Indoor Sex Work in New York City,* Sex Workers Project at the Urban Justice Center, 2005, Global Network of Sex Worker Projects, https://www .nswp.org/resource/member-publications/behind-closed-doors.

11. Young Women's Empowerment Project, "Girls Do What They Have to Do to Survive."

12. Katherine Koster, "17 Facts About Sexual Violence and Sex Work," *Huffpost*, December 4, 2015, updated December 6, 2017, https://www.huffpost.com/ entry/16-facts-about-sexual-ass_b_8711720.

13. Though updated in 2001 to include trafficking, Federal Victims of Crime Act (VOCA) Compensation guidelines prohibit federal victim compensation dollars from being provided to people who "have committed a criminal act or some substantially wrongful act that caused or contributed to the crime," including people who trade sex and people under the influence of illicit drugs. Furthermore, many states' rape shield laws, which limit the extent to which a person's sexual history can be brought into question in sexual assault trials, do not include participation in the sex trade.

14. Anonymous personal experience, used with permission.

15. These approaches are discussed more in the next chapter, "Compassion, Not Criminalization."

16. Find out more about Pros Network Chicago at http://www.prosnetworkchicago .org/.

17. Katy Grimes, "Immunity from Arrest for California Sex Workers Passes Senate," *California Globe*, Legislature May 2, 2019, https://californiaglobe.com/legislature/ immunity-from-arrest-for-california-sex-workers-passes-senate/.

18. Dean Spade writes about how regulatory and administrative policies are truly

what contribute to poor health outcomes for marginalized populations. See Dean Spade, "Trans Law Reform Strategies, Co-Optation, and the Potential for Transformative Change," *Women's Rights Law Reporter* 30, Winter 2009, Rutgers School of Law, http://www.deanspade.net/wp-content/uploads/2010/07/rutgers .pdf.

19. I am going to get on my soapbox for a minute because this drives me up the wall: the power of patriarchy allows for a category where men can have fluid sexuality to allow for sound public health provision, but women can't. Misorienting within the health care system means many bisexual women and sexually fluid folx outside the gender binary don't feel safe or seen, so don't go get seen. Catch up, public health. Damn.

20. Katherin Koster, "10 Facts on HIV and Sex Work," *Huffpost*, December 3, 2015, updated December 6, 2017, accessed July 30, 2020, https://www.huffpost.com/ entry/hiv-and-sex-work-facts_b_8705476.

21. Spade, "Trans Law Reform Strategies."

22. Lindsay Roth, "PrEP: What It Is and How Sex Workers Can Use It," *Tits and Sass*, October 22, 2014, http://titsandsass.com/prep-what-it-is-and-how-sex -workers-can-use-it/.

23. Susan G. Sherman et al., "Correlates of Exchange Sex Among a Population-Based Sample of Low-Income Women Who Have Heterosexual Sex in Baltimore," *AIDS Care* 30, no. 10 (2018): 1273–1281, https://doi.org/10.1080%2F09540121.2018.1447078.

24. Nandita Raghuram, "'It's Destroyed People's Lives': The Shocking Rise in Hepatitis C-Related Deaths," *Vice*, Identity, June 16, 2016, https://www.vice .com/en_us/article/mbqj3x/its-destroyed-peoples-lives-the-shocking-rise-in -hepatitis-c-related-deaths.

25. Sex Workers Outreach Project, "Good Samaritan Law Expansion Toolkit."

26. Tara Boghosian, "COVID-19 and the Untenable Criminalization of Sex Work," *OnLabor*, April 29, 2020, https://www.onlabor.org/covid-19-and-the-untenable -criminalization-of-sex-work/.

27. Reframe Health and Justice and SWOP Behind Bars are two organizations that offer this training nationally. Many major cities have local sex worker–rights groups that provide training as well. This includes HIPS in Washington DC, St. James Infirmary in San Francisco, and the Rocky Mountain Sex Worker Coalition in Colorado.

28. Gabrielle Glaser, "Alcohol Harm Reduction: A World of Growing Possibilities," *Filter*, August 17, 2020, https://filtermag.org/alcohol-drinking-harm-reduction/.

29. Find out more about these policies in the first chapter of my memoir, *Half Turned On and Half Triggered*.

30. Koster, "10 Facts on HIV and Sex Work."

31. Sex Workers Outreach Project, "Good Samaritan Law Expansion Toolkit."

32. Find out more about the APP in Chapter 9 of my memoir.

33. Ayanna Pressley, Alexandria Ocasio-Cortez, and Jan Schakowsky, "The

Hyde Amendment Hurts Black and Brown Women the Most—And We Need To Repeal It Now," *Refinery29*, July 29, 2020, https://www.refinery29.com/en-us/2020/07/9938994/aoc-ayanna-pressley-repeal-hyde-amendment.

34. "Federal Funding for Syringe Services Programs," Centers for Disease Control and Prevention, Syringe Service Programs, accessed July 31, 2020, https://www.cdc.gov/ssp/ssp-funding.html.

35. "Police abuse of sex workers in the United States," Wikipedia, accessed August 3, 2020, https://en.wikipedia.org/wiki/Police_abuse_of_sex_workers_in_the_United_States.

36. Reframe Health and Justice, 2018. Unpublished data.

37. T. Burns, "People in Alaska's Sex Trade: Their Lived Experiences and Policy Recommendations," Sex Trafficking in Alaska, Research, http://sextraffickingalaska.com/pdfs/AKSWR.pdf.

38. Taylor Palmby, "It's perfectly legal for cops to trick prostitutes into having sex with them. Meet the women behind the fight to change this," *Babe*, July 11, 2017, accessed August 3, 2020, https://babe.net/2017/07/11/perfectly-legal-cops-trick-prostitutes-sex-heres-women-behind-fight-change-7778.

39. Molly Crabapple, "Special Prostitution Courts and the Myth of 'Rescuing' Sex Workers," *Vice*, January 5, 2015, https://www.vice.com/en_us/article/yvq9bx/sex-workers-and-the-city-0000550-v22n1.

40. Katherine H. A. Footer et al., "Police-Related Correlates of Client-Perpetrated Violence Among Female Sex Workers in Baltimore City, Maryland," *American Journal of Public Health* 109, no. 2 (2019): 289–295, https://doi.org/10.2105/ajph.2018.304809.

41. Burns, "People in Alaska's Sex Trade."

42. Carmen Phillips, "74 Bail Funds You Can Absolutely Support Right Now," *Autostraddle*, May 31, 2020, https://www.autostraddle.com/43-bail-funds-you-can-absolutely-support-right-now/.

43. Quote amended for legibility. "What Is Divest/Invest?" Divest/Invest: Criminalization, Funders for Justice, accessed May 4, 2020, https://divest.nfg.org/#what-is.

44. Zhana Vrangalova, "Do Sex Workers Have More Mental Health Problems?" *Psychology Today*, Sex, October 30, 2014, https://www.psychologytoday.com/us/blog/strictly-casual/201410/do-sex-workers-have-more-mental-health-problems.

45. Bella Chudakov et al., "The Motivation and Mental Health of Sex Workers," *Journal of Sex and Marital Therapy* 28, no. 4 (2002): 305–315, https://doi.org/10.1080/00926230290001439.

46. Saul Mcleod, "Maslow's Hierarchy of Needs," Simply Psychology, accessed August 4, 2020, https://www.simplypsychology.org/maslow.html.

47. Adam McCann, "States with the Most and Least Medicaid Coverage," *WalletHub*, accessed August 4, 2020, https://wallethub.com/edu/states-with-the-most-and-least-medicaid-coverage/71573/.

48. Emma Seppala, "Connectedness and Health: The Science of Social

Connection," Stanford Medicine, The Center for Compassion and Altruism Research and Education, May 8, 2014, http://ccare.stanford.edu/uncategorized/connectedness-health-the-science-of-social-connection-infographic/.

49. Sofia Barrett-Ibarria, "BSDM Can Provide Profound Healing Experiences," *Vice*, Health, August 29, 2017, https://www.vice.com/en_us/article/nee9yg/bsdm-can-provide-profound-healing-experiences.

50. Blake Eligh, "How Psychedelic Microdosing Might Help Ease Anxiety and Sharpen Focus," *Medical Xpress*, Psychology & Psychiatry, July 25, 2018, https://medicalxpress.com/news/2018-07-psychedelic-microdosing-ease-anxiety-sharpen.html.

51. Mostafa Langarizadeh et al., "Telemental Health Care, an Effective Alternative to Conventional Mental Care: A Systematic Review," *Acta Informatica Medica* 25, no 4 (December 2017): 240–246, https://doi.org/10.5455%2Faim.2017.25.240-246.

52. Liz Highleyman, "Use of Psychedelic Drugs May Reduce the Risk of Suicide in Female Sex Workers," NAM Aidsmap, Sex workers, May 24, 2017, https://www.aidsmap.com/news/may-2017/use-psychedelic-drugs-may-reduce-risk-suicide-female-sex-workers.

53. National Alliaance of State and Territorial AIDS Directors, *Modernizing Public Health to Meet the Needs of People Who Use Drugs: Affordable Care Act Opportunities*, October 13, 2015, https://www.nastad.org/sites/default/files/resources/docs/ModernizingPublicHealth-NASTAD.pdf.

54. One of the best jobs I ever had was working for the Harm Reduction Action Center (HRAC) in Denver, Colorado, where I was under the wing of two very powerful and brilliant women. At the end of every workday, they would say this as we walked out the door.

COMPASSION, NOT CRIMINALIZATION: ALTERNATIVES TO CRIMINALIZATION THAT REDUCE HARM IN THE SEX TRADE

1. Footer et al., "Police-Related Correlates of Client-Perpetrated Violence."

2. "HIPS: Advancing the Health Rights and Dignity of People and Communities Impacted by Sex Work and Drug Use," HIPS.org, accessed January 18, 2021.

3. Sydney Brownstone, "Meet the Sex Workers Who Lawmakers Don't Believe Exist," *The Stranger*, News, February 11, 2015, https://www.thestranger.com/news/2015/02/11/21689047/meet-the-sex-workers-who-lawmakers-dont-believe-exist.

4. "LEAD Support Bureau," https://www.leadbureau.org/.

5. Ryan Beck Turner, "Project ROSE and Oppression as 'Rescue,'" Human Trafficking Center, accessed January 18, 2021, https://humantraffickingcenter.org/project-rose-and-oppression-as-rescue/.

6. "Devastatingly Pervasive: 1 in 3 Women Globally Experience Violence," World Health Organization, News, March 9, 2021, https://www.who.int/news/

item/09-03-2021-devastatingly-pervasive-1-in-3-women-globally-experience-vi-
olence.

7. LEAD Seattle—King County, https://leadkingcounty.org/.

8. HIPS, https://www.hips.org/.

9. "Sex Worker Giving Circle," Third Wave Fund, https://www.thirdwavefund.org/
sex-worker-giving-circle.

10. Gays & Lesbians Living in a Transgender Society, https://www.glitsinc.org/about.

11. Collective Action for Safe Spaces, https://www.collectiveactiondc.org/

REMATRIATING DRUGS

1. Albizu Campos was a leader in the Puerto Rican independence movement who
was tirelessly stalked, imprisoned, and poisoned by the US government.

2. For prompts on how to analyze your drug consumption and practice conscious
drug consumerism, check out the chapter "Drug Policy for Breaking Intergenerational Curses" in Section 4.

3. Merianne Rose Spencer, Arialdi M. Miniño, and Margaret Warner, "Drug Overdose Deaths in the United States, 2001–2021," Centers for Disease Control and
Prevention, NCHS data brief, no. 457 (December 2022), https://doi.org/10.15620/
cdc:122556.

4. "Violence Against American Indian and Alaska Native Women and Men Fact
Sheet," National Indigenous Women's Resource Center, accessed August 15, 2023,
https://www.niwrc.org/sites/default/files/images/resource/niwrc_fact_sheet_
violence_against_native_women_men.jpg.

5. Spencer, Miniño, and Warner, "Drug Overdose Deaths in the United States,
2001–2021."

6. Aliza Cohen et al., "How the War on Drugs Impacts Social Determinants of
Health Beyond the Criminal Legal System," *Annals of Medicine* 54, no 1 (2022),
2024–2038, https://doi.org/10.1080/07853890.2022.2100926.

7. "Framing Evaluation in Our Communities," American Indian Higher Education
Consortium, 2009, https://portalcentral.aihec.org/Indigeval/Book%20Chapters
/1-FramingEvaluationInOurCommunities.pdf.

8. Such as Insight Timer.

PRINCIPLES OF HEALING-CENTERED HARM REDUCTION

1. "Principles of Harm Reduction," National Harm Reduction Coalition, accessed
July 6, 2021, https://harmreduction.org/about-us/principles-of-harm-reduction/.

2. "What Is Harm Reduction?" Harm Reduction International, accessed July 6,
2021, https://www.hri.global/what-is-harm-reduction.

3. "Principles of Healing-Centered Harm Reduction," Reframe Health and

Justice, October 14, 2018, https://reframehealthandjustice.medium.com/principles-of-healing-centered-harm-reduction-5e728cf20e56.

PLEASURE AS AN ACCESS POINT

1. National Harm Reduction Coalition, https://harmreduction.org/.
2. Amanda Arnold, "A Guide to the 'Walking While Trans' Ban," *The Cut*, July 22, 2020, https://www.thecut.com/2020/07/walking-while-trans-law-in-new-york-explained.html.
3. "The Matilda Centre for Research in Mental Health and Substance Use," The University of Sydney, https://www.sydney.edu.au/matilda-centre/.

FUCK MYSELF INTO HEAVEN

1. Find out more at https://thecspc.org/.
2. Erin Blakemore, "Ancient Hallucinogens Found in 1,000-Year-Old Shamanic Pouch," *National Geographic*, May 6, 2019, https://www.nationalgeographic.com/culture/article/ancient-hallucinogens-oldest-ayahuasca-found-shaman-pouch
3. Sarah Sloat, "The 'Stoned Ape' Theory Might Explain Our Extraordinary Evolution," *Inverse*, July 14, 2017, https://www.inverse.com/article/34186-stoned-ape-hypothesis.

DRUG POLICY FOR BREAKING INTERGENERATIONAL CURSES

1. Mark Johnston, "The Sugar Trade in the West Indies and Brazil Between 1492 and 1700," University of Minnesota Libraries, University Libraries. https://www.lib.umn.edu/bell/tradeproducts/sugar.
2. Stephen Glass, "Truth & D.A.R.E.," *Rolling Stone*, March 5, 1998, https://www.pbs.org/wgbh/pages/frontline/shows/dope/dare/truth.html.
3. Nicole M. Avena, Pedro Rada, and Bartley G. Hoebel, "Evidence for Sugar Addiction: Behavioral and Neurochemical Effects of Intermittent, Excessive Sugar Intake," *Neuroscience and Biobehavioral Reviews* 32, issue 1 (2008): 20–39, https://doi.org/10.1016/j.neubiorev.2007.04.019. "Numerous studies have found that sensitization to one drug can lead not only to hyperactivity, but also to subsequent increased intake of another drug or substance (Ellgren et al., 2006, Henningfield et al., 1990, Hubbell et al., 1993, Liguori et al., 1997, Nichols et al., 1991, Piazza et al., 1989, Vezina, 2004, Vezina et al., 2002, Volpicelli et al., 1991). We refer to this phenomenon as 'consummatory cross-sensitization.' In the clinical literature, when one drug leads to taking another, this is known as a 'gateway effect.' It is particularly noteworthy when a legal drug (e.g., nicotine) acts as a gateway to an illegal drug (e.g., cocaine) (Lai et al., 2000)."
4. Serge H. Ahmed, Karine Guillem, and Youna Vandaele, "Sugar Addiction: Pushing the Drug-Sugar Analogy to the Limit," *Current Opinion in Clinical Nutrition*

and Metabolic Care 16, no. 4 (July 2013): 434–439, https://doi.org/10.1097/mco
.ob013e328361c8b8. "One currently estimates that about 10–20% of people would present addiction-like symptoms toward hyperpalatable foods—a proportion that is not different from the proportion of cocaine or heroin users who go on to develop addiction. The widespread introduction of hyperpalatable foods during the 20th century could be likened to the introduction of distilled drinks (i.e., gins, whiskeys) in the 17th century or of injectable synthetic drugs at the end of the 19th century, each spurred its own addiction epidemics. Finally, people are as ill-prepared biologically to foods high in added sugar and/or fat, as they are to drugs in pure or highly concentrated form. In this regard, the ubiquity, ready availability, and affordability of those foods make them a serious modern hazard to public health."

5. "Sanho Tree on Columbus and Drugs," *A Secret History of Coffee, Coca and Cola*, January 19, 2013, C-SPAN2 BookTV, https://www.c-span.org/video/?c4624302/user-clip-sanho-tree-columbus-drugs.

6. Leo Beletsky and Corey S. Davis, "Today's Fentanyl Crisis: Prohibition's Iron Law, Revisited," *International Journal of Drug Policy* 46 (August 2017): 156–159, https://doi.org/10.1016/j.drugpo.2017.05.050.

7. The use of newly popular substances, typically associated with lower classes, raised concerns about economic productivity or, in the American South, about the African Americans "forget[ting] their assigned status in the social order" (Williams 1914 quoted in Nadelmann 1990: 506). Beyond class relations, the consumption that was to be the subject of regulation or prohibition could also be associated with the despised minorities and immigrant groups and the substances as weapons used to undermine the social order either from the outside or from the inside.

8. The words "men" and "women" are in quotation marks here because the gender identities included in this survey are limited to the cis male–female gender binary.

9. Substance Abuse and Mental Health Services Administration (2020). Key substance use and mental health indicators in the United States: Results from the 2019 National Survey on Drug Use and Health (HHS Publication No. PEP20-07-01-001, NSDUH Series H-55). Rockville, MD: Center for Behavioral Health Statistics and Quality, Substance Abuse and Mental Health Services Administration. Retrieved from https://www.samhsa.gov/data/.

10. "Global market value of alcoholic beverages 2012 to 2025," *Statista*, June 16, 2021, https://www.statista.com/forecasts/696641/market-value-alcoholic-beverages-worldwide#:%7E:text=The%20global%20market%20size%20of,1.75%20trillion%20dollars%20by%202024.

11. "The Encyclopedia of Psychoactive Plants: Ethnopharmacology and Its Applications: Balché," DoctorLib, accessed June 23, 2021, https://doctorlib.info/herbal/encyclopedia-psychoactive-plants-ethnopharmacology/138.html.

12. Daniel Bradburd and William Jankowiak, "Drugs, Desire, and European Economic Expansion," in *Drugs, Labor, and Colonial Expansion* (Tucson: University of Arizona Press, 2003).

13. Rosa Benabarre Ribalta in *New Pedagogical Challenges in the 21st Century—Contributions of Research in Education*, ed. Olga Bernad Cavero and Núria Llevot-Calvet, Revista de Sociología de La Educación (RASE) 11, no. 3, 501–503, https://doi.org/10.7203/rase.11.3.13047.

14. Steven Newcomb, "'Canada' and the 'United States' Are in Turtle Island," *Indian Country Today*, September 30, 2011, updated September 12, 2018, https://indiancountrytoday.com/archive/canada-and-the-united-states-are-in-turtle-island.

15. Bradburd and Jankowiak, "Drugs, Desire, and European Economic Expansion."

16. "A Social History of America's Most Popular Drugs," PBS, *Frontline*.

17. Curtis Marez, *Drug Wars: The Political Economy of Narcotics* (Minneapolis: University of Minnesota Press, 2004), 126–132.

18. Constanza Sanchéz-Avilés and Ondrej Ditrych, "The Global Drug Prohibition Regime: Prospects for Stability and Change in an Increasingly Less Prohibitionist World," *International Politics* 55 (2018), 463–481, https://doi.org/10.1057/s41311-017-0081-5. "This emphasis of prohibitionist approach had several unintended consequences, the most important of which was the emergence of international drug trafficking, controlled by criminal organizations which would soon acquire global dimensions and become one of the main sources of transnational illicit enrichment (as demand remained high while illicit production and distribution to meet it presented a major business opportunity)."

19. Ibid. "The movement led by the USA at that time could even be described as 'revolutionary' as it challenged the 2000-year long tradition of permissiveness toward cultivation, production, trade and consumption of psychoactive substances. Moreover, some of the major colonial powers of the time, mainly the British and the Dutch, had a strong interest in maintaining the free trade of these substances . . . "

20. Jaya Nayar, "Aerial Fumigation in Colombia: The Bad and the Ugly," *Harvard International Review*, December 9, 2020, https://hir.harvard.edu/aerial-fumigation-in-colombia-the-bad-and-the-ugly/.

21. By 2020, during the COVID-19 pandemic, cannabis dispensaries and delivery services were declared essential businesses across the country.

22. Bruce Barcott, Beau Whitney, and Janessa Bailey, "Leafly Jobs Report 2021," Leafly, https://leafly-cms-production.imgix.net/wp-content/uploads/2021/02/13180206/Leafly-JobsReport-2021-v14.pdf.

23. American Civil Liberties Union, *A Tale of Two Countries: Racially Targeted Arrests in an Era of Marijuana Reform*, 2020, https://www.aclu.org/sites/default/files/field_document/tale_of_two_countries_racially_targeted_arrests_in_the_era_of_marijuana_reform_revised_7.1.20_0.pdf.

24. Matej Mikulic, "Global Pharmaceutical Industry—Statistics and Facts,"

Statista, November 5, 2020, https://www.statista.com/topics/1764/global-pharmaceutical-industry/.

25. Ellen Chang, "Why Investing in Psychedelic Medicine Could Be Better than Cannabis," *US News and World Report*, September 11, 2020, https://money.usnews.com/investing/articles/why-investing-in-psychedelic-medicine-could-be-better-than-cannabis.

26. "Alexander T. Shulgin," Alexander Shulgin Research Institute, https://shulginresearch.net/about/sasha_shulgin/.

27. Konstantin Gerber et al., "Ethical Concerns About Psilocybin Intellectual Property," *ACS Pharmacology and Translational Science* 4, no. 2 (2021): 573–577, https://doi.org/10.1021/acsptsci.0c00171.

28. Ibid.

29. Courtney Connley, "Black and Latinx Founders Have Received Just 2.6% of VC Funding So Far in 2020, According to New Report," CNBC, Work, October 8, 2020, https://www.cnbc.com/2020/10/07/black-and-latinx-founders-have-received-just-2point6percent-of-vc-funding-in-2020-so-far.html. Reports emerged in summer of 2020 "that Black and Latinx founders raised $2.3 billion in funding, representing just 2.6 percent of the total $87.3 billion in funding that has gone to all founders so far 2020." In 2019, less than 3 percent of all venture capital investment went to women-led companies, and only one-fifth of US venture capital went to startups with at least one woman on the founder team.

30. Alnoor Ladha and Martin Kirk, "Psychedelic Communities, Social Justice, and Kinship in the Capitalocene," Kahpi: The Ayahuasca Hub, April 30, 2019, https://kahpi.net/psychedelic-communities-social-justice/.

31. "North America Psychedelic Drugs Market Could Exceed $6.8 Billion by 2027," PR News Wire, January 6, 2021, https://www.prnewswire.com/news-releases/north-america-psychedelic-drugs-market-could-exceed-6-8-billion-by-2027--301201636.html.

32. "United Nations Declaration on the Rights of Indigenous Peoples," United Nations, Department of Economic and Social Affairs: Social Inclusion, https://www.un.org/development/desa/indigenouspeoples/declaration-on-the-rights-of-indigenous-peoples.html.

33. Alex Thompson et al, "More Potential Biden Hires Penalized for Marijuana Use," *Politico*, March 30, 2021, https://www.politico.com/newsletters/transition-playbook/2021/03/30/high-times-at-1600-penn-492299.

34. Environmental and other resources that are accessible to all and stewarded collectively as opposed to being privatized, commodified, and transformed into property with exclusive access.

35. adrienne maree brown, *Pleasure Activism: The Politics of Feeling Good* (Chico, CA: AK Press, 2019).

36. adrienne maree brown, *Emergent Strategy: Shaping Change, Changing Worlds* (Chico, CA: AK Press, 2017).

37. "Ecologies of Transformation," Sandberg Instituut, accessed June 23, 2021, https://sandberg.nl/temporary-programme-ecologies-of-transformation.

38. "Alnoor Ladha—Mystical Anarchism: A Spiritual Biography," interview by Michael Lerner, New School Commonweal, November 5, 2019, https://www.youtube.com/watch?v=SiqzXSEKVlk.

39. Benjamin J. Pauli, "Pacifism, Nonviolence, and the Reinvention of Anarchist Tactics in the Twentieth Century," *Journal for the Study of Radicalism* 9, issue 1 (2015): 61–94, https://doi.org/10.14321/jstudradi.9.1.0061.

BLACK TRANS JOY: A LOVE LETTER TO POPPY

1. Peter Tarr, "Opioids, at Very Low Doses, May Provide a New Way to Treat Resistant Depression," *Brain & Behavior Magazine*, March 2019, https://www.bbrfoundation.org/content/opioids-very-low-doses-may-provide-new-way-treat-resistant-depression.

2. Amanda B. Namchuk, Irwin Lucki, and Caroline A. Browne, "Buprenorphine as a Treatment for Major Depression and Opioid Use Disorder," *Advances in Drug and Alcohol Research* 2 (February 2022): 10254, https://doi.org/10.3389/adar.2022.10254.

3. Opioid naive means someone who isn't using daily or who hasn't used in the past week. Vermont Department of Health, "Rule Governing the Prescribing of Opioids for Pain," March 1, 2019, https://www.healthvermont.gov/sites/default/files/documents/pdf/Opioid%20Prescribing%20Rule%202.1.19.pdf.

4. Svend Norn, Poul Kruse, and Edith Kruse, "Opiumsvalmuen og morfin gennem tiderne [History of opium poppy and morphine]," *Dansk medicinhistorisk arbog* 33 (July 26, 2013): 171–184, https://www.yumpu.com/da/document/view/18293804/opiumsvalmuen-og-morfin-gennem-tiderne-jydsk-medicinhistorisk-.

5. Bureau of International Narcotics and Law Enforcement Affairs,, "Fighting the Opium Trade in Afghanistan: Myths, Facts, and Sound Policy," US Department of State, March 11, 2008, https://2001-2009.state.gov/p/inl/rls/other/102214.htm.

ANCESTRAL HEALING FOR LIBERATION

1. Itzhak Beery, *Shamanic Healing: Traditional Medicine for the Modern World* (Rochester, T: Inner Traditions, 2017).

2. Jonathan M. Pitts, "West African religions Like Ifa and Vodou Are on the Rise in Maryland, As Practitioners Connect with Roots," *Baltimore Sun*, March 28, 2019, https://www.baltimoresun.com/maryland/bs-md-african-faiths-20190315-story.html.

3. Yvonne P. Chireau, *Black Magic: Religion and the African American Conjuring Tradition* (Berkely: University of California Press, 2003).

4. Refers to logic that relies on tangibility. Praised in US culture, this approach to reality is heavily influenced by Enlightenment thinkers.

5. Jeff Diamant, "With High Levels of Prayer, U.S. Is an Outlier Among Wealthy Nations," Pew Research Center, May 1, 2019, https://www .pewresearch.org/fact-tank/2019/05/01/with-high-levels-of-prayer-u-s-is -an-outlier-among-wealthy-nations/.

6. *Raba* is the feminine spelling for *rabbi*. I chose feminized references in this sentence for political reasons.

7. Antonio Regalado, "More than 26 million People Have Taken an At-Home Ancestry Test," MIT Technology Review, February 11, 2019, https://www .technologyreview.com/2019/02/11/103446/more-than-26-million-people-have -taken-an-at-home-ancestry-test/.

8. David Hill, "Peru's Ayahuasca Industry Booms as Westerners Search for Alternative Healing," *Guardian*, June 7, 2017, https://www.theguardian.com/travel/2016/ jun/07/peru-ayahuasca-drink-boom-amazon-spirituality-healing.

AFTERWORD

1. Sinnamon Love, "A Question of Feminism," in *The Feminist Porn Book: The Politics of Producing Pleasure*, ed. Tristan Taormino, Constance Penley, Celine Parrenas Shimizu, and Mireille Miller-Young (New York: The Feminist Press at City University of New York, 2013), 97–104.

2. https://sexualhealthalliance.com/

3. https://www.equitablecarecert.com/